EARLY MEDIEVAL SCOTLAND

EARLY MEDIEVAL SCOTLAND

INDIVIDUALS, COMMUNITIES AND IDEAS

DAVID CLARKE, ALICE BLACKWELL AND MARTIN GOLDBERG

National Museums Scotland

Published in 2012 by
NMS Enterprises Limited – Publishing
a division of NMS Enterprises Limited
National Museums Scotland
Chambers Street, Edinburgh EH1 1JF

Reprinted in 2015 and 2017.

Text and photographic images © National Museums Scotland 2012, 2015 (unless otherwise credited: see the Acknowledgements page at the end of this publication).

Format and additional material
© National Museums Scotland 2012, 2015, 2017.

No part of this publication may be reproduced, stored in a retrieval system or transmitted in any form or by any means, electronic, mechanical, photocopying, recording or otherwise, without the prior written permission of the publisher.

The rights of David Clarke, Alice Blackwell and Martin Goldberg to be identified as the authors of this book have been asserted by them in accordance with the Copyright, Designs and Patents Act 1988.

British Library Cataloguing in Publication Data
A catalogue record for this book
is available from the British Library.

ISBN: 978-1-910682-02-9

Book design and cover by Mark Blackadder.
Printed and bound in Spain by Novoprint, SA, Barcelona.

www.nms.ac.uk
www.glenmorangie.com

THE COVER

The cover illustration is a composite image arranged by Martin Goldberg from fragments of the Hilton of Cadboll stone. As the spiral panel is broken in half, a mirror image was used and other fragments employed to create the symmetrical image on the cover. This image, created by Mark Blackadder as part of the cover design, does not represent what the original stone would have looked like – it is not real, although it is assembled from the real fragments that survive.

The quotation attributed to St Columba was taken from the following source: T O Clancy and G Márkus 1995. *Iona: The Earliest Poetry of a Celtic Monastery.* Edinburgh: Edinburgh University Press, pages 85 (English translation) and 84 (original Latin).

IMAGE CAPTIONS

page VI: The Hunterston brooch.
page VIII: The spiral panel from a modern reconstruction of the Hilton of Cadboll cross-slab, carved by Barry Grove.

For a full listing of NMS Enterprises Limited – Publishing titles and related merchandise visit:

www.nms.ac.uk/books

Contents

✶

FOREWORD by Dr Gordon Rintoul CBE
NATIONAL MUSEUMS SCOTLAND VII

FOREWORD by Marc Hoellinger
THE GLENMORANGIE COMPANY IX

INTRODUCTION XI
Fragments of Early Medieval Scotland

EARLY MEDIEVAL SCOTLAND

CHAPTER ONE
Individuals by Alice Blackwell 3

CHAPTER TWO
Communities by David Clarke 69

CHAPTER THREE
Ideas and Ideology by Martin Goldberg 141

CONCLUSION 205
BIBLIOGRAPHY 207
INDEX 221
ACKNOWLEDGEMENTS 230

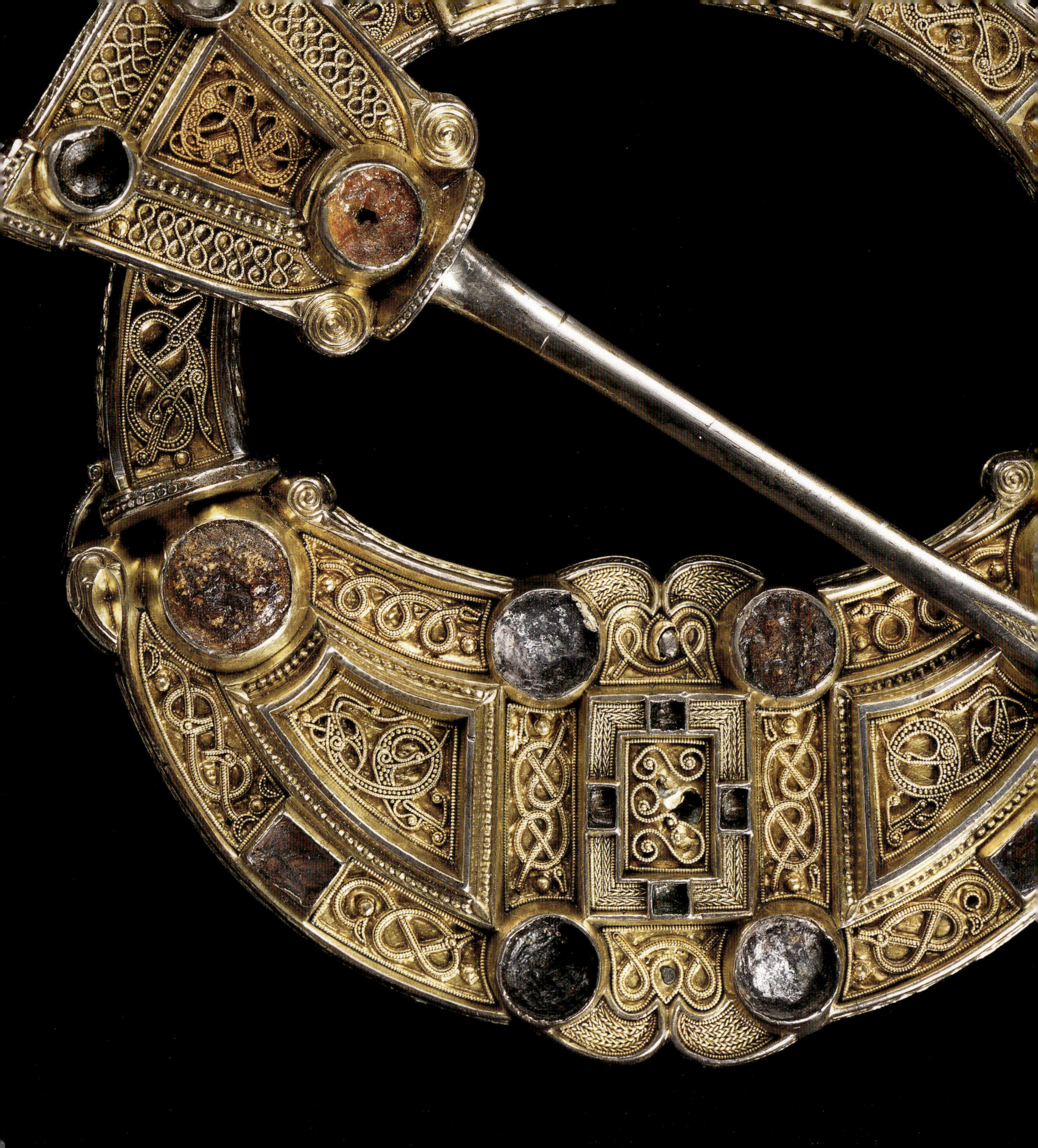

Foreword

✶

Dr Gordon Rintoul CBE
Director
NATIONAL MUSEUMS SCOTLAND

The pioneering partnership established in 2008 between National Museums Scotland and The Glenmorangie Company has supported a major programme of innovative research into the archaeology of Scotland during the Early Medieval period, AD 300–900. Some of the most treasured and enigmatic objects within the National Museum of Scotland come from this formative period of Scotland's past.

The support of Glenmorangie has enabled us to undertake an extensive re-evaluation of this key, but often misunderstood, period of Scotland's history. The findings of this research programme are revealed in this landmark book, which uses objects to explore the lives of individuals and communities in the Early Medieval period, as well as the ideas and ideologies that were important to them. We are extremely grateful to The Glenmorangie Company for their support and enthusiasm for our work. This partnership has provided an innovative means of supporting academic research and delivered a multi-award winning project of which we are all extremely proud.

EDINBURGH 2015

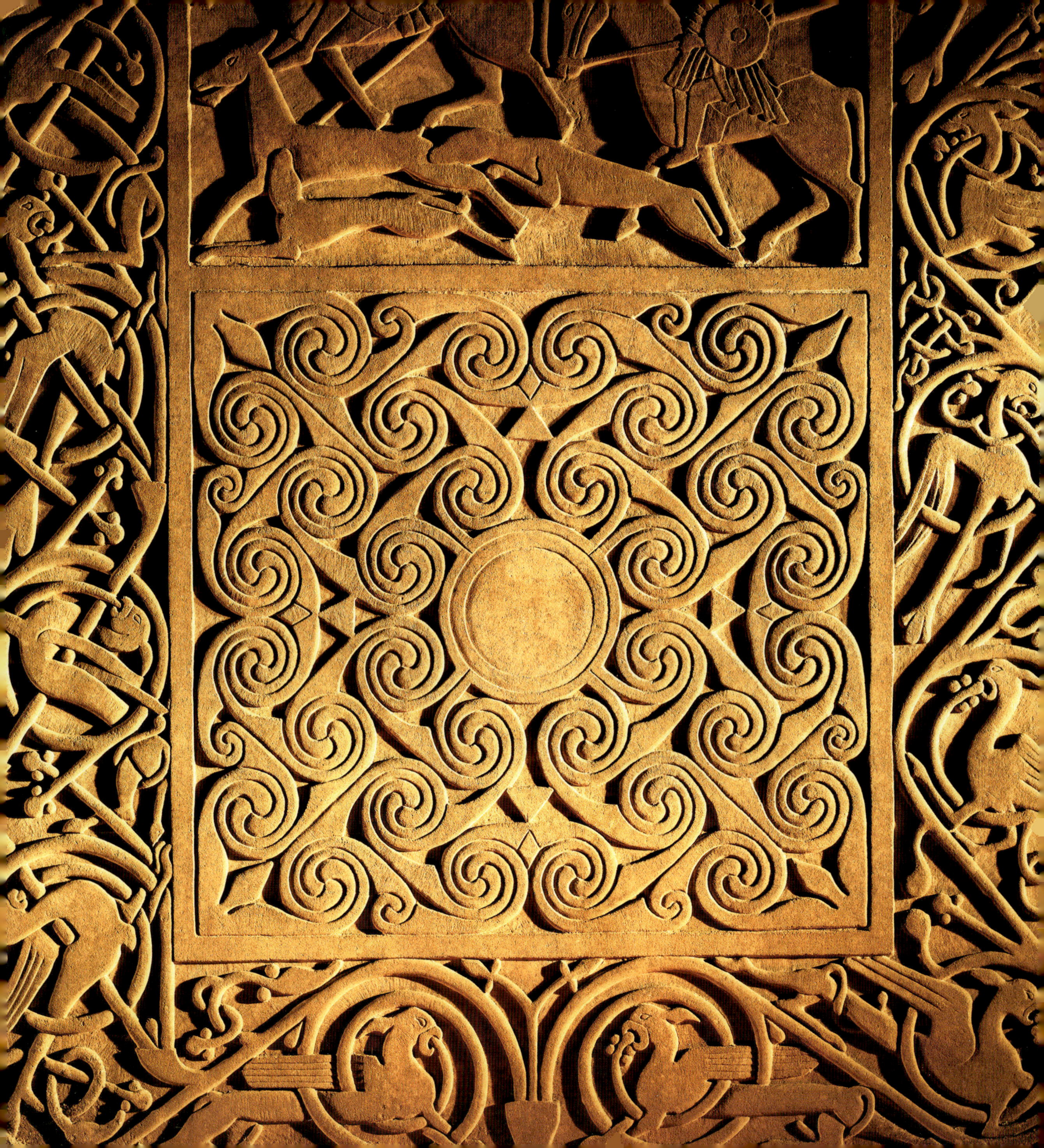

Foreword

✶

Marc Hoellinger
President and Chief Executive Officer
THE GLENMORANGIE COMPANY

At The Glenmorangie Company we are extremely proud of our Scottish roots, particularly the ancient art and culture of the Picts which is so much a part of our heritage in the north of Scotland. National Museums Scotland's collections include an 8th-century Pictish masterpiece, the Hilton of Cadboll stone cross-slab, which was discovered near our Distillery in Ross-shire and which provided the inspiration for the emblem that adorns Glenmorangie's bottles. This was the starting point for our partnership with National Museums Scotland.

Since then, the Glenmorangie Research Project has been furthering the study and understanding of Early Medieval Scotland, the fascinating period of Scottish history after the Romans left and before the Vikings arrived. This is a period that has many myths associated with it, when stunning treasures, the match of any in Europe, were produced. We are delighted to continue to be associated with this major study into Early Medieval Scotland, which has made intriguing revelations based on new discoveries by The Glenmorangie Research project. The need for a second printing of this delightful and fascinating book, first published in 2012, is a testament to the popularity of the original work and is an ongoing reminder of the important insights it set out to share.

EDINBURGH 2015

GLENMORANGIE
SINGLE MALT SCOTCH WHISKY

EARLY MEDIEVAL SCOTLAND

X

INTRODUCTION

Fragments of Early Medieval Scotland

During the Early Medieval period, a time that used to be regarded as the 'Dark Ages', treasures were made that still dazzle and astound today. Surviving objects demonstrate that people living in Early Medieval Scotland were part of sophisticated intellectual networks and had mastered complex technologies. And yet, to most people 'Early Medieval Scotland' is a vague and unfamiliar term – hardly a household name. It is not conveniently labelled with the name of a now (in)famous 'people', such as the Vikings or Romans. This is because surviving historical sources tell us that there was more than one group of people inhabiting the land – this is the time of the Picts, the Gaels, the Britons and the Anglo-Saxons.

The Early Medieval period, AD 300–900, marks the beginning of Scottish history, the end of a long pre-history when no written records were created. However, these early written sources are few and far between, and most were written by people outside Scotland, giving us a partial and often biased view of the period. On the other hand, new archaeological evidence continues to emerge: new sites are found and excavated, and stray finds continue to be discovered.

The material that archaeologists study is literally fragments of the past that have survived into the present. It can range in scale from tiny seeds recovered from the soil that tell us about the crops people grew, to large jewelled brooches, tools and pottery dishes made and owned by individual people, right up to monuments such as sculptured stones or ditches and ramparts of Early Medieval forts. All are testaments to the ideas that were important to the individuals and communities living in Early Medieval Scotland. Archaeology allows you to see the past and to populate it with the things that people made and gave away, wore and cherished, used and destroyed.

There has been a tendency in the past to concentrate on only a few topics – particularly warfare and kingship – when considering Early Medieval Scotland. However, these themes are only a fraction of what we *could* explore, and they are hard to study from the surviving archaeological

Opposite: A fragmented brooch. Only one terminal of this brooch survives; it was part of a hoard of objects from Croy, Inverness-shire.

evidence. Archaeologists have been heavily influenced by agendas and questions most suitable for historical texts, and particularly political history, but often these topics and questions are not appropriate to the material evidence. In this book we are not rejecting historical sources, but instead intend to redress the balance. The aim is rather to demonstrate the potential that archaeology has to help us understand the past when we ask the right questions of it.

Archaeologists are dependent on people deliberately burying objects (and human remains), or on the casual loss of things that, once dropped, end up being buried and preserved. With the deliberate burial of possessions we might be given a window onto *why* something was deposited: for instance, set in a house wall whilst being built, placed in a grave, or left in a wet place in the landscape. Such discoveries can tell us about attitudes towards material objects and their place in peoples' understanding of the world in life and in death. Casual losses, on the other hand, can be more difficult to interpret, but the objects themselves can tell us how they were made, used, decorated and mended in particular ways before being buried.

This publication takes three different perspectives to explore and to make sense of these surviving fragments of Early Medieval Scotland. The perspectives are 'Individuals', 'Communities' and 'Ideas and Ideologies', and each will be dealt with in turn within the three chapters that follow.

INDIVIDUALS

Most of our objects can reveal something about individuals, whether as creators or owners. These individuals are rarely named and even more rarely can they be linked to the historical record. However, they are people who have literally left their mark on the past through the survival of material culture. The objects themselves tell us about the people who fashioned, used, adapted, personalised and discarded the items that have survived in the archaeological record.

Archaeologists work closely with objects and spaces used intimately by individual people in the past – things made, loved and cared for; things that carried memories and personal associations; things that became irrelevant, were discarded or deliberately broken. Archaeology can provide us with opportunities to explore the lives, deaths, concerns and ambitions of individuals. But, as historian Paul Dutton has noted:

Too often we [as archaeologists or historians] *intellectualise the cultures we seek to recover, neglecting all the while the human and sensory experiences that once so enlivened them, that made them them.*[1]

People are inherent in everything we do as archaeologists, but rarely are they made explicit. There has been a tendency for archaeologists and historians to talk about Early Medieval Scotland in terms of groups of people or societies, and to follow broad themes such as the introduction of Christianity, the growth of distinct ethnic groups, the increasing hierarchy of society and the role of

Below: A brooch terminal from Dunbeath, Caithness. Although now fragmentary, this brooch would originally have been as impressive as the Hunterston brooch.

INTRODUCTION

Below: A tiny animal, made from beaded gold wire, adorns the front of the Hunterston brooch.

EARLY MEDIEVAL SCOTLAND

XIV

kingship. Broad themes like these tend to be depersonalised – there has been less attention given to how these kinds of issues affected individual people or what objects can tell us about them. Broad themes also tend to be concerned with long-term change. Archaeologists are used to working in terms of centuries because it can be difficult to give a precise date to archaeological remains. Rarely when we look at objects – a brooch or sculpted stone, for instance – do we manage to think in terms of people-sized blocks of time – a childhood, a lifetime, a generation.

And yet we know that objects could carry a vast range of associations and meanings to individuals in the past. In the Anglo-Saxon epic poem *Beowulf*,[2] material objects appear to have many different meanings. In a particularly poignant example, the booty from an old feud is worn by the victors, bringing up old animosity:

> *Then an old spearman will speak while they are drinking,*
> *having glimpsed some heirloom that brings alive*
> *memories of the massacre; his mood will darken*
> *and heart-stricken, in the stress of his emotion,*
> *he will begin to test a young man's temper*
> *and stir up trouble, starting like this:*
> *'now my friend, don't you recognise*
> *your father's sword, his favourite weapon …*
> *… and now here's a son of one or other*
> *of those same killers coming through our hall*
> *overbearing us, mouthing boasts,*
> *and rigged in armour that is by right yours'.*
>
> Beowulf, translated by Seamus Heaney[3]

Elsewhere in the poem, objects act as compensation when someone is killed; they also appear in the context of forging contracts and obligations between people, in forced allegiance, as rewards for loyalty and success, in honouring the dead, as offerings to idols, protection from monsters, indications of foreigners, and as symbols of power, respect, lineage, honour, dignity and regality. We need to remember this potential complexity in the meanings of objects to individuals in the past.

One path towards finding individuals in Early Medieval Scotland is to start by thinking about the concerns that were (and still are) important to people, such as those surrounding everyday life and death – that is, keeping one's family safe, warm, healthy and fed. These concerns were probably a mixture of conscious thoughts and unconscious 'knowledge'. They relate directly to how individuals understood their place in the world: for instance, their beliefs about the natural and the supernatural worlds, or what was needed to protect against demons and to appease the god(s) – and their place in relation to other people around them. In chapter one of this book, individuals will be sought in bodies, dress and protecting objects, in sickness, health and healing, in the sights, sounds and performance of early Christian rituals.

COMMUNITIES

Picts, Scots, Angles and Britons are central to historical accounts of this period, although they are less easy to define archaeologically. Beyond these ethnic groups, Early Medieval Scotland had two distinct types of communities, the secular and the religious. There were, of course, elements of each present in the other. But Christianity was, as far as we can see, the first religion to promote the establishment of communities devoted to religious practice. Over time, this division must have had a considerable impact on the control of land, but much less effect on how it was used.

These secular and religious communities of place were also participants in other, less precisely defined communities that can perhaps be seen as networks. Some of these can only be distinguished and explored effectively through material culture. Not all were new innovations, but rather adaptations of long-standing patterns of behaviour and social organisation.

In chapter two, four such groups are considered – communities of place, craft-workers, the wider world and memory. None of these is restricted to the Early Medieval world. We are all participants in contemporary forms of them.

Place has perhaps the strongest association with community. We often refer to the area where we live as 'our community', although we might find it difficult to define the social and geographical boundaries of that community with any precision. Indeed, we might well feel ourselves to be simultaneously a member of several communities of place – for example, neighbourhood, city, region, country. But how many different communities of place did people in Early Medieval Scotland feel that they belonged to?

The Early Medieval period is, more than most, summoned up for us by the creations of craft-workers. Elaborate metalwork, fine stone sculpture and magnificent illuminated manuscripts are the most evocative features of the time. The makers of these outstanding pieces shared the community of the workshop or *scriptorium*. Yet, as important was their participation in the wider networks that saw styles shared and developed. Through these styles, more intangible identities were promulgated and maintained. The networks that ensured their distribution and use may well have involved travel for the craftsman as much as for his products.

Awareness of the wider world is something we now take for granted. In Early Medieval Scotland it is likely to have been much more restricted, but it was by no means absent. Then, as now, knowledge was probably acquired from descriptions and images rather than through direct experience. For many the wider world may have been no greater than the distance possible in a day's walk from their settlement. For others, particularly merchants and pilgrims, it was a great deal larger. But even those who stayed at home could become aware of other places through unusual objects acquired through trade and exchange. No doubt encounters with objects and travellers provided many opportunities for storytelling involving myth, legend and distortion.

Memory in Early Medieval Scotland, where few were literate, probably had an importance for the communities that we would now find difficult to understand. It was one of the lubricants that enabled the maintenance of social

Below: This beautifully-decorated wooden box, found at Birsay, Orkney, contained the remains of a set of leather-working tools.

Below: This massive chain, made from solid silver, is one of a handful of portable objects that has Pictish symbols.

EARLY MEDIEVAL SCOTLAND

XVIII

life and structure, helping to legitimise the status quo. Most matters would still have relied on unwritten memories for resolution. Among the surviving material culture, there are pieces that were quite consciously created as monuments, and others that as heirlooms came to act as prompts that kept memories alive. But none would have prevented a re-versioning of memory over time.

IDEAS AND IDEOLOGIES

People are full of ideas and always have been. In chapter three, ideology is taken in its broadest sense as the way people communicated their ideas in the past, and consequently the way that we understand those ideas now. Ideas become ideologies when they are put into practice and these are capable of affecting both individuals and communities.

The big topics that have been used to characterise Early Medieval Scotland by archaeologists in the past – such as kingship and conversion to Christianity – can be thought of as ideas and ideologies. These important trends and concepts are derived from the historical record, but what is the material evidence for them? Such important ideas tend to be discussed from a long-term perspective across the entire period and often in an impersonal way, as powerful institutions. Sometimes these concepts are discussed almost as entities in themselves – the big ideas and unseen forces capable of shaping lives on a grand scale and developing over generations. But this runs the risk of distancing the study of Early Medieval Scotland from the material evidence and the people who created it. Archaeological evidence is difficult to link to specific historical events, especially in this period. Instead, each object represents the many voices of all those who could not leave a written historical record – people who nonetheless left their mark in the archaeological record through living, creating, dwelling, destroying and dying in Early Medieval Scotland. Approaching ideas and ideologies by analysing surviving objects will allow us to move away from a depersonalised perspective, and reveal how these concepts can be studied from the things that people created, used, treasured and destroyed.

Writing is a powerful ideological tool for communicating ideas and ideologies, but it is not the only one. We should not prioritise writing over other systems and means of communicating that survive. Art and symbolism feature strongly in chapter three. Pictish symbols were a means of communicating important ideas and one which changed in different contexts. Symbols were co-opted into complex pieces of Christian sculpture, where they feature amongst other types of powerful imagery that conveyed ideas drawn from many different places and times, but which were combined in a way entirely distinct to Early Medieval Scotland. In this context, Pictish symbols might be acting as a kind of script. But it is not just discrete symbols or designs that can act as powerful marks of ideology. Chapter three explores how a particular material – silver – and specific types of objects – such as hand-bells – can act as powerful manifestations of ideas and ideologies. Most important is how these things were used, so that even a sound, like the ring of a hand-bell, can communicate ideas and support ideologies.

Surviving objects can tell us different stories about

Opposite: A silver bowl decorated with a gilded and enamelled mount. It comes from the hoard of objects from St Ninian's Isle, Shetland.

the big ideas of the time and raise many questions that spring from our often partial or simplistic understanding of these issues. It is the how, when, and why objects are used, and the meaning and context of that use that can help us move from objects to ideologies. This approach encourages us to understand what can often seem like ephemeral (but powerful) ideas and ideologies through the real and tangible remains from the past.

A BEGINNING

The purpose of this book is to highlight some of the possibilities provided by archaeological evidence and to make this important period of Scotland's past more familiar, recognisable and appreciated. But in no way are we seeking to be definitive; in many places we highlight areas with both potential and problems. Of the three perspectives presented here, ideologies and ideas – the things that bind society together – has had the most attention in past scholarship, but here we will present some new topics and approaches to it. The other two perspectives, communities and individuals, and especially the latter, have been largely ignored to date, and so here we suggest the potential they provide and some of the themes they can help us explore.

We hope it will set in motion a resurgence of interest in the material culture of the period as a primary source of evidence. It is not an end in itself, but a beginning. It cannot hope to present a definitive picture, if such a thing is possible, but point towards a few new paths to follow.

NOTES

1   Dutton 2004, xviii.
2   Beowulf, translated by Heaney (2002).
3   Beowulf, translated by Heaney (2002), 52, lines 2041 onwards.

Throughout this book, carved stones and sculpture are referred to using the place-name and numbering system (e.g. Meigle 1, Aberlemno 3) developed by Allen and Anderson for their seminal (1903) publication, *The Early Christian Monuments of Scotland*.

*… The flame of God's love dwells in my heart
as a jewel of gold is placed in a silver dish.*

ATTRIBUTED TO ST COLUMBA

EARLY MEDIEVAL SCOTLAND

INDIVIDUALS, COMMUNITIES AND IDEAS

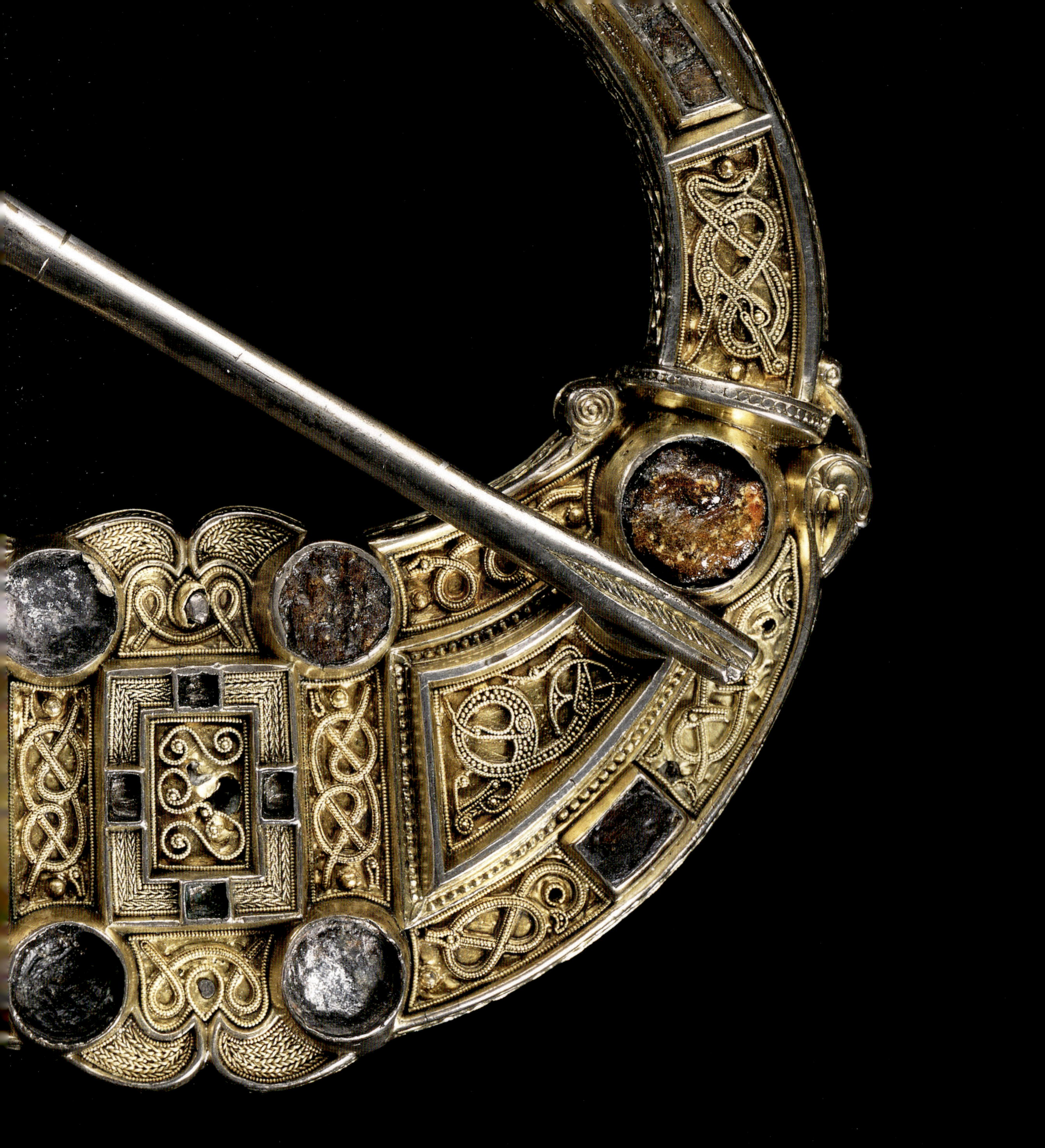

CHAPTER ONE

Individuals

Alice Blackwell

Objects have always been carried, sold, bartered, stolen, retrieved and lost. People have always given gifts. It is how you tell the stories that matters.[1]

★

The Hare with the Amber Eyes: A Hidden Inheritance,
Edmund De Waal, 2010

Some of the most evocative objects, those most easy to associate with people, also happen to be some of the rarest and most fragile – especially those made from organic materials, such as clothes, shoes or handwritten books. Irish bogs have yielded examples of all of these types of objects, in addition to well-preserved bodies (complete with styled hair). In 2006, an incredible discovery was made at Faddan More, County Tipperary in Ireland – a book of Christian psalms, written around AD 800, was carefully excavated from a bog and conserved [FIG. 1.2].[2]

We have a few comparable survivals from Scotland, such as the Orkney hood [1.7] – the sole complete piece of clothing to have survived. Things that were only ever meant to be transient or temporary can also be particularly evocative – for example, scribbles scratched to pass the time on a stone or piece of wood that was later discarded. The Springmount Bog tablets [1.3] from Ireland are a set of wax-filled wooden sheets that, amazingly, preserve two people's handwriting impressed in the wax – perhaps the hands of a pupil and a teacher. Given the fragility and temporary nature of writing on wax, it is breathtaking that these survive.

But we do not need to depend just on these rare and wonderful survivals to begin our approach to people in the past. We can, for example, look at the doodling of pictures and words on slates, explore the private and public meanings of brooches, look at the use of touch to convey the holy power of a reliquary, and ask when *is* a stone not just a stone but a healing relic. It is also helpful to consider what objects felt like to the touch, how they moved, smelled or even tasted. If we let an awareness of the body's senses pervade our thinking, we can better reconstruct how things were used and thought of – and these are still things that

Fig. 1.1 (opposite): A detail of the Hunterston brooch.

Fig. 1.2: Fragments from an early Christian book of Psalms found in 2006 at Faddan More, County Tipperary. The discovery of the manuscript in a peat bog was one of the most significant archaeological finds in Ireland in recent times.

Fig. 1.3: Part of a wax-filled wooden writing tablet from Springmount Bog, Ireland, which preserves the handwriting of an Early Medieval individual.

we can relate to today. Historical sources also provide rich material and can give us evocative glimpses of individuals, such as in writings that tell us about the sick visiting healing shrines.

There is only space here to cover a fraction of what is possible – there are many other opportunities for introducing individuals into Early Medieval Scotland that could be explored by others in the future. I cannot attempt to be definitive or comprehensive, if such a thing is possible. What follows are a few aspects, glimpses of individuals. Partly because of the weight of surviving evidence, but also because of the path my research has taken, much of this chapter concerns Christianity, directly or indirectly.

OTHER PEOPLE'S STORIES

Popular books on Early Medieval Scotland have tended to leave out children and women, and sick, old or otherwise dependent individuals. Even men are usually discussed in the rather limited terms of warriors, kings and clerics, rather than fathers or farmers. Historians are working with a limited number of texts, most of which concern important people and events, and from these sources political histories have been written. There have been few attempts to write a social history of the period, although some written texts – such as the stories of saints' lives – provide rich material. Such sources include accounts of a sick woman being brought by her parents to a healing shrine, as well as a mother and father together bringing a child for healing.[3] They hint at families travelling and acting together in order to protect and aid those most close to them.

Fig. 1.4: A doodle of a chicken scratched onto an Early Medieval slate from Jarlshof, Shetland.

Where women have featured in previous accounts of Early Medieval Scotland, it has usually been in discussions of a believed peculiarity of Pictish society. For a long time, scholars thought that the Picts practised matrilineal inheritance – that is, inheritance running by preference through the female rather than male line. The role of matrilineal inheritance has been downplayed in recent years in any case; far from being the normal means of inheritance, it is now seen simply as one possible strategy available to elites.[4] This brings the Picts in line with other contemporary groups and dispels much of their perceived oddness.

Beyond this, there has been little exploration of attitudes towards sex and gender in Early Medieval Scotland.[5] This is a vast area, where attitudes potentially affect a person's whole conception of the order, relationships and nature within their world. It is an area that is culturally determined, varying across time and space. A few basic questions that could be asked include: what did masculine and feminine mean to people; what things might be imbued with feminine qualities or associations (a cave, a god, a season, or a type of object, for example); and how did this affect how people interacted with places, objects and other people?

> *Sex and gender ... are fundamental categories that cultures use to conceptualise their world and to organise relationships between peoples in it. But we cannot assume that our categories for sex and gender held for prehistoric peoples. Instead, these need to be explicitly brought into our archaeological analyses, if we aim for any sophisticated understanding of prehistoric cultures.*[6]

The same need exists for the Early Medieval period.

How people think about their own body and the bodies of others is one of the most basic and central parts of our view of the world. The body is deeply personal: the body can become sick, and with sickness comes the possibility of death, a most basic human concern. In life, bodily ideals and taboos vary over space and time. How did people think about bodily appearance, or bodily workings, rhythms and substances in the Early Medieval period? For many, death was seen as a threshold to a new life beyond, with the body left behind to be disposed of with respect or without it, to be venerated or to be forgotten. Attitudes towards bodies are important, but they have not yet had the attention they deserve.[7]

How the body is treated in death has the potential to tell us about gender attitudes: at the simplest level, we can ask whether men and women were buried in the same ways?

INDIVIDUALS

Unfortunately, poor bone preservation across much of Scotland, caused by acidic soils, affects our ability to determine the sex and age of skeletal remains. The limited evidence that does survive suggests that women were not excluded from burial rites, and were sometimes buried within the most elaborate and complex types of grave.[8] For instance, an intriguingly-shaped complex of multiple burial cairns at a cemetery at Lundin Links, Fife, only contained adult female burials.[9] This might imply the relative importance of women to Early Medieval society: the loss of a woman, particularly of child-bearing age, could potentially cause significant disruption to the relationships and social obligations within a community. In other words, such a death might adversely affect social cohesion and, in order to avoid this, require a special burial effort on the part of those left behind.[10] This issue requires more work, but burial evidence has the potential to tell us about attitudes towards different genders, ages or life-stages, as well as attitudes towards the body in death.

Dress was an important (although not the only) means of expressing individual and group identities, including gender. This is not, by any means, unique to Scotland during this period – ostentatious display through costume was the norm across Early Medieval Europe. But while we have a rich body of artefacts from Early Medieval Scotland, we lack some of the most basic information concerning how objects were used and by whom. For example, while brooches are among the most elaborate and richly-made dress objects that survive, we do not know whether similar types of brooches were worn by both men and women. This represents a significant problem in understanding gender in the Early Medieval period.

Children have often been left out of the traditional archaeological accounts of Early Medieval Scotland – although this is by no means a problem restricted to this period of our past.[11] Fundamental issues concerning children – including age thresholds at which children were regarded as adult members of society – vary between different cultures and across time. These are vital attitudes towards life, death and age that require further attention. Stories of saints' lives suggest that children as well as adults could be taken to visit a holy shrine for healing. However, burial evidence suggests that children were treated differently in death to adults. Relatively few child burials have been identified in Scotland, in common with other parts of Britain during the Early Medieval period,[12] and indeed during most of prehistory. Given the undoubtedly high infant mortality rate, this absence must be significant. It seems that children were rarely given the same kind of burial as adults.

Excavations at a monastery at Inchmarnock suggested that monastic schooling had taken place on the site and this schooling may well have involved children and young adults.[13] The evidence was in the form of inscribed slates that were apparently used for learning to write and for memorising important Christian texts [1.5].[14] The pupils were practising two types of scripts, Latin and ogham. The slates are rare examples of writing in the everyday hand of learners, and possibly children [1.6].[15] They provide a glimpse of individuals' sketches and doodles perhaps, and one slate might even be the remains of a worktop covered in scribbles by the pupils who used it – the Early Medieval equivalent of a graffiti-covered school desk?

Fig. 1.5 (above): An Early Medieval writing practice preserved on a slate from the monastic site of Inchmarnock, lying off the coast of the Isle of Bute.

Fig. 1.6 (below): Horses and riders, perhaps drawn by a child, on a slate from Inchmarnock.

DRESSED BODIES

Specked, specked, Dinogad's coat,
I fashioned it from pelts of stoat.
Twit, twit, a twittering,
I sang, and so eight slaves would sing.
When your daddy went off to hunt,
Spear on his shoulder, club in his hand,
He'd call the hounds so swift of foot:
'Giff, Gaff – seek 'im, seek 'im; fetch, fetch …

Anonymous lullaby, 7th century[16]

People clothed their own bodies and would be immediately aware of the clothed appearance of the other people they interacted with on a daily basis. Personal dress objects constitute a major part of the surviving material culture from Early Medieval Scotland. This is not unique to Scotland, but it makes clear that, at this time, significant attention and resources were devoted to personal appearance. Dress may be used to make statements about the wearer, although it is not the only way, of course: people might also express their identity, allegiance, ideas or memories in the use of domestic space for instance, or in how they behave.

There are very few surviving Early Medieval clothes because of the fragility of organic textiles. Some limited textile remains survive on the reverse of objects because of the way the surrounding metal has corroded. These tell us more about the types of fabrics used than the clothes they were made into. However, in 1867 a unique discovery was made – a small woven fabric hood was found in a bog in Orkney.[17] This hood [1.7] has been radiocarbon dated to some time between AD 250–615 and is the only piece of

INDIVIDUALS

Fig. 1.7 (left): The Orkney hood, found in peat bog in 1867, is the only complete item of fabric clothing to have survived from Early Medieval Scotland.

Fig. 1.8 (below): Several gaming pieces, like this example from Mail, Shetland, preserve hints of faces from the past.

clothing (aside from shoes) to have survived intact from Early Medieval Scotland.[18] It gives us a fascinating insight into the type of clothes made and worn. Recent study of the hood, combined with the making of a replica version, suggests that it is a very significant object for another reason – because it was intended for a child.[19] The hood was very carefully made from several different recycled pieces of fabric, one of which was of an amazing quality and fineness. The fabric was old but cherished, and care was taken to make good small deficiencies resulting from this re-use.

There are more surviving leather remains: many are scraps, but several complete and near-complete shoes also survive. Shoes today have come to have powerful associations.[20] Unlike other clothing, shoes keep their shape when they are not worn, and this must be a big part of why they 'often stand for something not physically present'.[21] Of course, it is actually *someone* rather than *something* that they bring to mind. A complete and matching pair of leather shoes radiocarbon dated to the 5th–9th centuries[22] is a very unusual and poignant survival [1.9]. Shoe fragments of a similar design were excavated from the crannog at Buiston in Ayrshire.[23] This was not the only type of shoe made during the period – different designs survive from Iona, Argyll, and Dowalton Loch in Dumfries and Galloway, and a highly decorated shoe was excavated from the fort at Dundurn, Perth and Kinross.[24]

Pictures drawn, carved or scratched onto other objects can give us valuable glimpses of people from the past. Some of the images demonstrate exotic influences or particular conventions in the depiction of some figures. These may be idealised and might not always tell us about how people

Fig. 1.9 (below): The unique and poignant survival of a pair of Early Medieval shoes from an unknown location in Scotland.

Fig. 1.10 (right): A portrait of a man scratched onto a slate, from Jarlshof, Shetland.

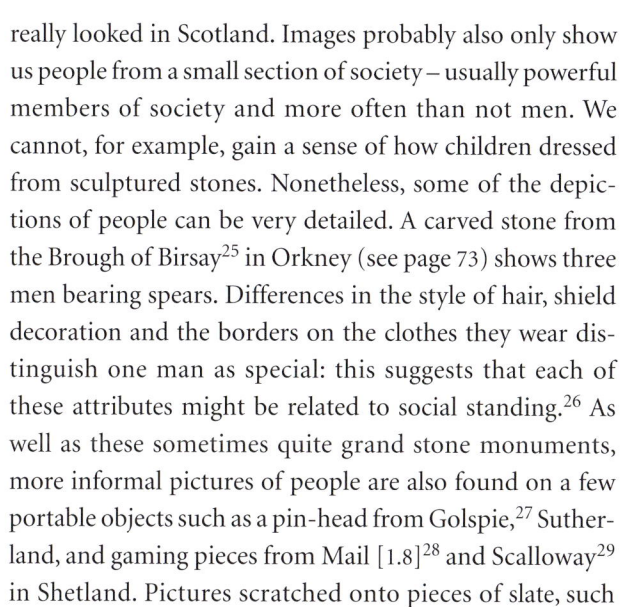

really looked in Scotland. Images probably also only show us people from a small section of society – usually powerful members of society and more often than not men. We cannot, for example, gain a sense of how children dressed from sculptured stones. Nonetheless, some of the depictions of people can be very detailed. A carved stone from the Brough of Birsay[25] in Orkney (see page 73) shows three men bearing spears. Differences in the style of hair, shield decoration and the borders on the clothes they wear distinguish one man as special: this suggests that each of these attributes might be related to social standing.[26] As well as these sometimes quite grand stone monuments, more informal pictures of people are also found on a few portable objects such as a pin-head from Golspie,[27] Sutherland, and gaming pieces from Mail [1.8][28] and Scalloway[29] in Shetland. Pictures scratched onto pieces of slate, such as a portrait of a bearded man with curly hair from Jarlshof,[30] Shetland [1.10], provide an impression of informality more akin to a quick sketch. Some may have been carved by children.

The Pictish sculptured stones show quite a wide variety of styles of clothing, including long and short tunics, long and short cloaks and short trousers for men, flowing robes for a woman on the Hilton of Cadboll[31] stone, and a shawl over a tunic for a female figure on a stone from Wester Denoon.[32] Some of these garments are plain, while others have decorated borders or fringes, or carved decoration suggesting patterned fabric. Despite these depictions on sculptured stones, the lack of surviving textile remains leaves us with a huge gap in our picture of the people of Early Medieval Scotland. First, we lack a sense of the range of types of clothes worn, for instance, by women of every

INDIVIDUALS

Fig. 1.11 (below): A type of dress accessory called a latchet fastener which was unique to Early Medieval Ireland.

Fig. 1.12 (opposite): Massive solid silver chains are only found in Early Medieval Scotland.

background, social status and age. Second, we have very little information about the colour of clothes. We know colour symbolism was important during the Early Medieval period – for example, clothes in purple were reserved for royalty (earthly or divine)[33] – but beyond this we know little about how colour and colour symbolism was used in everyday clothing. Colour can be a bold statement, read instantly rather than contemplated at close range in the way that details on a brooch might be, for instance. 'Colours can be a compelling, exact and calculated medium for producing and reproducing power and for transmitting knowledge.'[34] Colours may also be imbued with a quality or 'spirit' that is obtained by those using (or wearing) them.

More plentiful than the survivals of cloth and clothing are those of the objects used to fasten and to ornament clothing. The range of dress objects found in Early Medieval Scotland includes some kinds of objects that were found across Britain and Ireland at this time, as well as some that are unique to Scotland. For instance, certain types of brooches and pins are found in Scotland, Ireland and England, whereas massive silver chains are only known from Scotland [1.12]. Scotland is not unusual in having this mix of shared and unique types of objects – similarly there are objects such as lachet fasteners [1.11] that are really only known from Ireland.

Who designed and made dress objects is a fundamentally important question for archaeologists. If we attempt to read the meaning or significance of objects on the basis of their shape, material or decoration, then we need to ask who made these choices? Was the eventual wearer of a brooch free to specify what size or decoration they wanted, or would the repertoire of the maker dictate what was possible? Were some designs, materials or types of brooch reserved for certain people – kings or princesses, perhaps, or church leaders? Was the production of objects such as brooches controlled centrally by a powerful figure – a local lord or king – and did he dictate the designs of objects made for his followers?

The question of how the production of metal objects was organised during the Early Medieval period remains debated. Archaeologists excavating high-status centres of power have found quantities of metalworking evidence, such as moulds for the casting of objects like brooches. This suggests that the production of metal objects was controlled – restricted to those power centres, from which the resulting objects would be redistributed to those people loyal to the centre. This is a form of gift-giving where the bestowing of a precious object creates a bond of allegiance or obligation, binding the recipient to the giver. However, recent work has identified more evidence for metalworking on lower status sites than had previously been appreciated.[35] This sheds some doubt on the extent to which

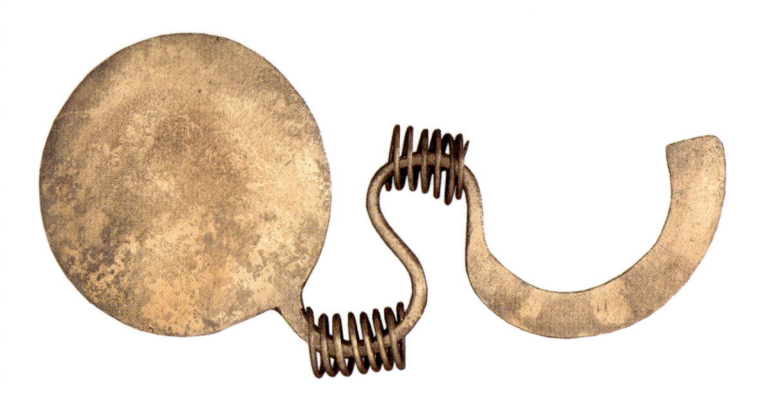

EARLY MEDIEVAL SCOTLAND

10

INDIVIDUALS

11

Fig. 1.13: The design of an elaborate brooch, like that from Hunterston, has been sketched out on a slate from the Early Medieval fort at Dunadd, Argyll.

Fig. 1.14: A detail of the back of the Hunterston brooch, found in Ayrshire, which features both old spiral designs and newer interlace decoration.

Fig. 1.15 (opposite): The massive silver chain from Whitecleugh, Lanarkshire. While the chains were likely to have been worn around the neck, the diameter of surviving examples suggests that they were intended for adolescents or women.

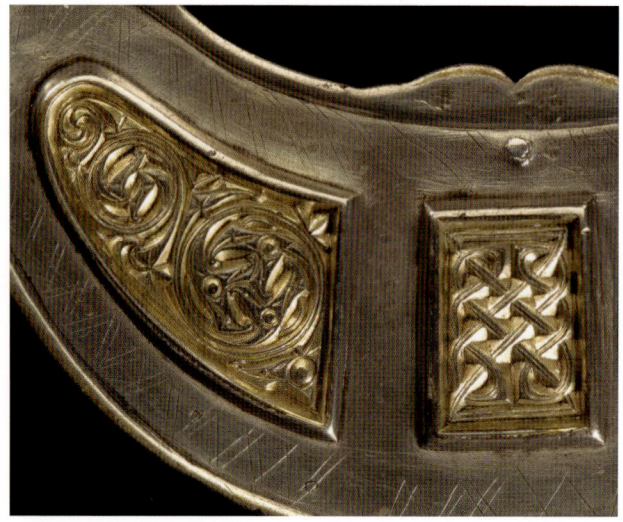

metalworking was controlled – it may be that different types of sites were producing objects such as brooches, or that the organisation of metalworking varied between regions.

We have very limited information about how most personal dress objects were used and by whom. In Early Medieval England and across much of Europe, people often chose to bury a wide variety of objects in the grave with their dead. This means that for these areas we can begin to assess the conventions that governed dress – what types of clothes and objects were worn by women, for example, and how and where on the body they were used. In Scotland, people were very rarely buried with objects, thus we lack this important type of evidence for the use of objects.

There is another side to this difference in burial traditions. In areas following Anglo-Saxon burial customs, a large number of objects would be committed to the ground with the body for burial, effectively removing them from circulation. In Scotland, objects were not routinely disposed of in this way. Unless they were specially put out of use – buried as part of a hoard or thrown into a river or lake perhaps – the vast majority of personal possessions would have been available to be given away to family or members of the community upon the death of the owner. These objects might be kept by their new owners, or recycled (in the case of metal objects, melted down and made into new objects). If they were kept, this type of burial tradition means that there would be a great potential for the circulation of 'old' objects in Early Medieval society.

This has broad implications: for example, in the role of objects in the creation and maintenance of memories, a role more often associated with written documents. Objects could be used to keep memories of the dead alive, such as their acts in life and rights to land. Elsewhere in Britain and

EARLY MEDIEVAL SCOTLAND

Europe where more written documents survive, wills record the giving of gifts to churches to preserve the memory of particular (important) individuals.[36] Objects could also play an active role in justifying the status or rights of their new owners. The maintaining of old objects in circulation would keep old motifs and types of object alive and mean that they were available to be copied, imitated and changed, then applied in turn to new objects. This might explain how some very old motifs, such as triskele spirals, came to be combined with newer designs like interlace and entwined animals in Early Medieval art [1.14]. We need to bear this in mind when dating objects, and when using what might be very old objects by the time they were buried to date archaeological sites.

The extent to which we do not understand who wore some of the most important Early Medieval objects is underlined by the group of massive silver chains [1.12, 1.15]. Clearly these were hugely important objects, using the greatest weight of silver (several kilograms in each case) of any object from the period. It would be tempting to associate them with important kings or warriors recorded in historical sources. However, if we are right in thinking that these chains were worn around the neck, the small diameter of some of the most complete examples suggests that they were intended to be worn by women or adolescents.[37] These must have been extremely valuable objects. If the silver chains were handed down as heirlooms, they would be likely to require alteration to fit the neck of the new wearer, either by the addition or removal of rings. While technically possible, the method of manufacture means that this is not a simple task and none of the surviving rings appears to show the kinds of strain that this would inflict.[38]

INDIVIDUALS

Fig. 1.16 (left): Glass beads from an Anglo-Saxon grave at Hound Point, Dalmeny, City of Edinburgh. Part of the rim from a Roman glass vessel has been re-used and worn alongside the beads.

Figs 1.17 (below): Two silver coins, pierced so they could be worn as pendants, from the hoard of Early Medieval metalwork and beads from Croy, Inverness-shire.

Glass beads are sometimes found during excavations at Early Medieval sites in Scotland, but again we have very little evidence to tell us how they were used. Some of the most distinctive beads seem to have been imported, possibly from Continental Europe or Anglo-Saxon England. In Anglo-Saxon graves, beads are usually found in female burials, worn around the neck or strung between brooches. An Anglo-Saxon burial from near Dalmeny, City of Edinburgh, included a group of different coloured glass beads [1.16].[39] Most burials from Scotland do not include objects and so we do not know how popular the wearing of necklaces was. Beads can be used in many different ways – they might be sewn onto clothes or attached to boats, buildings or weapons for good luck. Unlike brooches, no beads appear on the depictions of people on Early Medieval Scottish sculpture (perhaps not surprising, given their size). Nor does there appear to be any evidence about the use of beads within surviving Irish text sources.

What might beads have meant to those who saw and owned them? It has been suggested that Anglo-Saxons regarded their beads as amulets with protective properties.[40] As well as glass, beads were also made from natural materials such as rock crystal and amber. There is a reference within the heroic poem *The Gododdin* to a warrior winning amber 'beads', although the word in question has also been translated more generally as amber 'jewellery'.[41] *The Gododdin* is a text that contains many references to the appropriate activities and properties of warriors, and the mention of amber suggests that objects made from it may have been endowed with elite martial significance. The electrostatic properties of amber may have been significant in this context. Other objects could also be used as pendants, such as coins with holes for suspension, as in a hoard from Croy, Inverness-shire [1.17].[42] These might be worn alone or in combination with beads, such as in the Dalmeny necklace which included a re-used glass vessel rim.

While there seems to have been conventions in the composition of Anglo-Saxon bead strings, the opportunity to combine an array of different coloured, shaped and patterned beads offers some scope for expressions of individuality. It is interesting to ask whether beads were collected over someone's lifetime, with different beads carrying associations with varying stages of life, social positions and relationships; or whether a string of beads, and perhaps any associations it carried, was acquired in a single act. Given that each bead is a single object, necklaces can easily be broken down and turned into something quite different, providing significant scope for re-use in various ways. As a result, beads might be seen as more flexible than decorated metalwork and perhaps more readily translatable across social, cultural or political boundaries.

EARLY MEDIEVAL SCOTLAND

BROOCHES: PUBLIC AND PRIVATE

We can use one type of object – brooches – to explore the range of potential personal dimensions to Early Medieval artefacts. Brooches have come to dominate study of Early Medieval metalwork in Scotland. This is partly because of the numbers that survive, and partly because they are richly decorated, attractive objects to work with. Brooches could be used to fasten clothes in place of modern buttons or zips, or worn simply to embellish clothing. Brooches vary greatly in size and robustness: while some may have been suited to the fastening of a heavy cloak, others are too large or too small to have been used realistically in this practical way. For example, the Hunterston brooch,[43] as well as being very large, weighs 325 grams – a heavy weight perhaps for fabric to support.

A penannular, or horse-shoe shaped brooch is a very effective clothes fastener. The wearer would thread the pin through the fabric, then pass the pin through the gap in the terminals and swivel the brooch to hold the pin in place.[44] At some point this design of brooch was modified and the gap between the terminals of some brooches was closed by adding a panel, as on the Hunterston brooch [1.19]. This fundamentally changed how the brooch worked, although the visual resemblance to penannular brooches remains. Once the gap has been closed, the brooch is essentially a pin with a large head which no longer plays an active role in securing the brooch in place. But why change the design so as to sacrifice an effective fastener for one that was more awkward? Other means of securing seem to have been needed to compensate – these include metal chains and places for sewing the brooch onto the fabric. The Tara brooch from Ireland[45] has several alternative means of fastening, although these are lacking on the Hunterston brooch. Was the Hunterston brooch made to be worn or was it an object to be handled? No wholly satisfactory suggestions as to why the gap was closed on some brooches have been made.[46]

We can look at brooches from several different, though inextricably linked, points of view: from an outward or public-facing perspective, looking at how objects like brooches were used to express a person's place in the world; and from an inward-facing or private perspective, looking at the meanings brooches had for those who wore them.

WHO WORE BROOCHES?

Before we can begin to approach what brooches meant, we need to ask who wore them. One owner of the Hunterston brooch incised their name on the back. This person owned the brooch when it was already an old object. Scandinavian runes were used to spell out a Celtic personal name, *Malbriþa*, and the most likely reading of the runic text is the formula '*Malbriþa* owns this brooch' [1.20].[47] The spare space around the runic inscription has been filled with further rune-like decoration, perhaps a deliberate decision to leave no space for others to write their names and claim ownership of the precious object.[48] In this respect the Hunterston brooch is very unusual; normally we have no direct indication of who wore or owned a particular brooch. It acts as a reminder that objects might have very long use-lives – that is, be owned by many people over a long period of time. Brooches might be hereditary objects,

Figs 1.18 (left) and 1.19 (below): Two brooches shown at actual size illustrate the spectrum of scales of brooch worn in the Early Medieval period – the tiny brooch from Castlehill, Ayrshire (left) and the massive Hunterston brooch (below). The elaborate silver brooch with gold and amber decoration from Hunterston, Ayrshire, is at the other end of the scale of surviving brooches

EARLY MEDIEVAL SCOTLAND

16

Fig. 1.20: Unlike many Early Medieval brooches, even the back of the Hunterston brooch is decorated with intricate designs. In the spaces between, Scandinavian runes spell out the name of one owner of the brooch.

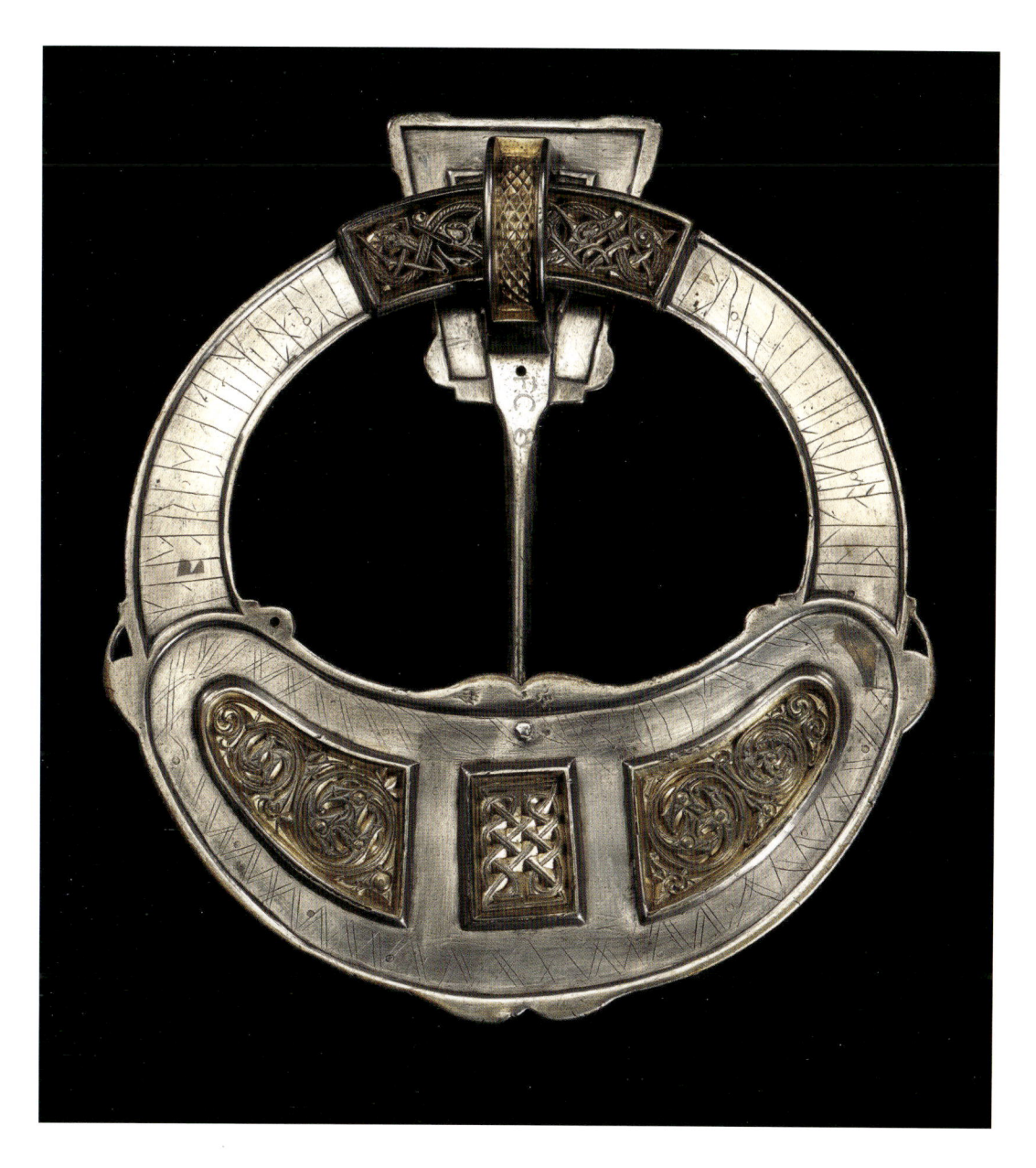

INDIVIDUALS

Fig. 1.21: An important figure, often identified as a woman, faces the viewer of the Hilton of Cadboll cross-slab. Although the stone is now very worn, it is still possible to make out a penannular brooch worn on the figure's chest.

handed down through generations,[49] and they might mean different things to each of these people. This multiple use of objects can be described as an artefact's biography. The biographies of many objects are lost to us and we cannot get to the specific individual(s) who wore or used artefacts. But worse than this, we also lack even a basic understanding of the sort of person who might have worn them.

Were brooches worn by both men and women? If so, were different types worn by each gender? Or were the same types of brooches worn by men and women, but in a different way perhaps – on different parts of the body, for instance, or with different clothes? Even in the rare case where we have a named owner of a brooch, we cannot be sure whether the *Malbriþa* who at one time owned the Hunterston brooch was a man or a woman – the name could be appropriate for either sex. Outside Scotland there were different customs for brooch-wearing. In Anglo-Saxon England, brooches were worn by women and not by men. Irish written sources tell us that brooches were worn there by both sexes, but that they were to be worn in different ways – by men on their shoulder and by women on the centre of their chest.[50]

Unfortunately we lack equivalent text sources or burial evidence to tell us about the wearing of brooches in Scotland, although archaeologists have tended to assume that brooches were worn by both sexes. However, we do have some evidence in the form of a handful of images of people shown wearing brooches. These were carved on Christian sculptured stones and have usually been identified as women by archaeologists and art historians. On the Hilton of Cadboll cross-slab, a person in flowing robes fastened by a centrally-placed brooch, and with carefully depicted long hair, rides sideways on a horse [1.21]. The identity of this person is a matter of debate. Is it a secular figure, an important Pictish woman, perhaps even a queen, out watching elite society hunting deer nearby? Or is this religious symbolism invoking the Virgin Mary?[51] On a sculptured stone from Kirriemuir, a person is seated next to what is probably a loom. This figure too has been suggested to be the Virgin Mary, with the loom referencing her association in biblical writing with the spinning of thread. This is, however, a rare type of iconography typically not found until the later Medieval period.[52] In the *Book of Kells*, a set of intricate illuminated gospels probably made at Iona around AD 800, the Virgin Mary wears a diamond-shaped brooch [1.22].[53]

While we have tended to assume that brooches were worn by both sexes, the limited evidence from Scotland (in contrast to that from Ireland) all appears to concern

EARLY MEDIEVAL SCOTLAND

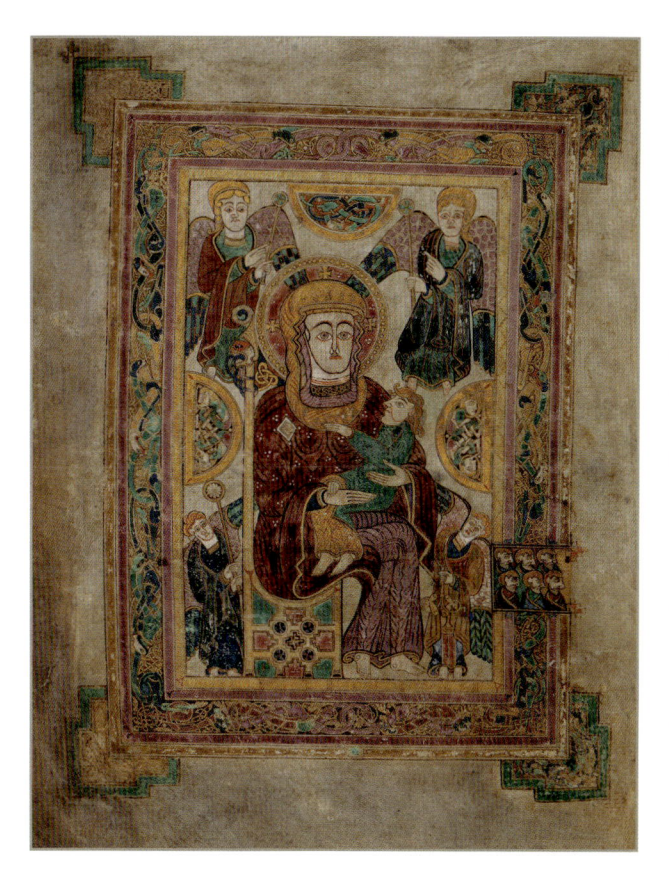

Fig. 1.22: In the *Book of Kells*, the Virgin Mary wears a lozenge-shaped brooch on the right side of her chest.

women, and perhaps specifically the Virgin Mary, wearing brooches.[54] Were men simply not shown wearing brooches (in these Christian contexts), or does this lack of depictions reflect the reality of who wore brooches in Scotland? Had brooches become an artistic convention, perhaps representing Early Medieval ideals of female gender or virtues associated with the Virgin Mary? If so, then brooches could be seen as having a role in projecting gendered identities.

PUBLIC: EXPRESSING YOUR PLACE IN THE WORLD

Gender is not the only way in which objects like brooches might be used to express a person's place in the world. In the past, archaeologists have tended to regard brooches in rather a one-dimensional way as relatively straightforward emblems of power and social standing.[55] The wearing of brooches to indicate status originated in the Roman period where they could signify the rank or office that an individual held.[56] Written sources from Ireland describe rules for *who* was entitled to wear various types of brooches: gold with gems for the sons of the kings of Ireland, silver for the sons of kings of territories.[57] However, this text is idealised – painting a picture of the way things should be rather than necessarily how they were in practice – and may in fact date to the 11th or 12th century.[58]

It would be simplistic to 'read off' someone's social standing from the nature of their brooch, as if it were part of a formal uniform. Brooches (and other objects) cannot be read as a crystallization of someone's identity, or an aspect of it such as their gender, social rank or ethnicity. They might be able to tell us about aspects of someone's identity, but they are unlikely to be used in the same way as badges. In any case, it is highly possible that people could own multiple brooches. An Irish text suggests that even a King of Tara could wear a small brooch for everyday use.[59] The king met his bride on a journey and said to her, 'You shall have this little brooch', which she accepted as her sole bride-price.[60] The message that a small brooch (though owned and worn by a king) gave about his status, would have been very different to a grand brooch on the scale of the Hunterston brooch, for example, which might perhaps be worn only on special occasions.

Much has been written on the importance of gift-giving in creating and maintaining social hierarchy, that is keeping society together and functioning. In this system a

INDIVIDUALS

EARLY MEDIEVAL SCOTLAND

Fig. 1.23 (opposite): Two silver brooches from Rogart, Sutherland. They were part of a hoard of Early Medieval objects found in 1868 which was mostly destroyed.

gift would be given in order to create an obligation on the person who received it – they would be expected in some way to support or to help the person who gave the gift. If brooches were given as gifts, then this complicates how we interpret them. Rather than simply reflect how rich the wearer of the brooch was, in this case the brooch would tell us more about the wealth of the person who *gave* them the brooch, or perhaps about how much that person valued the obligation and relationship that the gift created. Might the literal weight and value of a gifted brooch correspond to the weight of expectation, or the burden of obligation, that resulted from the giving? The recipient of the gift might be proud of this relationship and want to wear the brooch to publicise it, or they might be reluctantly bound by it. In either case, in gift-giving, objects like brooches tell us as much about the social relationships between people as the social status of the owner.

If brooches were involved in expressing social rank or status, then we might well expect them to be handed down through the generations. If so, possession of the brooch could demonstrate the legitimacy of the future owners to occupy the previous person's rank or status, or it could create chains of dependency with future generations inheriting obligations that were represented by the brooch. Alternatively, obligations and social standing might not be transferable: in some cases objects might be returned upon the death of the recipient, symbolically reflecting a release from obligation. New relationships and obligations might need to be established – those who are left after a person died would need to revise their relationships to each other.

Can we suggest specific occasions where gifts might be given, either to create obligations or to cement a verbal pledge or action? Previously there has been an emphasis on the gift-giving between kings and their followers. However, beyond this, an obvious occasion for the giving of gifts in order to create or represent relationships is on the occasion of a marriage. Work on Anglo-Saxon England suggests that there the groom had to pledge a substantial sum, a bride-price, and that the bride received a 'morning-gift' from the bridegroom the morning after the consummation of the marriage.[61] Irish texts refer specifically to the use of brooches as part of a bride-price.[62] Gifts could both symbolise the relationship between the bride and groom – the equivalent of modern wedding rings – but also the wider relationships established between the two halves of the new family. In times when marriages could be politically motivated, the linking of the wider families was of prime importance. An Irish story implies the dishonourable nature of a marriage where the bride-price, in this case a small brooch given by the King of Tara, was accepted by the bride without consulting the families involved.[63] This should warn us that convention may be discounted and that we might expect illicit gifts and relationships to be represented among archaeological remains.

The use of brooches to cement a relationship through marriage is not very different to the use of brooches in gift-giving to cement a relationship between a lord and follower. Irish texts also tell us that brooches could play a legal role, in acting as surety or guarantee for verbal pledges.[64] In this context, brooches were again used to cement an invisible obligation or a relationship between people. The brooch would be temporarily handed over and held as surety until the obligation or pledge had been fulfilled, at which time it would be returned to its owner.

INDIVIDUALS

The words for brooches often had double meanings in Irish and Anglo-Saxon written sources – literally they meant things like stake, nail, sharp end or thorn – but these were a symbolic reference to the sharpness of brooch pins.[65] In a literal sense, brooches fasten clothes together. But did this literal fastening also carry symbolic significance, the symbolic fastening of people together, perhaps at marriage or in other obligation-based relationships created through the giving of brooches? Penannular brooches were cast in clay moulds, and there are a few examples, including two brooches from the St Ninian's Isle hoard, where different brooches appear sufficiently similar to each other to suggest that one may have been used as the model for making the mould to cast the second. Might this strategy be used to reflect social dependence of the owner of one brooch on the owner of the second?[66]

Rather than see brooches as straightforward statements about the wearer's social rank – their power and wealth, perhaps – a more nuanced interpretation is that they may represent relationships, for instance between lord and follower, father and son, or husband and wife. A broader community may or may not 'read' these relationships from a brooch (they might instead reduce its meaning to social status, for example), but to the individuals involved the objects could represent their most important social relationships and ultimately their place in the community and society around them. There might also be an inward-facing dimension in this respect – in this context, objects such as brooches would provide physical proof of invisible relationships and social position.

PRIVATE: PROTECTING YOUR PLACE IN THE WORLD

While brooches have usually been seen from a public point of view – as public statements about social standing – there are hints that elements of brooch design might have had a different intention.[67] In the Early Medieval period, some types of objects, inscriptions and motifs were believed to protect from ill luck, spiritual or bodily harm, or indeed to undo their negative effects, that is to heal.[68] For example, on Anglo-Saxon shields particular types of ornamental mount were added in order to increase the protective ability of what was itself essentially a protective object. Could Early Medieval brooches have had protective qualities?[69] One use of brooches was probably to fasten cloaks – an outermost, protective garment. Might brooches have assumed some kind of symbolic significance from the fastening of cloaks, drawing on the garment's ability to hide – literally to cloak – and to protect? No surviving brooches have protective inscriptions, but ornament orientated towards, or sized appropriately for, the brooch wearer rather than a wider audience, might be protective[70] – as might some specific types of decoration.

The belief in the ability of complicated or never-ending designs such as knots and knotwork to catch or divert malign forces seems to have been very long-lived.[71] Both plain interlace and interlacing beasts are prominent among Early Medieval decoration, especially that on brooches, and it might be that they played a protective function. Some brooches feature such minute detail – particularly very fine filigree decoration in the shape of interlace or entwined animals – that it would not be possible for a viewer to

Fig. 1.24 (left): The back of the Hunterston brooch features interlace or knotwork decoration which may have been believed to hold protective qualities.

Fig. 1.25 (right): The scale of the intricate decoration on the front of the Hunterston brooch might suggest that it was intended for the wearer of the brooch rather than to be appreciated by others.

Fig. 1.26 (below): Spiral designs, already old by the time they appear on Early Medieval objects, are found on the back of the Hunterston brooch, as well as on other similar large brooches. They may have had protective attributes or other associations that required they be kept out of full view.

INDIVIDUALS

23

Fig. 1.27 (opposite): One of the twelve brooches from the St Ninian's Isle hoard, Shetland, features the heads of two animals that bare their teeth at each other, joined together by the brooch hoop.

appreciate it unless they were themselves handling the brooch. Given the role of brooches in pledges, it is possible that this is an occasion when the fineness of brooch decoration could be appreciated in this way. However, an alternative interpretation might be that it was more important for the decoration to be *on* the brooch than for it to be *seen by others* to be on the brooch. If they had protective qualities, then the presence of knotted designs would be more important than whether other people could see them easily. From a practical point of view, the smaller the size of the knotwork, the more could be fitted onto the surface of the brooch. The smaller the size of the interlace designs, the more difficult they are visually to untangle – perhaps this also made it more difficult for malign influences to escape, thus increasing its protective efficacy?

A number of brooches also have decorated backs, which would not be visible when worn. This may be another example – like the extreme fineness of filigree decoration – of features intended to be seen when a brooch was being handled, such as if it were used as a pledge. But again, perhaps the sheer presence of the decoration was more important than its visibility. Indeed, if this hidden decoration had protective qualities, then they might actually have been increased by being on the back of the brooch, for when worn the decorated back would be in physical contact with the person wearing the brooch. Was this perhaps thought to be more potent than protection on the front outward-facing surface of a brooch?

On the largest and most elaborate brooches – the Hunterston [1.19, 1.20] and Tara examples – the types of decoration on the back are different to those on the front. On the reverse are spiral-based designs [1.26], already very old motifs by the time the brooches were made, with roots stretching back into Iron Age art. This type of decoration does not occur on the front of penannular brooches, where instead interlace is most common, sometimes combined with animals. Were the spiral designs an old type of protection that was kept hidden from most eyes? If so, why was it appropriate to use spiral designs to decorate a Christian carved stone monument or illuminated manuscript? Many examples of this use of spiral designs exist, and it is not clear why they were not used on the fronts of brooches.

Like many of the more practically sized brooches, the backs of the examples from the St Ninian's Isle hoard are not decorated. However, several examples feature very light scribbles.[72] They are rare and informal additions to metalwork objects that have the look of doodles. They resemble a very rough example of an interlace knot, but are unfinished and too poorly drawn to be a trialling of motifs used on the front of the brooch – in any case, the basic decoration would have already been cast into the front of the brooch by the time the scribbles were made on the back. They might perhaps be a type of maker's mark, but they are barely visible and seem to be very inexpertly made. Or perhaps the person had seen more elaborate brooches with formal decoration on their backs and wished to emulate it. However, the quality and faintness of the scratched designs suggest that they are not primarily an aesthetic creation.

Perhaps, as with the very fine filigree interlace and animals, and the formally decorated backs of brooches, the presence of the interlace scribbles was more important than their visual appreciation. Could they be an attempt by the brooch owner to increase the protective power of the brooch?

A few penannular brooches, like one of the examples from the St Ninian's Isle hoard [1.27], have animal heads for terminals. Elsewhere in Early Medieval Europe, animal motifs could have protective qualities, partly explained by their association with different pagan gods and later with Christian stories, characters and attributes.[73] Penannular brooches with animal-head terminals can be 'read' as a two-headed animal, the two heads joined by a single body formed by the brooch hoop. The two-headed beast motif seems to have had protective qualities. It appears, for example, on the Anglo-Saxon Franks casket in scenes featuring the defence of buildings and their occupants.[74] Two inward-facing beasts' heads joined by a single body adorn the roofs of house-shaped reliquary caskets such as the Monymusk reliquary (pages 36–42).[75] A newly-identified reliquary roof-mount has a particularly fierce pair of joined animal heads [1.29].[76] The animals are bearing their teeth, some of which are fang-like. Are they preparing to defend the holy contents of the reliquary?

The St Ninian's Isle sword chapes,[77] U-shaped mounts attached to the bottom of a sword scabbard, are also formed from two inward-facing animal heads joined by a single curved body, producing a very similar effect to the animal-head penannular brooch. The function of sword chapes was to protect the scabbard from the tip of the weapon it contained, while the scabbard in turn protected the weapon inside. Ultimately, the weapon itself can be seen as a protective object. It is particularly appropriate that the chapes take the shape of the protective two-headed animal motif. One of the chapes [1.28][78] has a protective Christian inscription[79] which has been translated as 'in the name of God the highest', and continuing on the other side of the mount, 'property of the son of the holy spirit'. The inscription is orientated so that the wearer of the chape

Fig. 1.28: One of a pair of sword chapes – mounts that protect a leather scabbard from the point of a sword – incorporating vicious animal heads from the St Ninian's Isle hoard. This chape carries a protective Christian inscription.

Fig. 1.29: A pair of opposed beast heads on a mount from an early Christian reliquary give the impression of protecting the holy contents within.

can glance down to read it; for anyone else, the writing would be upside-down. The inscription on the front of the chape should have been protected from casual wear, against clothes for instance, by three raised bosses placed in the middle and at either end of the phrase. However, this is not the case – the inscription here is very worn. One possible explanation is that it was caused by the wearer of the chape touching the sacred words for luck or protection.

While there are relatively few animal-shaped brooches such as the example from St Ninian's Isle [1.27], some brooches appear to echo them by integrating abstract beasts into their shape and design. The placement of decorative amber insets on the Hunterston brooch [1.30, 1.31] and on the Dunbeath brooch terminal, for example, follows the placement of the major features, the eyes, ears and curled lips, of the beast on the St Ninian's Isle animal brooch. The Dunbeath brooch terminal features a tiny beast made from gold filigree on the brooch hoop, immediately adjacent to the terminal. The design of the beast's head can be seen as an explicit version of the hidden beast inherent in the design of the brooch terminal. What have usually been interpreted as very stylised eagles heads (consisting of an eye and beak) on the Hunterston brooch might also be intended to bring to mind the prominent teeth of the St Ninian's Isle brooches and sword chapes. The shape of the panel in the middle of each terminal simulates the shape of the open jaws of beasts on the chapes. On the Hunterston brooch, the gap between the two brooch terminals has

EARLY MEDIEVAL SCOTLAND

26

Fig. 1.30: The design of the Hunterston brooch features a hidden pair of beast heads which reach towards (perhaps striving to bite) a small rectangular panel. This panel originally had four small gems forming a Christian cross motif.

Fig. 1.31: The beasts hidden in the decoration of the Hunterston brooch are picked out by the amber settings. They have a rectangular eye, circles marking the top and bottom of a gaping jaw and a large circular piece of amber at the cheek.

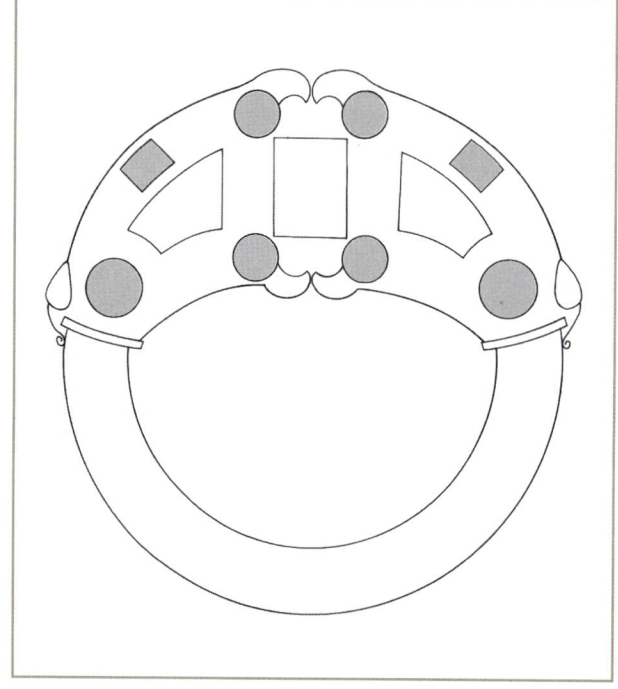

been closed by a rectangular panel, which the hidden animal-shaped terminals might be biting. Several ring-headed pins – such as an example from Armoy, Ireland, and a fragmentary example from Birnie, Moray – have pairs of opposed animals that reach to bite a shape between them. Are these explicit versions of the inherent design of brooches such as Hunterston?

Aside from the hidden animal heads in the design of brooch terminals, the Hunterston brooch features a menagerie of tiny beasts made from gold filigree. They form a kind of procession, flanking a cross created by the (now missing) gems set in the rectangular panel.[80] There are also similarities with the collections of filigree animals on church objects, such as the Derrynaflan chalice from Ireland. The birds, beasts, and snakes with fish tails on the Hunterston brooch might be identified with the creatures of Genesis, the three orders of living creatures – on land, sea and air – that surround Christ.[81] This might seem very subtle and perhaps far-fetched, but much Christian symbolism on metalwork from the Early Medieval period is similarly subtle or hidden. Even explicitly Christian objects – such as the Monymusk reliquary – do not feature obvious Christian symbolism. It is there, although subtle, in the cross hidden inside a knotwork panel, and in the arrangement of decorative mounts on the box and lid in the shape of a cross, and in groups of three recalling the Christian Trinity [1.45, 1.46].

In common with objects like the Monymusk reliquary,

INDIVIDUALS

27

Fig. 1.32 (right): Three-dimensional creatures reach into circular pools containing Christian cross motifs on one of the two brooches from Rogart, Sutherland.

Fig. 1.33 (below): Two simple bird heads, with (now empty) gem settings for eyes and curved beaks, reach towards a gem in the middle of each square terminal on this brooch from the St Ninian's Isle hoard.

EARLY MEDIEVAL SCOTLAND

28

Fig. 1.34: Many Early Medieval brooches, such as this incomplete brooch from the Croy hoard, carry subtle Christian symbolism such as cross shapes and other four-pointed motifs.

Christian decoration seems to have been well integrated into the decoration of Early Medieval brooches. For instance, simple crosses appear among other elements of the design of the terminals and pin-heads of brooches from the Isle of Mull, Argyll, and Rogart, Sutherland [1.23]. The shape of the terminal, made from four lobes, of one of the incomplete brooches from the Croy hoard [1.34], seems designed to reflect the simple cross-shape of the knot in the middle of the terminal.

Even when viewed from a wearer's perspective, much of the fine detail of the Hunterston brooch gold-work is lost. The structural features and colour insets would still stand out when the wearer glanced down to look at the brooch – some of these insets appear in the shape of a cross.[82] Perhaps this was a reassuring motif to be able to glance down and see.

Animals, like the birds that 'drink' from the central glass inset on the Rogart brooch [1.32], have also been suggested to have Christian significance.[83] There are other less obvious examples of birds and beasts reaching towards decorative gems, such as the single abstract bird head on one of the St Ninian's Isle brooches leaning into the centre of each terminal [1.33]. The tops of these animal heads are very worn; unlike the surrounding areas, the raised heads have lost their gilded surface. What might have produced this wear? Clothes may have rubbed the thin layer of gold away, but because the wear is on the front of the brooches, this would mean that the brooches were habitually covered by another layer of clothing, instead of fastening outer cloaks as has often been assumed. An alternative explanation for the wear could be the result of extensive handling or touching of specific parts of the brooches. If some of the brooches were venerated objects – associated with a saint perhaps – then we might expect them to have been touched and rubbed extensively: this appears to be the case with the Monymusk reliquary (see below), where specific areas of gilding have been completely worn away. Alternatively, perhaps the touching of a brooch whilst wearing it was a sign of good luck, a means of warding away evil. Such deliberate and repeated touching might explain the number of missing glass or gem insets from the St Ninian's Isle hoard. On not one of the twelve brooches have all the insets survived [1.51].

Amulets, protective objects and symbolism seem to have been fully integrated within Early Christianity; indeed they were still an acceptable part of Christianity in the Late Medieval period.[84] Christian symbolism on personal objects was not simply an expression of devotion, or a badge to show others that you were Christian, but part of wider beliefs in the power of signs and symbols to protect.

INDIVIDUALS

CHRISTIAN INDIVIDUALS

Early Christianity had not yet developed the fixed doctrines, practices, liturgy or indeed familiar Bible text of the modern Church. There was space for variation in the Early Christian mindset: for example, in the selection and interpretation of holy texts, the nature of practices and rituals,[85] and how the old (pre-Christian) world order might (or might not) be combined with Christian beliefs. This variation might exist between regionally powerful Church foundations, but also among different individuals. Material expressions of different Christian inheritance and development are recognisable in the design and layout of religious centres, their decoration and elaboration (for example, their sculptured stone monuments), or in the objects they produced (such as illuminated books).

The way in which Christian ideas and objects spread was also very personal: individuals set off on pilgrimage and travelled or wrote letters – some of which survive – to other Christians. Each Christian monastery or community can be seen as having a unique intellectual biography, composed of what texts it possessed, where its members had travelled, who and what they had seen, and the connections it had with other areas, communities or individuals (through letter-writing, for example). Each person had their own Christian biography too, part of their identity and personality on other levels. Special individuals (saints) developed cults of devotion, based on their performance of miracles (in life or after death). In many respects therefore, it is possible to see Early Christianity operating on an individual level. Indeed, during this early period, it is perhaps more appropriate to think about individual and community aspects of Early Christianity than to think about it as a single institution.

The physical church has been at the centre of many archaeologists' attempts to identify and understand Early Christianity in Scotland. In fact, we have only limited information about church buildings in Early Medieval Scotland as few have been identified or excavated.[86] It has been assumed that the majority lie underneath the later parish church buildings, and have either been obliterated over centuries of rebuilding and renovation, or are at least unavailable to archaeological excavation. Rather than focus on the architecture of Early Christian practice, the sections below will explore some sights, sounds, hopes and beliefs of Early Christianity in Early Medieval Scotland: the glimmering light of a lamp-lit church, a vigil to cure the illness of a child, the marvel of a floating pebble.

While discussion of Christianity in Scotland tends to assume it was practised communally, there was also scope for very individual Christian practice. For instance, written sources tell us about hermits and ascetics who sought to practise their faith away from the gaze of others. Written stories of saints' lives speak of visits to the homes of the sick, and the use of blessed objects hung above a bed at home.[87] A surviving Early Medieval manuscript, the *Book of Deer*, suggests that priests visited the sick at home to administer rites to the dying (see pages 48–49). We also need to be aware that Early Christianity in Scotland might not always have operated within the confines of dedicated church buildings.[88] In Rome, Early Christianity could be practised in the home, with daily domestic prayer and reservation of the Eucharistic bread for use during the week.[89]

Fig. 1.35: The Christian cross-slab from Papil, Shetland, shows four churchmen carrying staffs. As with other possessions belonging to saints, these staffs, or crosiers, could become holy relics.

Saints acted as channels of God's divine power and were sought for their miracles. Objects imbued with the divine power of holy people or places – known as relics – are one means of approaching the beliefs and practices of individuals in Early Christianity. The word 'relics' (Latin, *reliquiae*) literally means things 'left behind'. Relics could be a saint's bodily remains, or objects that had come into contact with the saint, either in life (their possessions) or in death (objects or substances that had touched their corpse or shrine). Relics were objects in which individuals, as well as communities and indeed Christianised societies, placed a huge emotional investment. These were objects that could contain and convey spiritual power – literally divine powers made material.[90] They lie at the intersection of matter and belief and were believed to be simultaneously treasures on earth and in heaven. The physical remains of saints' bodies maintained a link to their holy soul in heaven, and because of this they acted as divine conduits for holiness.[91]

Relics can be seen as an intuitive and personal response to the need to give a material presence to the spiritual. Individuals experienced relics in tactile and sensory ways – they could be seen, touched, kissed, even consumed – and through these practices the holy power was conveyed from object to individual. The veneration of relics was practised but not taught, and is a personal element of Early Christianity which could complement institutional Church practice and doctrine.[92] Relics maintained their holiness after removal from a shrine, or after breaking up, and as such were both portable and possessable. Relics could be privately owned and used in the home, as well as owned, promoted and controlled by the Church. Many different types of miracles were attributed to saintly relics – including healing, raising of the dead, bringing fertility to land and people, restoring things that had been stolen, and delivering divine judgement on sinners or unbelievers.

INDIVIDUALS

Fig. 1.36 (left): The Kells crosier. A wooden crook or staff was encased within bronze plates around the late 9th or 10th century, with silver plates added in the 11th century.

Fig. 1.37 (top): The inscription on the Kells crosier asks for a prayer to be said to the individuals involved in its refurbishment.

Fig. 1.38 (above): This mount was originally from the end of the crook head of a crosier, found at Aberlady in East Lothian. The Kells crosier is missing the equivalent mount.

The cult of saints and their relics was practised across the Early Christian world, although there were differences in their use and particularly in attitudes towards the unearthing and enshrining of the bodily remains of holy people. Some areas of Christian Europe appear to have begun moving corpses from their original resting-place to purpose-built shrines or elaborate portable containers at an early date. Once exhumed, these bodies were often said to be miraculously preserved (uncorrupted) – even in some cases to have radiated sweet-smelling perfume as a sign of their sanctity and holy power. The places to which these remains were moved and enshrined could in themselves become holy places, and time spent inside the shrine in proximity to the relics could have miraculous effects.[93] In other areas, including Brittany, Wales and perhaps Scotland and Ireland, there seems to have been a reluctance to promote bodily remains as relics, and a preference instead for the veneration of objects that belonged to the saint during their lifetime.[94] In these areas, a saint's hand-bell or staff were commonly venerated in place of the saint's corpse.

Carved stone monuments are one of the most important sources of archaeological evidence for this period. There has only been relatively limited exploration of how Christian sculpture was used, or what it meant to the contemporary makers and audiences. Some people have suggested that the large cross-bearing monuments were boundary markers, a focus for preaching, or simply communal expressions of devotion to their beliefs. Rather than seeing sculpture as purely 'communal' monuments – products of Christian communities – might some pieces also have had a more personal dimension?

The monastery at Iona provides a hint – no more – of a more specific and personal interpretation of some Early Medieval sculptured stones. The large stone crosses from the island are now named after saints: St John's Cross [1.39], St Oran's Cross, St Martin's Cross.[95] It is difficult to trace the origins of the associations of large sculptured crosses on Iona with individual saints – and they may well be only Late or Post-Medieval legends[96] – but they hint at a tantalising possibility: Early Medieval sculptured crosses might, in some cases, be associated with specific people (such as saints), or events (a miracle or a death perhaps). A sculptured cross might be erected to mark important events in a saint's life, such as the site of a miracle, where a saint rested on a journey, or where they died. Written stories of saints provide us with examples of places, at which events like these happened, becoming sacred. In telling the story of St Columba, the monk Adomnán says that on Iona,

> ... *where he* [St Columba] *rested halfway, a cross was later set up, fixed in a millstone; it can still be seen today at the roadside. As the saint was sitting there for a few minutes' rest (for he was weary with age, as I have said), behold a white horse came to him ... and it began to mourn like a person, pouring out its tears in the saint's bosom and weeping aloud with foaming lips ....*
>
> Adomnán's *Life of St Columba*[97]

Several cross-bases at Iona are in the form of boxes made from stone slabs (rather than solid blocks of stone) [1.39].[98] These may have been intended to contain objects (relics) or to protect the area immediately around the cross. Saints' stories tell us that the earth upon which events like miracles or the death of a saint occurred could be revered as contact relics. Perhaps these stone boxes were designed to 'enshrine' the earth around a holy place, which was in turn marked by the sculptured cross? Several carved crosses – the St Orland's cross-slab at Cossans, and freestanding St John's cross at Iona – have recesses in their decorated surfaces which appear to have been intended to accommodate (now missing) metalwork bosses. Might the space behind these bosses have contained saints' relics?[99] If so, the saintly powers would be absorbed by the protective boss in particular, but presumably also by the whole stone monument, turning it into a contact relic.[100] Unfortunately most pieces of stone sculpture are so weathered that it is impossible now to assess whether there is any evidence of focused areas of wear – the kind of wear that might be caused by repeated touching by visiting pilgrims.

Relics were frequently enshrined in portable containers called reliquaries. Reliquaries could be moved within a church building as part of Christian rituals, as well as taken out into the surrounding landscape and communities. A study of the lives of Irish saints suggests that reliquaries could be used to the advantage of the church that owned them in many different ways, including helping in the gathering of dues, imposing the authority of their bishop, or in making oaths sworn upon them binding.[101] Presumably reliquaries would, for most of the time, be kept within a church, and the elaborate nature of surviving

EARLY MEDIEVAL SCOTLAND

Fig. 1.39 (opposite): A concrete replica of St John's Cross, Iona, standing within the grounds of the abbey. The replica is set into a hollow box-shaped base that is likely to be Early Medieval in date. The original 8th-century stone cross survives in fragments.

Fig. 1.40 (right): The depiction of the temple in the *Book of Kells* closely resembles Early Medieval house-shaped reliquaries, particularly in the use of animal-heads at either end of the building's roof.

examples suggests that this would be somewhere conspicuous, perhaps the altar.[102]

Some reliquaries from other parts of Christian Europe carried ornament or inscriptions that link the box with a particular saint or relic. In practice, a reliquary could be any object that housed relics – and even this was not its original purpose. There is therefore an element of difficulty in identifying reliquaries, particularly if they are now empty. Bede, a Northumbrian monk writing around AD 731, tells us that St Germanus

> *… tore from his neck the little bag which hung close to his side, containing relics of the saints. Grasping it firmly, he pressed it in the sight of all on the girl's eyelids; her eyes were immediately delivered from darkness and filled with the light of truth. The parents rejoiced while the people were overawed by the miracle.*[103]

In reality, the reliquaries that have survived are not so humble as St Germanus's relic pouch. Most are very elaborate and precious objects, although purse-shaped reliquaries might have enshrined original fabric bags, perhaps some considerable time after their earliest veneration.

Many reliquaries from across the Early Medieval Christian world consisted of small caskets, some with a pitched (or roof-shaped) rather than flat lid. Today we describe these reliquaries as house-shaped shrines, although some have argued that this name is misleading; as they are Christian objects, it might be more appropriate to call them church-shaped shrines. Others have argued that the shrines allude neither to the shape of churches nor houses, but resemble larger stone tombs or sarcophagi – themselves perhaps modelled on the shape of a house for the dead.[104] The most common analogy, however, remains the depiction of the tabernacle/temple in the Temptation page of the *Book of Kells* [1.40]: the temple even has animal-head terminals at the ends of the roof, that are mirrored on the house-shaped reliquaries by decorative animal-headed mounts.

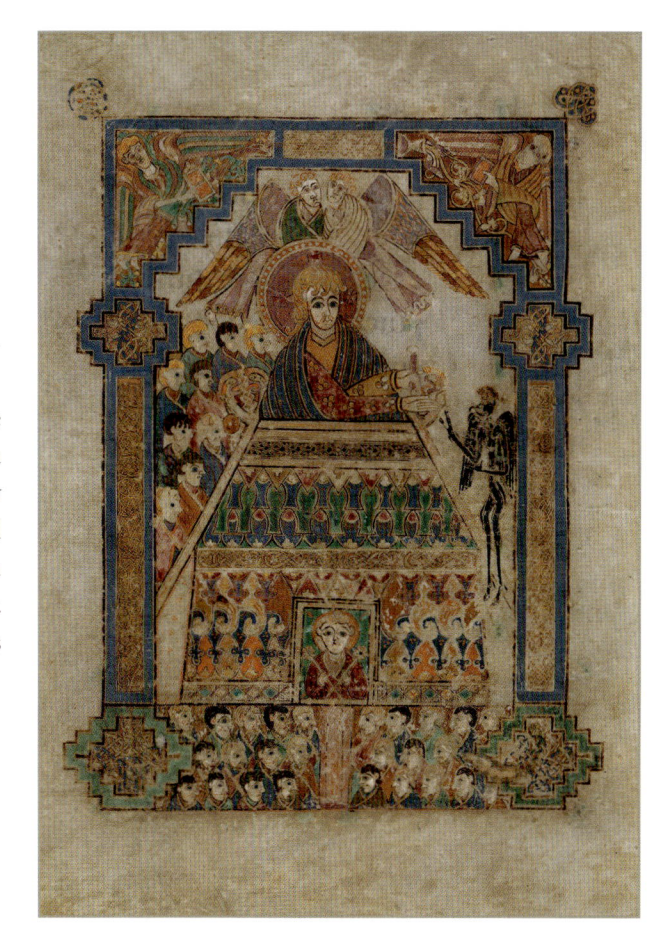

A different tradition of reliquaries exists which sought to enclose objects within precious metal cases shaped like the relic, rather than containing them within a box. Examples from Scotland and Ireland include enshrined bells and crosiers (a bishop's crook or staff). The date of the visible 'encasement' is not necessarily a guide to the origins of the contents. From the 9th century onwards, reliquaries

INDIVIDUALS

were made in the shape of the body parts they were thought to contain – such as arm- or head-shaped reliquaries – although they might in reality only contain a small fragment rather than an intact limb.[105]

As reliquaries were in close proximity to the relics they contained, they became holy in their own right. The materials from which reliquaries were manufactured, and particularly the use of precious metals and gems that introduced colour and light, were thought to enhance the power and majesty of the holy contents.[106] This hints at the paradox inherent in the concept of reliquaries – that the relics inside were precious and required a special, dedicated container which preserved the relic, while often totally obscuring it from view.[107] In the same way that access to a saint's shrine within a church could be controlled, so could access to portable relics and reliquaries. It is not clear how often reliquaries were opened[108] – it is conceivable that the ritual opening of a reliquary might be performed at special points on the Christian calendar (such as a saint's day). However, in the case of both shrines and reliquaries, the fact that the sacred contents were usually hidden did not detract from their power. The containers of both (and indeed substances that came into contact with the containers) could transmit the divine power of their contents.

THE MONYMUSK RELIQUARY

Although the Monymusk reliquary [1.41] is one of the most important Early Medieval objects from Scotland, it is perhaps best known for its (doubtful) identification as the battle standard later carried at the battle of Bannockburn.[109] The reliquary itself has only had very limited specialist attention,[110] and much of this has focused on comparing its decoration to other reliquaries, or to discussing its date. Dating the reliquary is more complicated than has been recognised, as it is made from many different components that could have been made and added to the reliquary at widely different times. The decorative mounts, for example, seem to have been manufactured in different ways: the circular mounts are made from two pieces, one with a neat cut-away portion, indicative perhaps of removal from another object, while the rectangular mounts were cast in one piece. Were the circular mounts made to accommodate metalwork from another object, and the rectangular mounts made to match? It is even possible that the roughly carved internal wooden box was originally a saint's possession, precious in its own right, which was only later clad in metal plates to protect and venerate it.[111]

Although now empty, Monymusk and other similarly-shaped caskets have conventionally been identified as reliquary boxes. There are no surviving records listing what the Monymusk reliquary originally contained. It is a small box – the internal space is only eight centimetres long by three centimetres wide by four centimetres deep – and so could only have accommodated little objects, perhaps small bones, stones or pieces of cloth. Reliquaries enabled holy

Fig. 1.41 (below): The Monymusk reliquary is the only house-shaped reliquary to have survived in Scotland. The reliquary consists of a wooden box and lid, encased within silver and bronze plates and elaborated with gilded and enamelled mounts, some of which are now lost.

INDIVIDUALS

Fig. 1.42 (opposite, above left): Unlike the front of the Monymusk reliquary, which is covered by silver plates decorated with lightly punched entwined animals, the back, sides and bottom of the reliquary are encased within plain bronze plates.

Fig. 1.43 (above right): The reliquary is now empty and no information about its original contents survives. The inner wooden box is in fact surprisingly roughly carved. This might originally have been concealed by a fabric lining.

Fig. 1.44 (below): The reliquary would have been carried by a strap or chain attached to the decorated side-plates. One set down, the side-plate would have been lowered, and an iron rod drawn out from the side of the box to release a hidden clasp allowing the box to be opened.

remains to be portable and the Monymusk reliquary would have been carried by either a strap or chain (now lost) attached to decorative hinged plates on the side of the box (only one of the two survives). The box would have been opened by drawing a small rod out of the left side of the box (as you view it), thereby freeing the two halves of a clasp hidden inside the front wall of the box and the lid. Unlike some reliquaries with small windows, when Monymusk is closed the contents are hidden from view. One can imagine the opening of such a box and the revealing of hidden and holy contents as a performance, and part of other Christian rituals. Monymusk is easy to open, which might suggest it was intended to be opened frequently, although some other kinds of reliquaries (book shrines, for example) appear to be sealed and not intended to be opened.

Perhaps house-shaped boxes like Monymusk were not originally used as relic containers. Recently it has been suggested that they might instead have been used as chrismals – containers for the Eucharist.[112] In some ways, these two types of containers might be thought of as not so very different: in the same way that saints' relics were thought literally to embody the saint, so the bread was thought literally to embody Christ. Wherever it was carried, Eucharistic bread created 'spaces of particular sacredness'[113] and might even have had protecting or healing power. The ease of opening might perhaps be more suited to a chrismal box which would have been opened regularly. Monymusk may have served multiple purposes during its lifetime.

The decoration of the Monymusk reliquary emphasises the front face of the box and lid. Here, and here only, silver (rather than copper) plates are used that dramatically reflect light. Early Christianity used shining precious metals and gleaming gems on reliquaries as both a metaphor for divine light and sanctity, and as a means of radiating these to the faithful.[114] Clusters of stones on reliquaries 'would have sparkled with rays of light considered to be powerful instruments of healing, possessing powers that were similar and complementary to those of saint's relics'.[115] It is these two silver parts of the reliquary – the front of the lid and box – that separate to reveal the contents when it is opened. And yet the decoration is most impressive and coherent when the reliquary is closed. When the box is open, the lid is tipped back and the roughly carved inside surface is exposed and the lugs and pins fastening the mounts are revealed [1.43]. When the reliquary was carried, the decorative side-plate is viewed to best advantage; when it is put down and the box opened, these plates were also lowered, therefore hiding their intricate decoration [1.44]. The reliquary is best appreciated when it is closed, viewed from the front, and when being carried.

Unlike some other Early Christian reliquaries, there are no figural or narrative scenes on Monymusk; no specific decoration relates to the saint or objects enshrined in the box. This is also true of the other house-shaped boxes that were probably made in Ireland or Scotland. It was a deliberate choice to opt for abstract designs such as interlace and entwined animals, rather than explicit imagery concerning the purpose of the box. There also appears to be a general lack of explicit narrative scenes or depictions of holy figures on portable objects from Scotland more generally. This contrasts with carved stones, which carry pictures of people and events from the Scriptures, albeit less frequently than sculpture from Ireland and Anglo-

INDIVIDUALS

Saxon England.[116] The reason for the lack of comparable portable images is not at all clear – they are found fairly widely elsewhere in the Early Christian world.

It might seem strange that such an important Christian object as the Monymusk reliquary should appear to carry no overt Christian decoration. The archaeologist Robert Stevenson was the first to recognise Christian imagery on the reliquary – a subtle Christian cross formed by the spaces between the interlace strands on the central panel on the roof-bar.[117] The forming of crosses 'in reserve' between interlace strands is now widely recognised as a common feature of Early Medieval illuminated manuscripts, metalwork and sculptured stones. Colour may be used to highlight these subtle features, as is the case within the art of the illuminated manuscripts, and perhaps on sculptured stones through the application of pigments. Subtle and complex imagery like this characterises much Early Christian art from Britain and Ireland; this is what we would expect, given the prominence of contemplation and rumination of Scripture within Early Christian thought. It demands the viewer to take time to look, untangle and contemplate. Individuals would need to take more than a glance at Monymusk to find the symbolism for the first time, although its prestige and importance would be immediately apparent.

When the reliquary is closed, the whole series of decorative mounts on the lid and the box (when originally complete), together with the interlace panel on the roof-bar, can be read together as a Christian cross [1.45, 1.46]. The mounts can also be read as two separate groups of three: three circular mounts and three rectangular mounts, both arranged at the points of a triangle. The design of each of the two types of mount also emphasises these decorative principles in miniature: the circular mounts have three panels of enamel, while the rectangular ones have four, with the spaces in between forming a subtle cross-shape. The top of the decorated side-plate features a motif of three interlocking spirals, a common design among Early Medieval art.

An obvious Christian interpretation for these designs composed in sets of three is an allusion to the Holy Trinity of Father, Son and Holy Spirit – although three is also a significant number in many other respects within Christianity). The central and interwoven Christian themes of the Crucifixion and the Trinity are here visually combined by the arrangement of the six mounts on the face of the reliquary in a cross-shape. This symbolism would be particularly appropriate if the box were originally intended to be a chrismal, containing the bread representing Christ's Incarnation and Resurrection.[118]

On Pictish sculptured stones, animals and animal-based interlace frequently occur around the outside of the cross, but the decoration *within* the body of the cross is almost always geometric, comprising interlace, key-pattern or spiral designs. This choice of what was appropriate to elaborate the body of the cross might also be reflected in the decoration on the Monymusk reliquary. The mounts that together form the shape of a cross are decorated with interlace, whereas the silver plates surrounding them feature faint, lightly punched, entwined animals. A pair of birds' heads, interlacing around a central jewelled setting, act as a terminal to each end of the reliquary's roof-bar. These birds face inwards, towards the central interlace panel on the roof-bar – the panel with the 'hidden' cross.

Figs 1.45 (below) and 1.46 (right): The Christian symbolism on the Monymusk reliquary is very subtle. For example, the rectangular mounts, together with the small rectangle in the middle of the roof-bar, form the shape of a Christian cross.

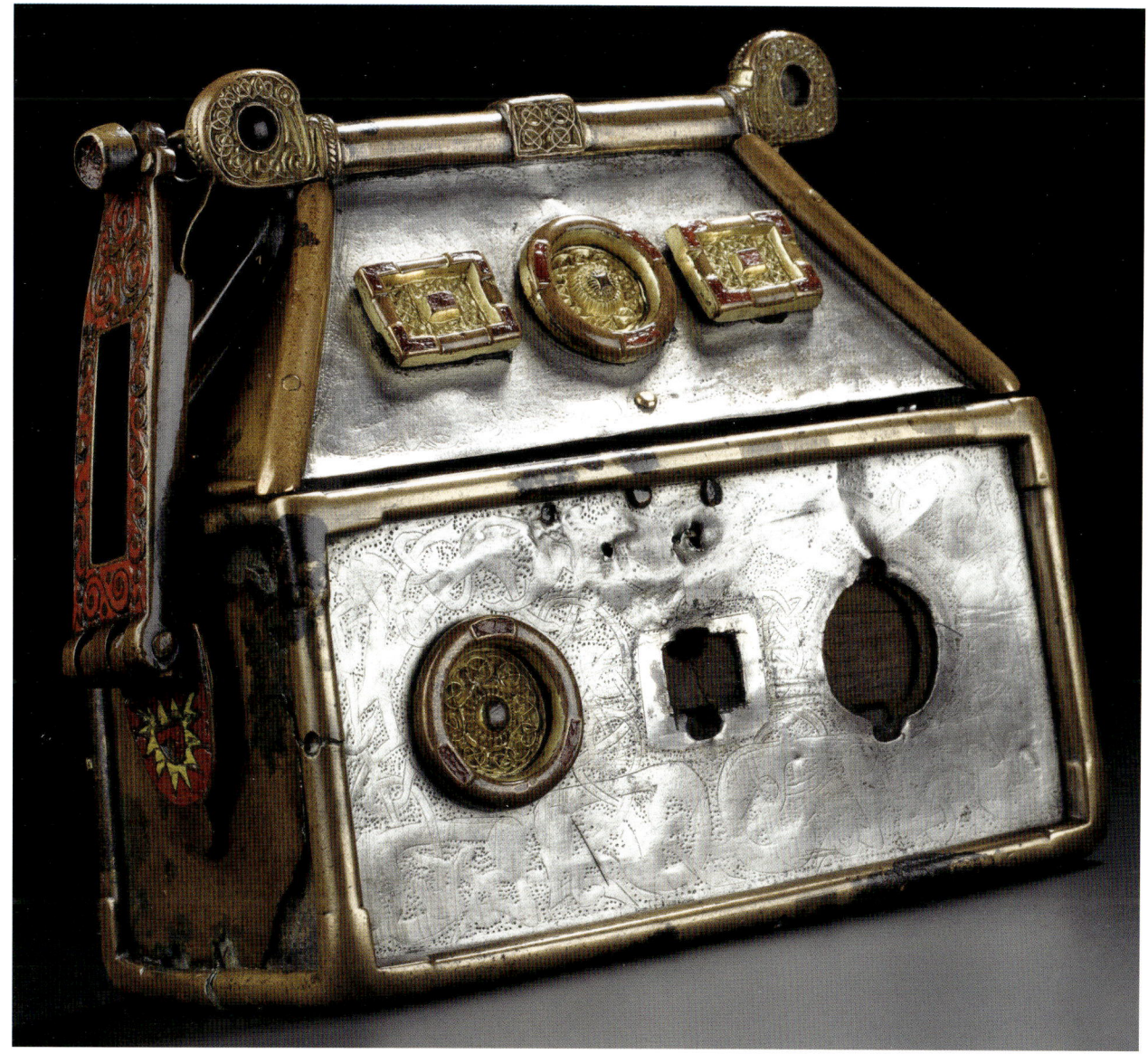

INDIVIDUALS

41

In Early Christian art, images of the faithful being drawn to Christ could be represented by a central cross flanked by two identical creatures, often peacocks – and it is possible that a similar meaning was intended for this aspect of the reliquary's decoration.[119] These are only some of the possibilities,[120] but it shows that we can explore the iconography of objects such as the Monymusk reliquary and adopt approaches more usually applied to sculptured stones and illuminated manuscripts.

Reliquaries were powerful objects. Hints of the personal belief in the holiness of the Monymusk reliquary survive in specific areas that are very worn, where the gilded surface has almost completely been removed. The most touched places seem to be the roof-bar (originally completely gilded, only traces of which remain), and the decorative mounts, especially the outer frames and the bosses in the middle. Other reliquaries also have foci of wear suggesting heavy touching: on the newly-identified roof-mount mentioned earlier, the golden surfaces of the fierce animal heads are almost completely worn away. This restricted wear suggests the repeated touching and rubbing of certain parts of the reliquary, perhaps those deemed to be particularly effective or symbolic.

SICK BODIES

Cures are one of the most frequent types of miracles recorded in stories surrounding early saints and their relics. This quest for divine healing is one area where we have evidence for the participation of apparently ordinary individuals and, unusually among written sources concerning Early Medieval Scotland, these stories feature women and children as well as men. They also tell us about cures obtained in the home, as well as those gained at holy shrines within churches. Beyond this, these stories concern the deeply personal subject of the sickness and healing of people's bodies and minds. It relates to belief in how to achieve and maintain bodily well-being – to extend life, alleviate pain and to deliver children safely. Texts like these can help us better understand the places and objects that could be involved in curing:

> *… for crushed by chronic illness many come hurrying here,*
> *eagerly accepting what is given to obtain a saving cure,*
> *and in all their new members, by the same saint's power,*
> *they are made new.*[121] *…*
> *the darkness of blind folk he changed into brightest light,*
> *he cleansed from scaly bodies their leprous swellings,*
> *he cured for many the lameness of their feet,*
> *and deaf ears he penetrated with his piercing voice.*[122]
>
> *The Miracles of St Nynia (Ninian) the Bishop,*
> 8th-century text

Healing stories give us sometimes vivid descriptions of diseases and afflictions. All of the information of course comes from a deeply Christian point of view. There may be particular problems or biases inherent within these sources: for instance, they may wish to promote a particular saint's shrine, perhaps for political or economic reasons. However, the somewhat incidental information – such as the particular way in which a disease is described, who it was said to have affected, the means by which they received a cure, who accompanied them to the shrine – remains very valuable.

The 8th-century Anglo-Saxon text *The Miracles of St Nynia the Bishop* contains stories of the powers of a saint whose remains were associated with Whithorn in Dumfries and Galloway. The *Miracles of St Nynia* mostly concern miracles delivered after the saint had died, and because of this they promote Whithorn as the burial-place of the saint. The accounts of the miracles praise the power of the saint, and therefore the importance of the location of his bodily relics. In several places the shrine is described as a 'famous sanctuary': these Anglo-Saxon texts are clearly at pains to promote the cult at Whithorn. Analysis of hagiography from Wales and Brittany suggests that written saints' lives were created for 'intrusive' cults – in other words, those brought in from elsewhere. Established saints' cults did not require written lives to mediate between the saint and the community that believed in them and visited their secondary relics and holy springs.[123] The written *Miracles of St Nynia* are therefore, in part at least, political propaganda: Whithorn had been taken under the control of the Anglo-Saxon Church of Northumbria in the early 8th century.[124] Nonetheless, the texts can give us a hint of the types of practices that those visiting such a shrine might have taken part in.[125]

Within this text, and a hymn celebrating the life of the saint, there seems to be a particular focus on healing miracles and on Whithorn as a place to seek healing. Four different people – a man, woman, a child of poor parents, and a king – are portrayed as receiving miraculous healing through the sanctity of St Ninian. Only the king was cured during the saint's life; the other three individuals sought healing at the saint's tomb. This suggests that healing sanctuaries or shrines could be open to all kinds of individuals, regardless of gender, age or social standing.

Several different practices at the tomb are described. The parents of the disabled child brought him to the shrine and begged and prayed on bended knees for a cure. At sunset they left their child alone in the shrine and shut the gate. At midnight the saint appeared to the child and cured him by placing his hand on its head. The child is named and said to have lived as a monk in the monastery.

A man with 'leperous elephantiasis', which caused 'discoloured limbs', 'deformed flesh' and 'corrupted frame', visited the tomb 'where the blessed bishop's body lay in furrowed marble'. At the saint's feet he prayed in supplication and was quickly healed. Here proximity to the saint's remains and prayer was sufficient to cure his ills.

A blind woman suffering 'chaos of the mind' sought the shrine. The unnamed woman was cured by praying and throwing her body down: '… with her brow she pressed the ground, she lay in the hollowed cavity.' It seems unlikely that pilgrims would be allowed to lie *in* the tomb with the saint's remains – perhaps instead this passage implies a niche in which the tomb was set, or a sunken cavity allowing closer proximity to the tomb, or indeed a worn hollow caused by frequent prostration by visiting pilgrims.

In this last miracle, the tomb is described as 'where the bowels of the hollowed rocks hold fast the holy body in their stony inner parts'. This almost suggests a rock-cut tomb, perhaps hollowed out of the bedrock, although this would be at odds with the 'furrowed marble' tomb already described.

The Whithorn shrine does not survive, but a number

Fig. 1.47 (left): Exquisitely carved stone panels from St Andrews, Fife, have traditionally been interpreted as part of a box-shaped shrine or sarcophagus. Recent research suggests that they are more likely to be architectural features, perhaps from a decorated chancel screen or altar.

Figs 1.48 (middle) and 1.49 (below): This sarcophagus from Govan, Glasgow, was carved from a single block of stone. A space for the body was hollowed out and the outside surfaces covered with decoration.

EARLY MEDIEVAL SCOTLAND

44

Fig. 1.50: This silver Byzantine votive plaque was intended as a gift to a church in return for divine help or healing. The eyes depicted on the plaque suggest that sight was a concern for the individual seeking aid.

of other possible stone shrines or shrine-fragments from Scotland have been identified by archaeologists.

There are, however, a number of problems with this interpretation of the evidence. The group of shrine pieces were identified on the basis of their construction as panels with small tenons, fitted into grooved posts to create a kind of stone box. It is clear, however, that this technique could be used to build different types of structure – and on the Continent it was used to build chancel screens to divide and define different parts of a church building. Perhaps the best known Scottish 'box shrine' is the St Andrews sarcophagus [1.47]. Although it is currently displayed as a box shrine, the various pieces that make up the monument were not found together. None of the pieces fits well together and it may be that archaeologists have 'made' a box shrine out of pieces that originally came from several different monuments. The only clear example of a stone coffin is the Govan sarcophagus [1.48, 1.49]. Like examples from the Continent, it is carved from a single piece of stone that has been laboriously hollowed out inside (unlike 'box-shrines' constructed from separate posts and panels).

In addition to tomb shrines, the church also housed saints' relics within the altar. Some churches had more than one altar; each time a new one was created, relics had to be found to be included within it. Within St Ninian's *Miracles* a priest 'at the altar stood in prayer, where rests the buried body of bishop Ninian'. It is not clear, however, whether the altar referred to would have been the main altar of the church or a separate altar within a separate shrine. An altar excavated at St Ninian's Point, Bute, and possibly dating to the Early Christian period, seems to have had a box-like cavity that presumably would have contained relics.[126]

Promotion of the healing cult at Whithorn seems to have been an important aim of the author of the text of the *Miracles of St Nynia*. While the saint is said to have performed other miracles, there are more healing cures than other kinds of miracle, and three of the four cures happen at the shrine itself. An important cult might benefit a church foundation in several ways. It might help to make it a more important church than others in the area, but it would also bring in material wealth.

Elsewhere in the Christian world there is evidence of pilgrims bringing gifts to try to procure, and give thanks for, divine aid. There is no mention among the Whithorn miracles of the giving of votive offerings by grateful pilgrims, but it would seem strange if this were not the case. In other parts of Christendom, votive offerings could take a variety of forms. Most were items intended to be used – such as incense, or oil or candles for the giving of light within the church[127] – thus rendering them almost invisible to archaeologists. Silver was also given, and while usually it would be melted down, some votive plaques have survived, including Byzantine examples shaped like the body part that required a cure [1.50].

It is also possible that, rather than give purpose-made gifts to the church, people in Scotland tended to give

INDIVIDUALS

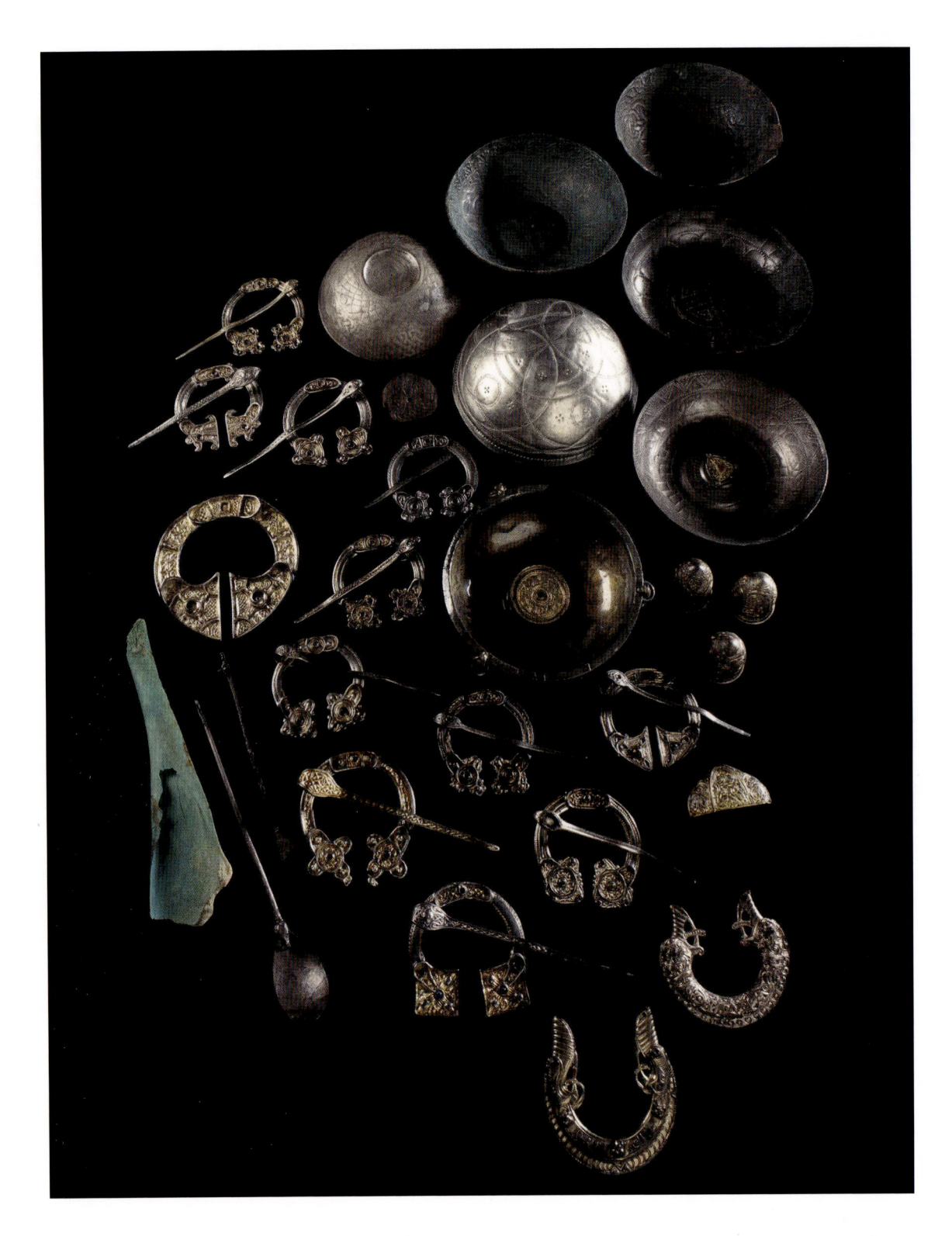

EARLY MEDIEVAL SCOTLAND

Fig. 1.51 (opposite): The hoard of silver objects from St Ninian's Isle, Shetland. The hoard is made up of twelve brooches, a set of six thin silver bowls and one hanging-bowl, a spoon and forked utensil, two sword chapes and a sword pommel, three cone-shaped mounts and part of a porpoise jaw bone.

ordinary objects, providing problems of identification for archaeologists. Coins might be one example: they could be of precious metal and many carried the symbol of the cross, perhaps making them particularly appropriate offerings to a church or saint. Coins recovered during the excavation at Whithorn were interpreted as representing a 'contact zone' between the church community and visiting pilgrims.[128] Some may have been intended to be votive gifts to the church, although those recovered by archaeologists will be limited to the objects that the church had failed to retrieve. However, alternative interpretations for the presence of coins are possible – they may represent the use of monetary wealth by those within or communicating with important monasteries.

More substantial objects given to a church might include the collection of silver brooches, bowls, sword fittings and other objects found buried within a church building at St Ninian's Isle, Shetland [1.51]. The inclusion of a porpoise jaw bone among these precious metal objects is difficult to explain. It must have been valued to be part of the hoard, although its value is not apparent to us now. Was it included because it was a rarity, or perhaps because of stories or associations attached to it? Might it even have been a holy object, perhaps believed to have been associated with a saint or with miracles?

In some cases, saints' stories provide an insight into the perceived causes of illness. Among the miracles attributed to St Columba are two stories where the cause of an illness is described. In the first, the disease was attributed to a poisonous well, worshipped as a god by heathens – contact with the water caused people to become leprous, half blind or crippled, struck down by the devil's art.[129] In the second, illness was brought by a 'heavy storm cloud to the north rising from the sea on a clear day'. St Columba foretold that the cloud would bring great harm to people and livestock, shedding a 'deadly rain', 'a rain that will raise awful sores full of pus on the bodies of people and the udders of cattle'.[130] Interestingly, both of these stories concern water as the cause or transmitter of illness. As we will see below, water is commonly described in a positive way in Scottish saints' lives as a medium for the transfer of healing powers of holy relics to those that needed aid.

The evidence discussed here all comes from explicitly Christian sources. The Northumbrian monk Bede also wrote about the types of cures that pagans used – or at least what he *thought* they used:

> ... some of them too, in times of plague, would forget the sacred mysteries of the faith into which they been initiated and take to the false remedies of idolatry, as though they could ward off a blow inflicted by God the Creator by means of incantations or amulets of any other mysteries of devilish art.[131]

It is worth noting, however, that Bede's 'incantations and amulets' might be seen as having a lot in common with (Christian) prayers and (Christian) relics.

Some of these saintly stories also mention medical treatments that either failed, or were used in combination with holy power. For instance, the life of St Cuthbert, Prior of Melrose in the Scottish Borders, written by Bede, provides a detailed description of a young man with a tumour on his eyelid which grew daily until it threatened the loss of his eye.

Though the doctors sought to reduce it by applying formentations and ointments, they could do nothing. Some thought it should be cut away, while others opposed this course for fear of doing greater harm.

The man was eventually cured by applying some of St Cuthbert's hair.[132]

In this case, medical treatments had failed, but there is also evidence from the hagiography of Bishop John of Hexham (later of York) of saints calling for the services of doctors to help cure those in their care. The patient was a man who had fallen from a horse, causing a broken thumb, skull and 'vomiting blood because some internal organs had been ruptured'. The bishop kept overnight vigil and discovered that the man had been improperly baptised. After the bishop breathed on his face, the man immediately felt better. John is then said to have called for a doctor and had him set and bind the man's fractures,[133] demonstrating in theory at least the interaction of saintly and prosaic healing practices. There may be some evidence for this combining of medicine and the divine at the church site at Whithorn, the focus of the cult of healing centred around St Ninian. Here excavators recognised coriander, dill, black mustard, chickweed and dog rose seeds from a latrine pit. All have, at some time or other in the past, been used for medicinal purposes, and many were associated with curing digestive problems. A very small knife blade excavated from an Early Medieval context at Whithorn was tentatively identified as a surgeon's knife, akin to a modern scalpel.[134]

Skeletal material could provide an important source of evidence for illness and some of the treatments and interventions intended to help and heal. However, the combination of poor bone preservation across much of Scotland due to acidic soil conditions, together with limited large-scale study of the pathology of surviving skeletal remains, means that this potential has not yet been realised. One example of the burial of a young man at Skaill, Orkney, demonstrates what is possible. His skeletal remains suggested that he had congenital anomalies in his back, had carried heavy loads in his youth and possibly used a crutch.[135] This burial was radiocarbon dated to between the mid-6th century to late 7th century and is a rare insight into real physical suffering and attempted alleviation in the burial record.

The 10th-century illuminated *Book of Deer* gives us an insight into the church's treatment of the very sick in Scotland. This compact book was not intended for use within a church, but as a portable – literally 'pocket sized' – set of gospels. Three of the four gospel texts within the *Book of Deer* have been abbreviated, and in the choice of text there seems to be an emphasis on healing and sickness: the Gospel of Matthew ends with Christ's warning against false prophets and false healers, while the Gospel of Mark ends with his teaching that healing comes through faith.[136] After the Gospel of Mark is the 'Office for the Visitation of the Sick', spelling out rites and rituals to be administered to the very sick. Healing certainly seems to have been an important concern – although not the only one – for the scribe who selected the text excerpts and designed the layout of the *Book of Deer*.

The portable size of the volume, combined with an emphasis on healing, implies that it would have been used by a cleric when visiting the sick in their homes.[137] Not only can the text act as a written document to illuminate the church's attitudes towards the sick, but the book itself is an important material object that was intimately involved in the management of illness. These rites are, however, less concerned with promises of healing than with spiritual preparation of the very sick for death and the next world. A single blank page was left between the end of the Gospel of Mark and the text of the Office for the Visitation of the Sick, allowing the rites for the sick to run over two facing pages. This seems a very practical arrangement that would have left the hands free to administer the Eucharistic bread given to the dying as food for the journey into the next world.[138]

POSSESSING CHRISTIANITY

In the section on brooches, we touched on the potential power of Christian symbols and holy words and how they were integrated into the decoration of dress objects. The Talnotrie hoard from Dumfries and Galloway [1.52] is a group of objects that have been interpreted as the property of a metalworker.[139] But an alternative interpretation (or an extra layer to the existing interpretation) might see it as a personal collection of Christian objects: the majority carry cross-based motifs. They include a cross-shaped mount, coins (with crosses), a pair of pins with geometric decoration that forms a simple cross-shape, and a lead weight decorated with a piece of re-used metalwork, with a cross-shaped motif similar to that on the pins. Were these objects collected because of the cross-motifs that embellish them? A piece of beeswax was also probably part of the hoard and might well have been used in metalworking.[140]

However, this is not the only interpretation that is possible – given the amount of cross-based symbolism among the other hoard objects, might the beeswax have been taken from a church site or shrine and kept because of these associations?

If so, it would fall into another category of holy objects that offer exciting opportunities to see personal Christianities. These are contact relics or *eulogiae* – otherwise mundane objects or substances that have become holy through blessing by a saint in life, or proximity to holy relics. Examples of contact relics include substances gathered by visitors to the shrines of saints: oil from adjacent lamps, wax from the shrine's candles, dust from the tomb, earth from the floor, and cloth touched to the shrine are just some of the recorded possibilities. While relics such as body parts or saint's possessions were closely controlled by the church, contact relics could be collected and owned by ordinary people. Contact relics have the advantage to the church of being renewable – dust will continue to accrue, lamp oil can be refilled. The advantage to the pilgrim is that they could be collected and taken home, to be used privately or kept and inherited. They could enable sick people to receive the healing power of a Christian saint without visiting the shrine in person. Contact relics could join the public and domestic, as pilgrims brought personal domestic needs into the public sphere at holy sites, and returned home taking something conveying holy power with them.[141]

The child brought to Whithorn for healing (as discussed above) is said to have been brought to visit the saint's 'body and dust'. It seems likely that this presents the opportunity for pilgrims to procure for themselves a small but

EARLY MEDIEVAL SCOTLAND

50

Fig. 1.52 (opposite):
The hoard of objects from Talnotrie, Dumfries and Galloway. The hoard includes a broken cross-shaped mount, a silver tag for the end of a leather strap or belt, three spindle-whorls for making thread, two matching silver pins, a lead weight decorated with a re-used gilded mount, a piece of beeswax, a piece of cannel coal and a piece of agate, some fragmentary coins, a spherical pin-head, some thin scraps of wire and a thin gold finger-ring.

significant holy contact relic. In Byzantium, 'dust' or holy earth was made into cakes, stamped with healing Christian imagery, to be taken away from the site for later use. These tokens were later broken up and either eaten or applied to the body, implying that the sick did not need to be present at the shrine to gain healing. The Byzantine contact relics are identifiable as such because of the stamps they carry – showing pictures, symbols or inscriptions associated with particular saints or healing cults. Other examples from elsewhere in Christian Europe, where iconography allows recognition of a holy substance, include flasks from the shrine of St Menas, an Egyptian saint with a well-known healing cult. Several examples are known from England, presumably brought back by pilgrims from abroad, including one from Meols, Cheshire, although none has been found in Scotland.[142] These flasks were containers for holy water or oil taken from the healing shrine.

A variety of posthumous contact relics are known from northern British literature, which tells us that the practice did occur. These are difficult to identify in the archaeological record. Examples of posthumous relics include earth from the place of St Oswald's death, which when added to water was believed to cure sick people and animals.[143] Even water in which his bones were washed, when poured away, made the surrounding soil curative. An abbess took some of this soil, wrapped in cloth and put in a casket, to cure a man possessed by a devil.[144] St Aidan died leaning on a wooden buttress – splinters from this wood when dipped in water were thought to be curative.[145]

There are also stories about objects or substances blessed and used during a saint's lifetime as conduits of their holy power. Adomnán's *Life of St Columba*[146] contains stories of blessed pebbles, bread and salt – all used with water – producing miraculous cures. Salt was a precious substance. Roman soldiers were paid partly in salt, and this is the origin for the word 'salary' ('salt' in Latin is *sal*) and phrases such as 'worth her salt'. Both bread and salt carried Christian significance – bread as symbol of nourishment drawn from Christ, and salt as preserver of this nourishment and relationship with Christ. Salt was also thought to have purifying power, as in a miracle from the Old Testament where salt was added to a contaminated well to purify it.[147] Neither bread or salt are likely to survive for long, even if they could be identified by archaeologists as blessed objects.

Pebbles or stones, on the other hand, might well survive, although they are potentially very difficult to recognise as 'special' rather than naturally occurring stones. The *Life of St Columba* tells of a white pebble, perhaps a piece of quartz or rock crystal, that the saint picked up at the River Ness, 'through which the Lord will bring about the healing of many sick people …'.[148] The pebble was used to cure a king who at first refused the saint's demand to free a slave, but later agreed after having been struck down by a seizure. The pebble was said to float 'in defiance of nature' because '… that which the saint had blessed could not be made to sink'. The account tells us that the pebble was henceforth kept in the royal treasury, confirming private ownership of contact relics.

A number of small stones or pebbles that had simple crosses carved onto them might perhaps have been powerful holy objects. Examples include stones from St Ninian's Cave, near Whithorn [1.53], and from the early church site at Hoddom, both in Dumfries and Galloway.[149] A stone

Fig. 1.53: A cross-marked pebble from the St Ninian's cave, near Whithorn, Dumfries and Galloway.

Fig. 1.54: A pebble from the fort at Dunadd, Argyll, with a Christian phrase scratched onto the surface.

Fig. 1.55: A piece of near-flawless rock crystal, carefully cut and polished and possessing magnifying qualities, from a crannog at Lochspouts, Ayrshire.

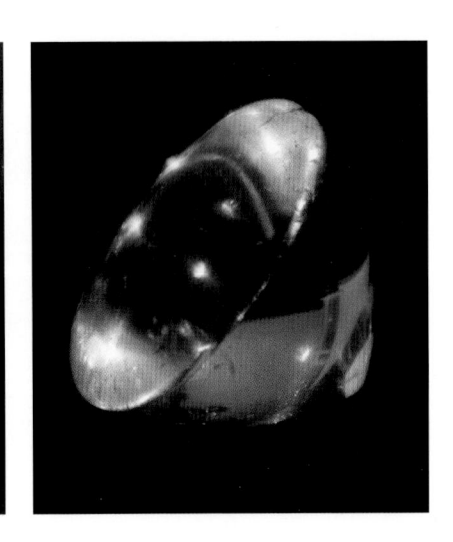

from the Early Medieval fort at Dunadd, Argyll, was carved with the Latin words '*I nomine*' [1.54].[150] This inscription translates as 'in the name of' and was part of an early invocation 'in the name of the Lord', which might indicate it was a blessed object with healing or protective powers.

But holy or blessed objects might not always be marked in this way – they could be unmodified or polished pebbles without symbols, inscriptions or decoration. A wide variety of unusual stones and pebbles were found during excavations at the pilgrimage site of Whithorn. These included pieces of rock crystal,[151] including one crystal with a blood-red tip and two carefully cut pieces of smoky quartz. A range of small 'exotic' pebbles with polish, not readily identifiable as serving practical purpose, were suggested as 'keep sakes or talismans', and included rose and banded quartz as well as granite and sandstone.[152] A small piece of translucent mica, sometimes used to create windows in reliquaries, and a highly polished belemnite brought from the east coast, were also found. Perhaps this collection represents objects brought to the site by pilgrims in the hope that they would be blessed.[153]

Early Christian writers ascribed particular qualities, associations and powers to gemstones, drawing on Classical tracts.[154] Rock crystal, believed to be petrified water, symbolised purity and was often associated with Christ and with the water of baptism.[155] Rock crystal was not commonly used to decorate Early Medieval objects, but does occur on some of the most elaborate Early Medieval liturgical vessels that survive: the Ardagh chalice and the Derrynaflan strainer, both from Ireland. Both of these objects were intimately associated with Eucharistic wine, the 'blood of Christ'. Rock-crystal balls are found in some female Anglo-Saxon graves, often associated with strainers. This suggests a wider cultural association between (and perhaps curative powers of) straining liquids over rock crystal. A piece of near flawless rock crystal of almost

EARLY MEDIEVAL SCOTLAND

Fig. 1.56 (below): A glass *tesserae* inlaid with gold leaf found at Dunadd, Argyll, but likely to have come from a mosaic in the Mediterranean region.

identical size and shape to that on the base of the Ardagh chalice[156] was found on a crannog at Lochspouts, Ayrshire [1.55]. It is of such a high quality – both in terms of the flawless crystal and the cutting and polishing of the stone – that it would have been a prized possession in its own right. It could perhaps have decorated an Early Medieval liturgical vessel like the Ardagh chalice, or had protective or curative associations.

Is a church or shrine the only type of place we should expect to find contact relics or *eulogiae*? Given that these objects allowed divine blessings to be taken away from a holy site, clearly not. They might, for example, be carried upon the person to provide protection and the warding off of malign powers or illness. Archaeological context might not be much help in identifying blessed objects – they may have been used, or dropped, anywhere. For example, a glass tessera inlaid with gold leaf, excavated from Dunadd [1.56], is of a type more commonly found in splendid mosaics, such as those at Ravenna or in Byzantium.[157] Might this be a pilgrim's memento from a visit to an important church, brought back to Argyll because it was thought to carry divine power?

Written sources from elsewhere in the Early Christian world tell us that holy objects were often used in the home, particularly around the bed and at thresholds.[158] They could be humble objects used by families in everyday domestic life. The written miracles of St Columba provide some evidence for similar beliefs, relating a story of a block of blessed salt hung above a bed.[159] In this context, blessed objects hung above the bed might have been 'in use' every night, rather than reserved for special occasions (such as during illness, for example). This association with curative or protective relics used in the night-time strikes a chord with the practice of night-time vigils at shrines – this is described in the miracles of St Ninian which is discussed above.

Evidence for the use of relics in Scotland at thresholds is harder to find. An interesting parallel might be provided by the hagiography of the Irish St Brigit. A contact relic of the saint – a millstone – was moved to the gate of the walls around her sanctuary. Touching the stone cured disease, and only when this had happened could the individual pass into the body of the sanctuary. This suggests a concept of theological hierarchy which would prevent 'catechumens, sinners and those who were chronically ill from entering the most important spaces of the church'.[160] Such a concept is not found among sources for the healing shrine at Whithorn, as discussed above, where the chronically ill were apparently allowed to come into close proximity with the saint's bodily remains.

The use of liquid as a vehicle to transfer holy powers from relics and make it easy to consume is a widespread phenomenon, found across the Early Christian world (and indeed non-Christian areas). While also common elsewhere, water does seem to be particularly prominent among written accounts of Scottish saints' miracles. St Columba himself was said sometimes to use blessed water alone to bring about cures, and in another instance an

INDIVIDUALS

unnamed blessed object carried in a pine box, dipped in a jar of water.[161] The Northumbrian sainted King Oswald brought cures after his death through splinters of a wooden cross (that he had erected before a great battle) which were dipped in water – this was either drunk or sprinkled onto sick people or animals.[162]

Wells and springs associated with saints are a feature of the Early Christian hagiography of Wales and Brittany, and several examples occur among the Scottish miracles. It is, however, notoriously difficult to identify early healing wells or holy springs. In many instances it is nearly impossible to demonstrate that the well's place-name or saintly association is of Medieval, let alone Early Medieval, origins. St Columba was said to have miraculously 'cured' a poisonous and evil well that was causing illness. The well had supposedly been worshipped as a god by the heathen population 'because the devil had clouded their sense'.[163] The saint washed his hands and feet in it, thereby turning it into a curing well. Wells believed to have been blessed by a saint provide a naturally replenished source of holy water that was not under direct church control in the same way that access to shrines or portable reliquaries were. They might be understood as a primary means by which a community connected with their local saint, albeit one that is difficult to identify and not always recorded in written sources.[164]

Early Christian relics were perhaps the most powerful of objects, capable of bringing healing (and other miracles) to individuals. Bodily relics, portable reliquaries, contact relics and blessed objects brought different levels of access to this divine power to ordinary people. Individuals were able to touch, and literally connect with, objects thought to be simultaneously on earth and heaven. They could be used in an intimate way – touched, applied to the body or eaten – in order to cure the body. Potentially they could be taken away from a church and into the home. Healing was an important aspect of how individuals interacted with Christianity and its establishments, objects and people. It is an aspect about which we have some written evidence, as well as a chance of identifying archaeological material.

PERSONAL CHRISTIAN EXPERIENCE

Reconstructing the emotional and sensory impact of interaction with Christianity through drawing in the senses allows us to engage further with individuals. A surviving 12th-century Italian text gives us a sense of the kinds of details about sensory experience that we lack for Christianity in Early Medieval Scotland. This account is about an important event in the Christian calendar, the lighting of the Easter candle:

> *The night before Easter Sunday all candles and lamps were extinguished. A new flame was struck and kindled and into the darkened church came a procession of clergy bearing incense and the new flame. In white robes, the liturgical colour for Easter, the deacon carrying the lighted taper chanted* Lumen Christi, *the 'light of Christ', in three different parts of the church, each time in a higher tone to which the congregation responded. He then sang, pressed grains of incense into the Easter candle in the form of a cross and finally lit the candle with the new flame. All other candles and lamps*

in the church were then lit from this flame and the 'night became as bright as day'.[165]

This text evokes the sounds, smells, lighting and performance of Christian rituals that were fundamental to people's experiences of Christianity, but which can be difficult to reconstruct from archaeological evidence. The role of Early Christian hand-bells – in creating atmosphere, bringing attention to important points of church rituals, signalling arrival, death or danger, for instance – will be explored in chapter three of this book.

Another important element affecting the experience of being in a church would have been the amount and kind of light provided. Lighting is a practical necessity, particularly for night-time church attendance. Unlike the home, a church would not benefit from the light of an open fire, but would depend upon dedicated means of light provision such as lamps or candles. Textual descriptions of early churches emphasise the splendour of brilliantly-lit churches. The luminosity of these interiors was an image of heavenly light.[166] About the gifts of gold, jewels and silken tapestries, beautifully picked out with gold and given to churches by the Northumbrian sainted King Oswald, Alcuin says:

> ... *Chandeliers and lanterns he placed throughout holy buildings,*
> *there to represent the starry heaven ...*[167]

Christian thought interpreted real light as a metaphor for the divine light of Christ, with candles and lamps central to rituals such as those surrounding the celebration of Easter. The account of St Columba's death recorded by the Ionan monk Adomnán relates that the divine light apparently emanated from the saint in a dark church where the lamps of the brethren had not yet been brought.[168]

Yet there is virtually no recognised evidence for artificial lighting dated to the Early Medieval period in Scotland. Surprisingly, given the importance of light to Christian celebrations, no lamps or candlesticks have been identified.[169] Has the evidence not survived, or are we simply missing it? Candles would be highly unlikely to survive because they would be made from organic materials and, once used, they would leave only residues of wax or scraps of the wick.[170] Many simple stone lamps have been recovered from excavations, but they are thought to be earlier in date than the Early Medieval period.[171] Bowls, such as elaborate metal 'hanging bowls' [1.57], might be used to contain burning oil, but no stains or areas of carbonisation have been identified, weakening the case that they were used as lamps.[172]

Glass lamps were certainly used elsewhere in the Early Christian world, and a tiny glass sherd from the Anglo-Saxon monastery at Wearmouth and Jarrow in Tyne & Wear, has been identified as being from the handle of a glass lamp, perhaps made in Byzantium.[173] Whithorn has produced one of the most important assemblages of imported Early Medieval pottery and glass vessel sherds. The imported glass vessels are usually assumed to have been drinking cups, although very similarly shaped glasses from Byzantium have been interpreted as lamps.[174] The most common shape from Whithorn is a cone-shaped beaker, which because of its pointed base means that it cannot be put down when full of liquid. Such beakers might perhaps have been used to hold oil for burning, although in this

Fig. 1.57 (below): A silver hanging-bowl from the St Ninian's Isle hoard, Shetland. The bowl would have been hung from rings held in the mouths of three boar-shaped mounts.

Fig. 1.58 (opposite): One of a set of thin silver bowls from the St Ninian's Isle hoard, Shetland. Each of the bowls is decorated with fine punched and inscribed designs, many of which feature Christian symbolism.

case they would require a suspension chain, bracket or a stand to hold them, and nothing of this sort has been confidently identified.

While little evidence of artificial lighting survives from Early Christian Scotland, there is some evidence for the manipulation of light and colour in the form of coloured window glass. Excavations at Whithorn have recovered the earliest coloured window glass fragments from post-Roman Scotland.[175] Indeed, the range of colours and the number of pieces found, exceeds that from many important church sites in England of a similar date.[176] We tend to take glazed and multi-coloured windows for granted, but they would have been a revelation to those seeing them for the first time. Dazzling light and colour would signal the importance of a building, as coloured glass windows were not at all common. And, as mentioned above, light was used symbolically in Early Christian art and thinking to represent and recall divine power.[177] There is insufficient evidence to understand the attitudes towards the provision of natural light in early Scottish churches generally, but Tomás Ó Carragáin has suggested that it was used sparingly in Irish churches. A generally dim interior might contribute to the sense of entering a 'sacred, almost otherwordly space'.[178] The drama and atmosphere of an early church

EARLY MEDIEVAL SCOTLAND

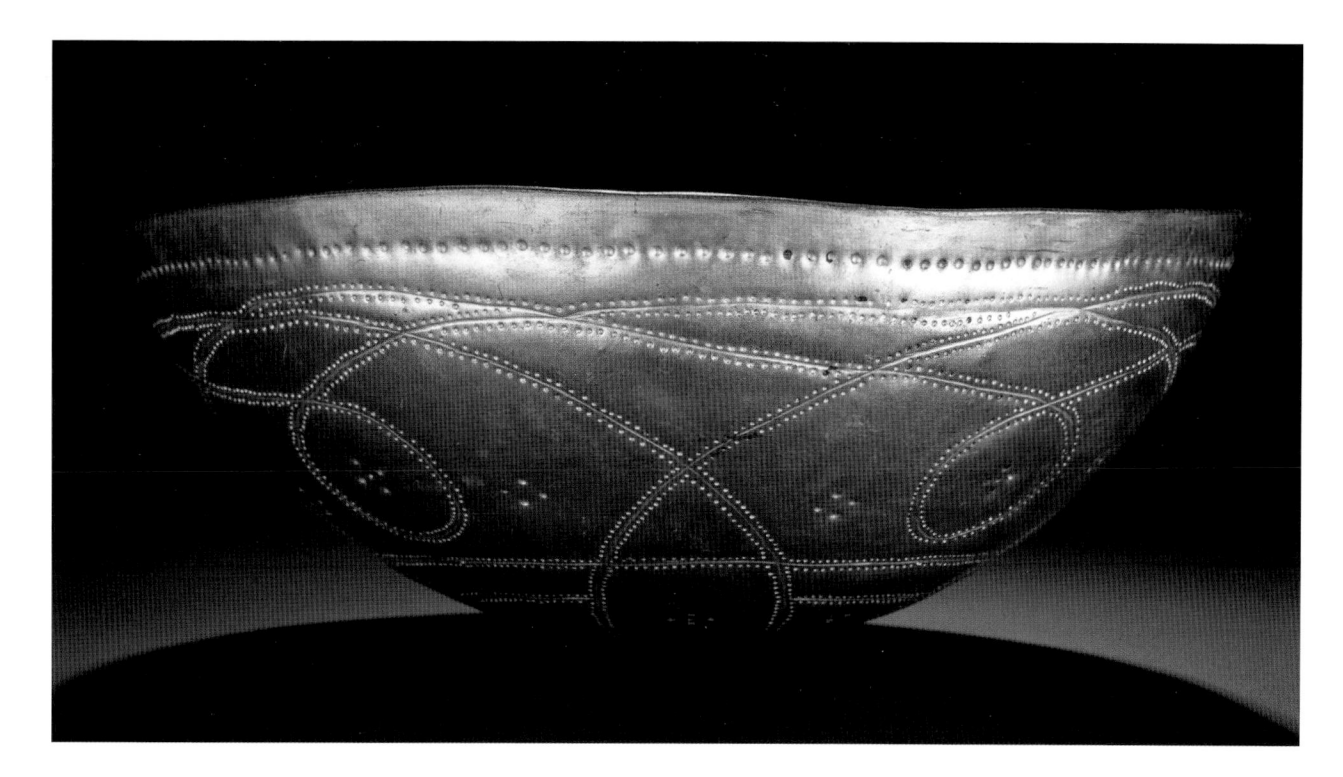

would be heightened by focal points illuminated in the gloom, whether by thin shafts of daylight (perhaps falling on an altar from an eastern window) or by artificial lighting. Colour was also important and could be used symbolically in Christian art. However, colour is also usually fragile and rarely survives – it can fade, flake or be deliberately obscured. Unfortunately we cannot reconstruct the design of the coloured windows at Whithorn. The sherds were concentrated around the southern and eastern walls of the burial chapel, although some were associated with the main church building. While it used to be thought that glass windows could only be found in stone buildings, it has now been recognised that they could also be a feature of timber churches.[179]

Written accounts of the miracles that occurred at Whithorn speak of lofty architecture, a gleaming church building and marble floors,[180] although this grandeur could be the result of artistic licence and a desire to promote the shrine. No remains of marble floors were found by the site's excavators, although it might not be as unlikely as it seems: the transportation of a slab of marble from Rome to Early Christian Britain during the 8th century is recorded in written Anglo-Saxon sources.[181] Other Early Medieval texts describe the paintings and precious textiles that adorned Northumbrian churches, neither of which are likely to survive.

It is possible that some of the many carved stones, including the grand crosses, were originally intended to be inside a church building (rather than out in the landscape). Certainly there is evidence for elaborate church interiors featuring expertly carved stone sculptures. A sculptured slab from Jedburgh, Scottish Borders [1.59], has been traditionally identified as a shrine fragment, but is more likely to be part of an elaborate church interior, perhaps an altar frontal or chancel screen fragment.[182] In either case, it was intended to be within a church, and as such formed part of the performative space used during the liturgy. The quality of the carving on the Jedburgh slab stands out amongst Northumbrian sculpture for its ability to communicate the liveliness of its subjects. It is decorated with a vine, with

INDIVIDUALS

57

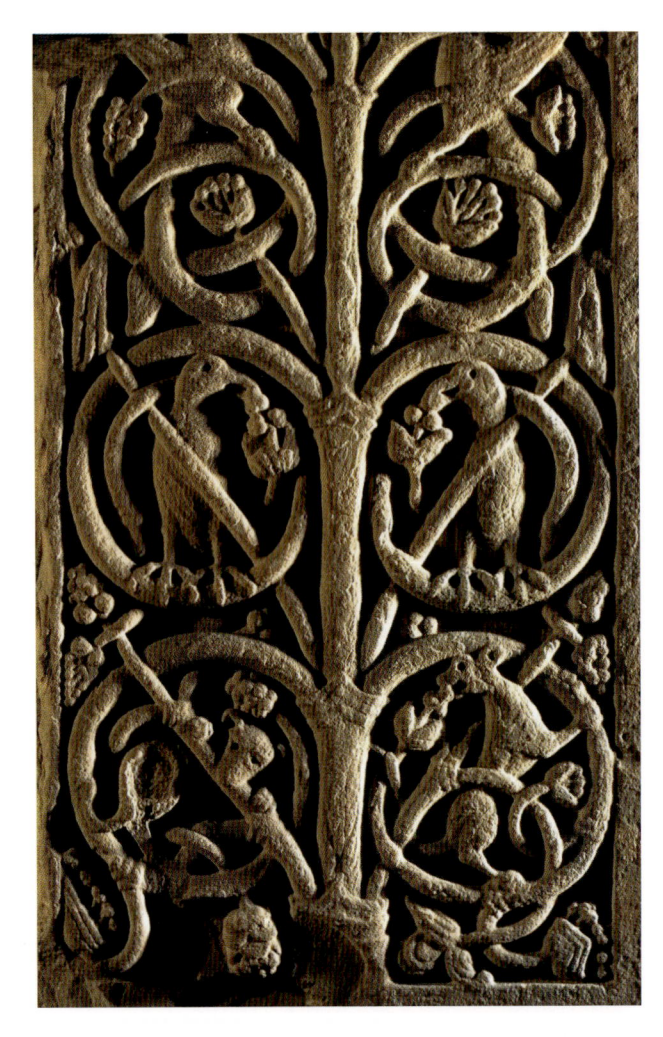

Fig. 1.59: An Anglo-Saxon carved stone, probably part of a decorated altar, from Jedburgh in the Scottish Borders. The creatures that sit within the vine, and in some cases nibble its fruit or stems, would have been originally even more life-like, having bright, shiny eyes made from small gems or pieces of glass.

animals and birds being nourished by its grapes – a clear and common allusion to the Eucharist, and to the nourishing of the congregation by the church – a design that would have been particularly appropriate for an altar.

Like many other pieces of Anglo-Saxon sculpture, the creatures of the Jedburgh slab have deeply carved eye-sockets that are now empty but would originally have contained insets – probably glass or semi-precious stones – to bring the eyes to life.[183] The impact of this carving might have been increased further with the judicious use of colour, and heightened by the flickering light and shadow of an interior space. If embellished with white gesso, gold leaf and bright gleaming eyes, its appearance might have evoked a response along the lines of a passage from an Irish Early Christian text, *The Evernew Tongue*. In describing the tree that produced the wood for Christ's cross, it says:

> *The brilliance of the moon and sun and the shining stars, shine from its blossoms. … Three-hundred and sixty-five birds, with the brightness of snow, with golden wings, with gleaming eyes, sing many songs in many languages from its branches.*[184]

The primary ritual of the Christian Church – the liturgy – requires special vessels: a chalice to hold Eucharistic wine, and a paten or plate on which to place the bread. An individual's participation in the Eucharist would have been central to their experience of Christianity, involving sight, sound and taste as they partook of the wine and bread thought literally to be transformed into the blood and body of Christ. Sources from the Continent suggest an individual church might have many precious vessels, often displayed on altars.[185] No Early Medieval liturgical vessels have been definitely identified from Scotland, meaning that at present we lack the material objects central to the most important Christian rituals.[186] Only seven liturgical chalices are known from the British Isles – five from Ireland and two from England.[187] The shapes of these vessels came to differ between regions and therefore they might not necessarily reflect the types of vessels used in the Early Church in Scotland.

Might precious imported glass vessels have played a role in the liturgy?[188] Fragile glass vessels were clearly high status objects – often found on sites with other imported objects, as well as evidence of precious metalworking.

Fig. 1.60: A detail from one of the silver bowls from the St Ninian's Isle hoard, Shetland.

They are more common on secular high status sites than monasteries, but these sites have also been more fully excavated than ecclesiastical centres. Uniquely, glass vessels were translucent and available in a range of different colours, some pale and subtle while others (from around the 8th century onwards) were bold and bright. Fragments of rare dichroic glass – glass that appears to the viewer to be different colours in transmitted and reflected light – were found at Whithorn.[189] These would have been splendid, highly prized and perhaps mystifying objects. Among this dichroic glass are sherds of a rare stemmed beaker or goblet in pale wine-coloured glass, perhaps a particularly suitable vessel for use in the liturgy?[190]

Fine pottery tablewares were also imported from the Mediterranean and are often found with imported glass fragments. African Red Slipware was imported from the Carthage region in modern Tunisia. This type of pottery is a fairly rare import, and in Scotland it has only been found at Whithorn and Iona. The sherds from Whithorn came from a bowl and a plate, as well as a possible flagon, and the Iona example is a single sherd from a plate. Might fine imported pottery vessels such as these have been used in the Early Christian liturgy?[191] One sherd from Whithorn had been ground down, perhaps suggesting it carried some talismanic value.[192] Among the imported pottery from Whithorn are types known to have contained olive oil and wine[193] – both necessary substances for church rituals.

If precious metals were being used to make Eucharistic vessels in Scotland, then the thin silver bowls (some decorated with cross-based designs) [1.58, 1.60], spoon and forked implement from the St Ninian's Isle hoard might be strong candidates.[194] Alternatively, they might have been votive gifts to the church, or have been used for secular feasting.[195] Feasting and drinking is a strong feature in Early Medieval secular poetry and forms a mainstay of our picture of the culture of the heroic hall. But the use of special and valuable containers for the ritualised and symbolic consumption of food and drink is something common to both the secular and the Christian worlds.

INDIVIDUALS

Fig. 1.61: Animals running around a silver bowl from the St Ninian's Isle hoard, Shetland.

DRAWING TOGETHER SOME INDIVIDUAL THREADS

'Looking after yourself' has featured strongly in this exploration of individuals, whether through the protective designs of objects worn on the body or the touching of holy bones and their caskets. Christianity has been a thread running through this chapter, either explicitly in the relics and saints' powers, or in a more subtle way in the drawing in of Christian motifs into the weave of older protective designs.

There has been a tendency among archaeologists to see Early Medieval objects essentially as badges that existed to be read by others – demonstrating to a community audience an individual's social standing, wealth, ethnic background or religious affiliation, for example. But not necessarily everything was intended for an audience: the size, orientation and wear on some motifs or inscriptions hints that they were aimed at the wearer rather than a wider audience.

The themes explored here are only some of the many different ways in which archaeologists can attempt to reconnect with people in their stories of the past. The potential range of circumstances, associations and meanings of Early Medieval objects to those who owned, wore, gave or saw them, are fleeting but fundamental issues.

EARLY MEDIEVAL SCOTLAND

NOTES

1. De Waal 2010, 348.
2. Kelly and Sikora 2011.
3. For instance, the miracles of St Ninian (see section 'Sick bodies').
4. Fraser 2009, 53–54 and references in his note 33; Woolf 2007, 28.
5. For a brief, general introduction to sex and gender in archaeology, and further reading on the topic, see Whitley 1998, 219–21.
6. *Ibid.*, 220.
7. See Coon 2008.
8. Maldonado 2011, 173.
9. Often described as the 'horned cairn complex' (see Grieg et al. 2000; Maldonado 2011, 233).
10. Maldonado 2011, 172.
11. This is gradually being addressed for other areas and periods: for example, recent work by Dawn McLaren (2012) on Bronze Age child burials, a 1999 study on Anglo-Saxon childhood by Sally Crawford, and work on Roman and Medieval childhood by Wiedermann 1988 and Shahar 1990, respectively.
12. Maldonado 2011, 174.
13. Only traces of a potential Early Medieval church building and no structures identified as the 'school house' were found during excavation at Inchmarnock. See Lowe 2008, 75–86, 257.
14. Forsyth and Tedeschi 2008, 130.
15. *Ibid.*, 132.
16. Clancy 1998, 94.
17. National Museums Scotland [NMS] accession no. X.NA 3.
18. Gabra-Sanders 2001.
19. Wood 2003.
20. For example, Kelly 2010 explores the emotional impact of shoes, and particularly how they have become a 'pregnant signifier of twentieth-century horrors', embodied in haunting images of the holocaust of piles of shoes in Nazi concentration camps.
21. Riello and McNeil, quoted in Kelly 2010, 59.
22. NMS X.TA 10 and X.TA 11: radiocarbon dated to 1350 BP, calibrated using OxCal version 4.1 to AD 439–937. See Crone 2000, 132.
23. Groenman-van Waateringe in Crone 2000, 129–133.
24. Barber 1981; Goubitz et.al. 2001, 390–91.
25. NMS X.IB 243.
26. Detailed attention was sometimes given to depicting hair on sculptured stones and evidence from Ireland suggests that it could be tightly bound with people's identities and wider symbolism. See Sayers 1991.
27. NMS X.FC 301.
28. NMS X.NS 36.
29. Sharples 1998.
30. NMS X.HSA 793.
31. NMS X.IB 189.
32. Reviewed in Ritchie 2005. There is also limited textile evidence from Ireland, and there too literary and sculptural sources have been drafted in to provide supporting evidence. See Fitzgerald 1997; McEnchroe Williams 2002; Whitfield 2006.
33. Dodwell 1982, 145–46; Henderson 1999, 122–35; Whitfield 2001, 223–25.
34. Young 2006, 180.
35. Heald 2010; Heald 2005.
36. For example, see van Houtts 1999, especially 93–120.
37. The chain from Hoardweel, Scottish Borders (NMS IL.2009.15.5), for example, has an internal circumference of 34 cm.
38. A major programme of analysis of the silver composition of the chains is currently underway at National Museums Scotland. It will examine the differences between each link of a single chain, as well as differences between each of the nine surviving chains and should help us to examine this question further.
39. NMS X.EQ 340.
40. Meaney (1981) regarded all Anglo-Saxon beads as having the potential to be amulets, whereas others have focused only on special or unusual beads.
41. Clancy (1998 [A4], 48) translates this as amber beads, although Koch (1997, 57) renders it as amber 'jewellery'.
42. NMS X.FC 12–X.FC 25.

43 NMS X.FC 8; Stevenson 1974, 1983.
44 For detailed discussions of the means of fastening penannular and pseudo-penannular brooches, see Whitfield 2001, 2004.
45 National Museum of Ireland R 4015.
46 See Stevenson 1974; Whitfield 2001, 2004; Blackwell (in press).
47 Barnes and Page 2006, 217–21.
48 Spearman and Ryan in Youngs 1989, 92.
49 Whitfield 2001, 226.
50 Whitfield 2004. However, some of the pictures showing people wearing brooches are more ambiguous than has been admitted. For example, Whitfield describes Muiredach's cross at Monasterboice as showing Christ wearing a brooch on his right shoulder. In actual fact, the brooch is only a little to the right of the centre of his chest – the two sides of his robes meet in the middle of his body.
51 See chapter three ('Ideas and Ideologies') for more discussion of the identity of this figure. Only Mary and Jesus are usually shown riding sideways on beasts in religious art. The female gender of the figure has usually been taken for granted, although some traditions of the depiction of Jesus emphasise his flowing hair, lack of facial hair, and what might be regarded as a fairly feminine appearance.
52 Trench Jellico 1999. There may be a second example of a seated figure depicted with loom on a piece of sculpture which comes from Kingoldrum (illustrated in Fraser 2008, 57), but the stone is incomplete and the surviving portion does not include the upper torso or head of the figure. It is unclear therefore whether the figure would have worn a brooch or had feminine characteristics.
53 Whitfield 1996. A brief summary of debate surrounding the date and place of origin of the *Book of Kells* is summarised in Meehan 1994, appendix I.
54 While Irish sources attest to men *and* women wearing brooches, we have tended to assume that men wore brooches in Scotland (although there is no evidence on sculptured stones for this) and yet require the female use to be demonstrated by evidence. Margaret Nieke noted the female figures with brooches 'indicates that they crossed the gender divide' (Nieke 1993, 129). To my knowledge it has not been suggested that the evidence supports a primary use of brooches by women in Early Medieval Scotland.
55 Nieke 1993; Whitfield 2001 and 2004.
56 Whitfield 2001, 226–27.
57 *Ibid.*, 226.
58 Etchingham and Swift 2004, 47.
59 Whitfield 2004, 98.
60 'The Wooing of Becfhola', Whitfield 2006, 97.
61 See Hough in Lapidge et al. 2001, 302–303 and refs therein.
62 'The Wooing of Becfhola', Whitfield 2006, 97.
63 Whitfield 2006, 97.
64 Etchingham and Swift 2004, 44–48; Whitfield 2004, 99.
65 Whitfield 2004, 93–94.
66 There is also the potential, although near impossible to confirm, that objects melted down for recycling transferred elements of the biography/associations/relationships to new objects made from them.
67 The ideas explored within this section are treated in more detail in Blackwell (2011).
68 Belief in protective objects and substances continued well beyond the Early Medieval period, as demonstrated by burial practices from the 11th to the 15th centuries. It was tolerated by Christianity, and pagan Anglo-Saxon practices, including charms and amulets, became 'thoroughly Christianised' (Gilchrist 2008).
69 During the Medieval period, brooches were often used as vehicles for religious inscriptions and designs, part of the role of which will have been Christian protection (Stevenson 1974, 38).
70 Nieke 1993, 132.
71 Kitzinger 1993, 3.
72 Identified by Martin Goldberg during the course of writing this book. NMS X.FC 294, X.FC 293 and X.FC 289.
73 For example, see Speake 1981, 77–92 for discussion of the significance of the boar, bird and snake motifs in Anglo-Saxon art.
74 Webster 1999, 235–36.
75 NMS H.KE 14.
76 In private possession.
77 NMS X.FC 282 and X.FC 283.

78 NMS X.FC 282.
79 Leslie Webster in Webster and Backhouse (eds) 1991, 223–24.
80 This panel has been likened to a book shrine and to a reliquary on a brooch from Belgium (although the Hunterston panel is not a reliquary – there is no space to contain a relic): see Stevenson 1974, 40. It may be intended to bring to mind these kinds of powerful and richly elaborated Christian objects.
81 Stevenson 1974, 39.
82 *Ibid.*, 39–40.
83 *Ibid.*, 40.
84 Gilchrist 2008.
85 There is a useful summary by Jane Stevenson in Warren 1987.
86 Recently summarised by Foster (in press).
87 *Adomnán of Iona: Life of St Columba*, trans. by Sharpe (1995), [II 7], 159–60.
88 Also raised recently by Foster (in press).
89 Domestic worship was supposedly renounced by a 4th-century church council, but a role for the home in Christian practice seems to have continued – particularly regarding women and notions of purity, sanctity, and virtue. See Bowes 2008, especially 76.
90 See the major volume on relics accompanying the exhibition *Treasures of Heaven* (Bagnoli et al. [eds] 2011).
91 Krueger 2010, 5.
92 The 2010 British Academy Raleigh Lecture on History, delivered by Julia Smith, 15 November 2010, in Edinburgh.
93 When unearthed or moved, parts of the body could be removed and used as portable relics. St Cuthbert's hair was cut when the body was unearthed and found to be uncorrupted. Bede tells us the hair was 'either to give as relics to their friends who asked for them, or to show as proof of the miracle'. He also tells us that the hair was kept in a casket. *Bede's The Ecclesiastical History of the English People*, trans. by Colgrave 1999, [IV 32], 232–33.
94 Edwards 2002; Smith 1990.
95 Fisher 2001, 131–34.
96 The names of St John's Cross and St Martin's Cross were first recorded in the 17th century. See Fisher 2001, 133.
97 *Adomnán of Iona: Life of St Columba*, trans. by Sharpe (1995), [III 23], 227.
98 Fisher 2001, 16 and 135.
99 Henderson, pers. comm. to D. Clarke.
100 Sally Foster notes recumbent stones at Meigle have recesses 'designed to hold things' and possibly acting as a reliquary (Foster, in press).
101 Lucas 1986, 13. Lucas argues that relics in Ireland could function as a sign of the importance of a bishop or abbot when travelling outside their church; to encourage payments due to the church and to protect those that travelled in order to collect them; to help bring into effect the Law of Adomnán, which forbade the killing of innocents; on the battlefield as holy talismans – for instance, the Irish psalter book known as the 'Cathach of Colmcille' – although it is difficult to know how early this practice began; to make oaths sworn on them binding; and to effect curses. This range of uses of relics has much in common with secular peripatetic kingship, whereby the king and immediate supporters would travel around their lands in order to enforce their power and collect dues.
102 *The Miracles of St Nynia the Bishop*, translated by Clancy 1998, [13], 136: '… so came the day, in the heights of the tall temple, when the suppliant at the altar stood in prayer, where rests the buried body of bishop Nynia …'.
103 *Bede's The Ecclesiastical History of the English People*, trans. by Colgrave 1999, [I 18], 31.
104 Whichever analogy is preferred, there has been a tendency to separate discussion of this small group of shrines from scholarship on other shapes of early Christian reliquaries. They are in fact not dissimilar in shape to another group of shrines, called purse-shaped shrines. These are slightly narrower objects and many are not intended to open, but they do feature the same pitched roof over a rectangular body.
105 See Bagnoli et al. (eds) 2011; Walker Bynum and Gerson, 1997, 4.
106 Bagnoli et al. (eds) 2011.
107 Some reliquaries have small 'windows', formed of mica, to allow the relics to be seen when the box is closed.

108 There seems to be a contrast between house-shaped reliquaries that essentially act as a box that can be opened and other types of reliquaries where the object is permanently encased in precious metals, meaning that the original object is not easily accessible.

109 Caldwell 2001.

110 Indeed there are a number of false assertions about even basic details of the reliquary in the limited published literature, including the number of surviving mounts (an image showing all mounts complete, with no mention in the text that two are in fact missing, was used by Alcock 2003, 328, fig. 133), the colour of the sole surviving inset of the roof terminal (Alcock gives this as red, when it is actually blue glass; Alcock 2003, 328), and the material of the metal plates (Blindheim says the front of the box has a copper-alloy plate underneath the visible silver one, but this is not the case: Blindheim 1984, 38). Interesting comments regarding reliquaries as a type of object or practices involving reliquaries generally have not been applied to specific examples such as the Monymusk reliquary.

111 See below for the possible identification of house-shaped shrines such as Monymusk as chrismals (containers for the host) rather than reliquaries – in this guise it could perhaps have belonged to a holy person before being encased in precious metals.

112 O'Donoghue 2011a; O'Donoghue 2011b. Thanks are due to Heather Pulliam for drawing these to my attention. Interpretation of the *Book of Deer* and its use by clerics when visiting the homes of the dying to administer the Last Rites suggests a context where special containers to convey the holy Eucharist would be needed – it was a sin to allow harm to come to these most holy viands. See Márkus 2008.

113 Bowes 2008, 221.

114 Bagnoli et al. (eds) 2011, 138.

115 *Ibid.*, 139.

116 When figural art and narrative scenes do occur on Pictish sculpture, they are almost entirely limited to Old Testament themes.

117 Stevenson 1983, 473–74.

118 The most commonly cited parallel for the shape of the house-shaped boxes is an illustration in the *Book of Kells* of the Temptation page (202v). This analogy would also be particularly appropriate if the house-shaped boxes are chrismals, given the context of this page and its focus on Christ and his Resurrection.

119 O'Reilly 1993, 110. Thanks are due to Heather Pulliam for drawing this to my attention.

120 Other possible routes of enquiry include exploring the use of colour on Early Christian objects. For example, yellow enamel is only used in one place on the reliquary, to depict a very rare motif, a kind of sunburst, on the side-plate. This restriction of yellow highlights the 'sunburst', if indeed more specific colour symbolism was not intended. It is possible the restricted use of yellow for this unusual shape was intended to represent divine light. Exploration of colour symbolism use in early Christian illuminated manuscripts is, surprisingly, a recent scholarly development, but one that is producing very interesting results (see, for example, papers by Heather Pulliam 2012 and 2013).

121 *The Miracles of St Nynia the Bishop*, translated by Clancy (ed.) 1998, [4], 128.

122 *Ibid.* [9], 132–33.

123 Smith 1990.

124 It has been suggested that St Ninian was an Anglo-Saxon rendition of a British cult of Uinniau (Clancy 2001) that Whithorn appropriated and made its own (Fraser 2002b). These texts gave the impression that what was probably a dispersed cult of Uinniau (two focuses of names) was instead focused on a single and therefore important church foundation. This may have been part of a justification for the ecclesiastical power of Whithorn over other church foundations.

125 There is likely to have been a significant amount of cult activity that did not take place within a church shrine, by analogy with Brittany and Wales where springs played an important role. See below for a discussion of the role of water and springs in early Christianity in Scotland.

126 Aitken 1955; Thomas 1971, 179, fig. 86.

127 Note that there is no identified archaeological evidence of lighting from Early Medieval Scotland.

128 Hill 1997, 352–54.
129 *Adomnán of Iona: Life of St Columba*, trans. by Sharpe (1995), [II 11], 162–63.
130 *Ibid.*, [II 4], 156–58.
131 *Bede's The Ecclesiastical History of the English People*, trans. by Colgrave 1999, [IV 27], 223.
132 *Ibid.*, [IV 32], 232–33.
133 *Ibid.*, [V 6], 242–44. For another instance of the successful combining of saintly and medical treatments, see [V 2], 237–38. For an example of Christianised healing folklore concerning the right and wrong phases of the moon in which to bleed a patient, see [V 3], 239.
134 Nicolson in Hill 1997, 427, cat. no. 66.60, fig. 10.104.
135 Daphne Home Lorimer in James 1999, 773.
136 Henderson 2008c, 49.
137 Márkus 2008.
138 *Ibid.*, 69.
139 Graham-Campbell 2001, 20–26; Graham-Campbell 1995, 4.
140 The identification of this object as decayed beeswax has been recently confirmed by scientific analysis (NMS unpublished report). The inclusion of what appear to be sea-worn glass fragments in the hoard suggests the possibility that later material might have been inadvertently incorporated when it was recovered in the early 20th century.
141 Leyerle 2008, 237.
142 Campbell 2007, 74.
143 *Bede's The Ecclesiastical History of the English People*, trans. by Colgrave 1999, [III 9], 124.
144 *Ibid.*, [III 11], 127.
145 *Ibid.*, [III 17], 136–37.
146 *Adomnán of Iona: Life of St Columba*, trans. by Sharpe (1995).
147 2 Kings 23: 25–21.
148 *Adomnán of Iona: Life of St Columba*, trans. by Sharpe (1995), 181–82.
149 Cross-marked stone from St Ninian's Isle cave, NMS X.IB 54. Cross-marked stone from Hoddom. See Lowe 2008, 131, cat. no. SF151.
150 NMS X.GP 209.
151 The rock crystal was suggested by the excavator as 'likely to have been imported as charms or relics, or for the manufacture of jewellery' (Hill 1997, 472–73). There is no evidence that rock crystal was used in secular jewellery in Early Medieval Scotland, unlike in Anglo-Saxon England, suggesting that an alternative purpose is likely.
152 *Ibid.*, 469–70.
153 *Ibid.*, 469. A wide range of different small collected objects such as pebbles, fossils, bones and teeth have been found in Anglo-Saxon graves and interpreted as (pre-Christian) keepsakes or talismans. See Meaney 1981.
154 See Lapidge et al. (eds) 2001, 278; Kitson 1978, 1983.
155 Bagnoli et al. (eds) 2011, 138.
156 Organ 1973.
157 Lane and Campbell 2000, 173, fig. 4.86, pl. 21.
158 Leyerle 2008, 236.
159 *Adomnán of Iona: Life of St Columba*, trans. by Sharpe (1995), [II 7], 159–60. The salt and the two pegs on which it hung were miraculously preserved, despite a fire that destroyed the rest of the house. This is paralleled by a 5th-century Syrian bishop who apparently slept with 'oil of the martyrs' hung above his bed and a holy cloak under his pillow. See Layerle 2008, 225.
160 Bitel 2004, 615.
161 *Adomnán of Iona: Life of St Columba*, trans. by Sharpe (1995), [II 5], 158–59. The saint also foretold how many more years the sufferer would live after being cured, and wrote this number on the lid of the box that carried the unnamed 'blessing'.
162 *Bede's The Ecclesiastical History of the English People*, trans. by Colgrave 1999 [III 2], 111–13. This is the cross that Oswald erected at a place known to Bede as Heavenfield. Bede tells us that monks of the monastery at Hexham came every year on the day before the king was killed to keep an overnight vigil, to sing psalms, and on the following morning to offer up 'the holy sacrifice and oblation on his behalf. And since that good custom has spread, a church has lately [i.e. soon before 731] been built there'.

163 *Adomnán of Iona: Life of St Columba*, trans. by Sharpe (1995), [II 11], 162–63.
164 See above concerning the use of written hagiography, which was not created for all saints, as many did not need written lives to mediate between their cult and community. Places such as wells and springs in the landscape provided deeply embedded places of contact between the saint and followers that were maintained by repeated use and oral traditions.
165 Freeman 1945.
166 Gage 1999, 44.
167 Godman (ed) 1982, 26–29.
168 *Adomnán of Iona: Life of St Columba*, trans. by Sharpe (1995), [III 23], 229.
169 Two iron wick holders found at Whithorn may possibly have been displaced from 9th- or 10th-century contexts, but perhaps are more likely to be Medieval in date (see Hill 1997, 430).
170 Candles might be formed in moulds – but none have been recognised – or by the successive dipping of a wick in molten wax or tallow.
171 Eckhardt 2002, 243. They are very similar in shape to simple open lamps from Roman Britain. A lamp carved from the soft stone steatite was found during excavations at Scalloway, Shetland, which also produced evidence of occupation during the Early Medieval period. See Sharman in Sharples 1998, 149.
172 A wide variety of uses for hanging bowls have been suggested – including lamps – but all remain speculative (for example, Peers and Radford 1943, 47). The author of the most definitive study of hanging bowls to date has argued that a function involving water is more likely – either as part of church rituals, for washing hands or the liturgical vessels, or in secular contexts (Bruce-Mitford 2005, 32).
173 Cramp 2006, 320, cat. no. GIV29 (supplementary catalogue of lost fragments not seen by Evison). Also see Crowfoot and Harden 1931 for a discussion of Byzantine glass lamps.
174 Crowfoot and Harden 1931.
175 Cramp in Hill 1997, 326–31.
176 *Ibid.*, 327.
177 Kessler 2004, 174–76.
178 Ó Carragáin 2009, 133.
179 Cramp in Hill 1997, 327–28.
180 *The Miracles of St Nynia the Bishop*, in Clancy (ed.) 1998, 128, 134, 135, 137.
181 Discussed in Dodwell 1982, 35.
182 Radford 1955; Webster and Backhouse (eds) 1991, 153, no. 14.
183 Recent scientific analysis of a piece of sculpture from Aberlady, East Lothian, has identified the remains of a tin lining in these deep eye-sockets. This confirms, as has been generally assumed, that the sockets originally contained decorative insets.
184 Carey 1998, 85–86.
185 See Ryan 1997, note 20, for a discussion.
186 In discussing the similar non-survival of Welsh liturgical objects, David Petts draws attention to 'the cumulative impact of Viking raiding, Norman ecclesiastical interventions, zealous promoters of the Reformation, the seventeenth-century puritan ideal and over-enthusiastic Victorian church restorers' (see Petts 2009, 79).
187 Ryan 1997, 1014.
188 Murray and Murray 1998, 280–81.
189 Campbell in Hill 1997, 298, 303–305.
190 *Ibid.*, 303–305. Glass sherds (as with other imports) were found in areas in the outer zone interpreted as representing domestic and potentially craft-related activities rather than around the church building. However, the inner sanctified areas of the complex were kept clean of debris and so we cannot rule out the use of prestigious glass vessels in the church itself: if a glass vessel was broken while in use here, it would be deposited elsewhere (322–23).
191 The possibility that this might have been the case in Wales, particularly as several types occasionally carry Christian symbols, was suggested in passing by Petts 2009, 80.
192 Campbell in Hill 1997, 316.
193 *Ibid.*, 317–18.
194 McRoberts 1961, 301–303.
195 O'Dell et al. 1959, 243; Small et al. 1973.

Below: A detail from one of the silver bowls from the St Ninian's Isle hoard, Shetland.

INDIVIDUALS

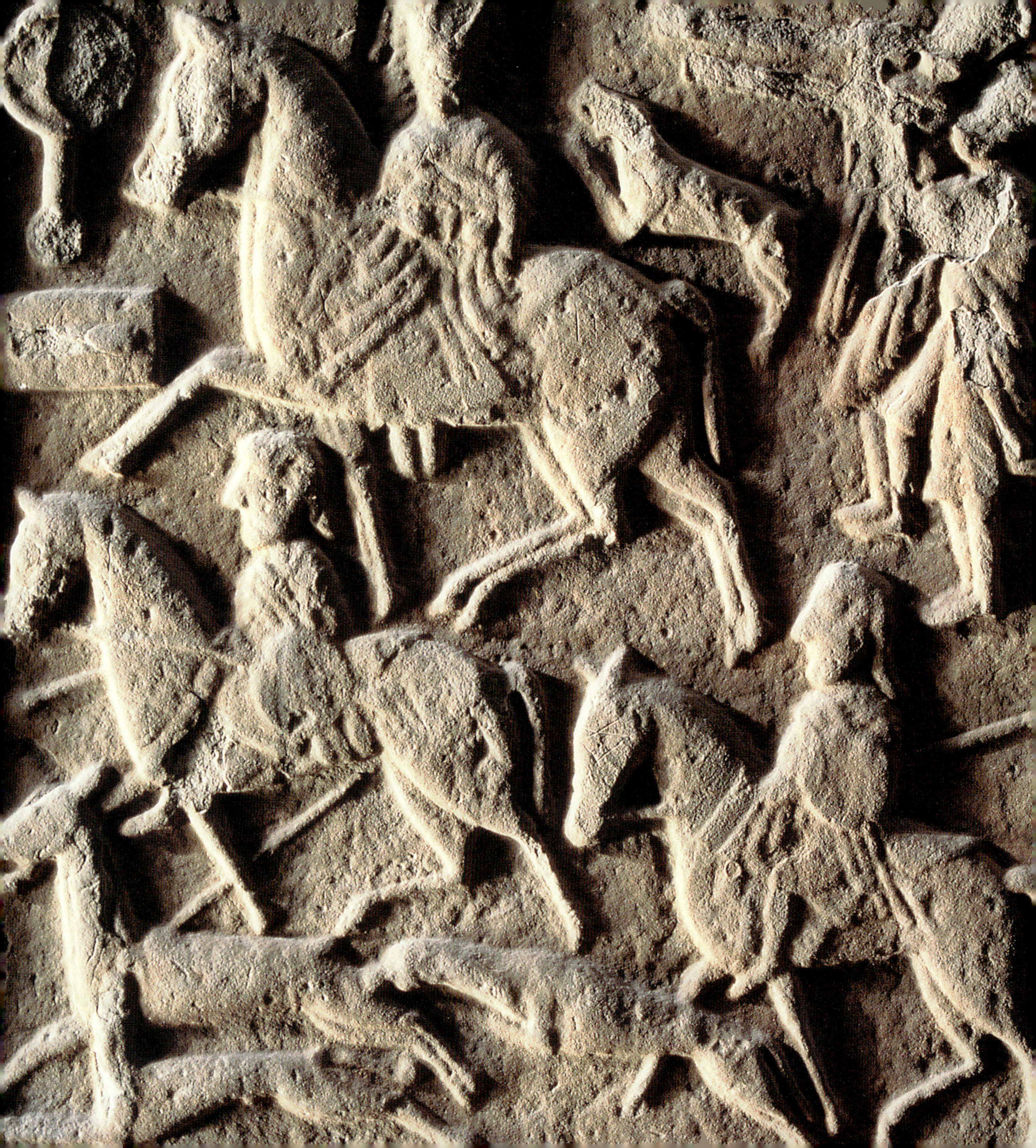

CHAPTER TWO
Communities

David Clarke

*Castles in the air, they're so easy to hide in.
And easy to build too.*[1]

★

The Master Builder,
Henrik Ibsen, 1892

At any point in time, or in any given location, numerous communities exist alongside one another. The emphasis here is given to four different communities that have left some trace in the archaeological record. The first are the communities of place that are forged and maintained around a geographic space. The second are communities of craftsmen where the links are shared skills. The third are the communities of the imagination reflecting an awareness of distant places that most people will know only though travellers' tales and objects that originated elsewhere. And fourth are the communities of memory, maintaining and using the past to negotiate the present. Aspects of all these communities are reflected in the sculptured stones of the period.

On the cross-slabs of eastern Scotland are pictures of a community. Moreover, they are depictions of the community created by some of its own members. Among the avowedly religious symbols of the new Christian beliefs are numerous images of human figures. They are not attempts at portraiture as we understand the word. Some might well be religious symbols in their own right. But their interest for us is that these human portrayals are expressed in terms of contemporary values and fashions. They are, in the effective absence of surviving texts written in Scotland, the only contemporary views from the inside rather than the outside. It is the first time we have any contemporary images, and the importance of that cannot be gainsaid.

It is not a comprehensive picture of the community. There are, for example, no slaves or peasants. The images are overwhelmingly male, making an important, if unsurprising, statement about who had power and status. The notable exception to this is provided by the female rider on the stone from Hilton of Cadboll, perhaps our only

Fig. 2.1 (opposite): Central panel of the stone from Hilton of Cadboll, Easter Ross. The female figure is the upper of the three riders.

contemporary image of a noble lady, perhaps a queen [Fig. 2.1]. The figures were never intended to illustrate a balanced cross-section of the community. Instead they show selected aspects of life in Early Historic Scotland. Essentially, they reflect the upper echelons of a hierarchical social structure. Among the images clerics are prominent, but the majority of the figures appear to be secular. For both, the emphasis is on the shared styles of the community, not a trumpeting of individuality. Because of this we can be more confident that the values and styles portrayed are those embraced and acknowledged by the wider community.

The dominant impression is of power shared by religious and secular groups. Interestingly, the contemporary religious figures – as opposed to figures of saints or those from biblical stories – are not shown engaged in overtly religious acts. The one exception is the slab from Papil, Shetland, presumptively a fitting of some kind from a church, showing both walking and mounted figures in procession towards a cross [2.2].[2] Otherwise, they are shown standing, seated or moving in poses that speak to the establishment and maintenance of authority and power. They do have some exclusive features, however. They alone, for instance, are shown with book satchels or crook-headed staffs (it is unclear whether these are appropriately termed 'crosiers' at this date). But many other aspects of their appearance are shared with undoubtedly secular figures. There is no reason to suppose that this sharing of power between secular and religious figures was a new introduction accompanying the adoption of Christianity. Adomnán's description of Columba's encounter with King Bridei certainly suggests that the wizard, Broichan, was an important figure in the royal household.[3]

The secular figures form a more diverse class, but again many elements overlap between the various groups. A simple distinction can be drawn between those who are riding – usually on a horse, but in one instance from Meigle, Perthshire, now lost, on a cart – and those walking. Some scenes involve both. These secular figures fall largely into three main groups. The first involves those bearing arms, normally a sword, shield and spear or lance. The second includes those taking part in, or watching, the hunting of deer. These may or may not be armed. In both circumstances hounds play a leading role. And the third embraces those individuals who appear to be just riding or walking but do not apparently bear arms. This last group may be clerics perhaps, although they are given no features that would identify them conclusively as such. These are three key categories in the representation of the secular com-

Fig. 2.2 (opposite): Stone slab from Papil, Shetland, showing clerics in procession towards a cross.

munity, but they do not provide a comprehensive description of all the figures.

Without these images on the stones, much of this detail would be largely absent from the archaeological record. In large part this is because burials furnished with objects were not part of the traditional practices of the groups occupying Scotland. We know, for instance, from early Anglo-Saxon burials in England, and subsequently from textual evidence, that the sword was *the* weapon to signal social status.[4] The same is suggested by the figures on the Scottish cross-slabs. The evidence from later Viking graves suggests that the sword retained its role as a status indicator throughout Britain and Ireland to well beyond the period we are reviewing here. This reflected the relatively large quantity of raw materials and the craft skills required to make a sword in comparison to other weapons such as spears. Yet swords, scabbards and their fittings are rare finds in Scotland. Spears are no more common. Confirmed shield fittings have still to be found. This provides a marked contrast with brooches that have also been interpreted as markers of social status. They are rarely shown on the stones, but are relatively common as archaeological finds. Much energy and effort has been invested by some in attempts to use the objects displayed as a basis for dating the stones. This assumes unwarranted levels of accuracy on the part of the sculptors in what are small-scale images created on the intractable medium of stone.[5] But more significantly, the focus on analysis of detail has left the bigger pictures largely uncommented upon except in terms of historical sources.

A good example of this is provided by the battle scene or scenes on the back of the Aberlemno churchyard stone, Angus [Aberlemno 2: Figs. 2.3, 2.4]. They have been regularly interpreted as images of the battle of Dún Nechtain[6] (often called the battle of Dunnichen) fought between the Picts and the Northumbrian Angles on 20 May 685.[7] This historically-based judgement has enabled ethnic labels to be applied to the figures: Picts are bareheaded, Anglo-Saxon Northumbrians wear helmets.[8] The evidence adduced in support of this is two-fold. First, Picts are not shown on any other stone wearing helmets. And second, from rare finds we know that some Anglo-Saxons had helmets – a particularly fine example has been recovered from Coppergate, York, within Northumbrian territory.[9] Yet the absence of helmets may only reflect the absence of other battle images of Picts. We certainly have no idea whether helmets were worn by either Britons or Scots. Even without the recent convincing demonstration that the battle of Nechtansmere took place much further north, severely weakening the link between the battle and the Aberlemno stone, there was very little justification for these historically-derived ethnic attributions.[10]

The sculptor has provided guides to help a reading of the scene. One side's arms are in relief, while the other side's are incised – this does not seem to be just an attempt at providing some perspective. The presence or absence of helmets could be a similar device for distinguishing between the fighting groups and it might not be any more significant than that. Nevertheless, the reading of the scene is far from straightforward. Modern commentators certainly cannot agree about it.[11] Much depends on whether the image is recording an actual battle, an imagined one, or providing a generic image of warfare. The levels of required realism might well be different in each case. Making a

Fig. 2.3: The rear face of the stone from Aberlemno, Angus, showing the battle scene.

Fig. 2.4: The cross face of the same stone from Aberlemno, Angus.

EARLY MEDIEVAL SCOTLAND

72

Fig. 2.5: A detail of the stone from the Brough of Birsay, Orkney, showing three warriors.

judgement will also need to take into account that this is our only portrayal of a battle scene except for the later Sueno's Stone at Forres, Moray.[12] Nor can its presence on a larger monument be wholly ignored. The key image on the other side of the stone is a Christian Cross in high relief. It is the dominant motif of the whole monument [2.4]. Of course, success in battle was regularly interpreted in Early Medieval texts as signifying the victor's enjoyment of God's support and so a memorial to a particularly significant battle success might not be inappropriately linked to an image of the Cross. But equally, we may be dealing with a generalised representation of an activity, familiar to all in Early Medieval Scotland, intended here to illuminate religious teachings. The latter may only require an illustration convincing in terms of the teachings but not necessarily accurate in all its details. This does not, of course, explain the presence of two apparently unrelated symbols in the panel above the battle scene.

The purpose then that lies behind the creation of any sculptured scene is probably critical to the amount of incidental information it can provide us with concerning the wider communities. This applies particularly to depictions with a unique or unusual subject matter. The reasons that lie behind the use of any of the apparently non-Biblical scenes is something that we have very little information about. Indeed, 'the function of the cross-slabs, other than as focuses of devotion to the Cross of Christ, is speculative'.[13]

Yet there are moments when we can be confident that we are grasping at least some of the messages embedded in the images. The fragmentary slab from the Brough of Birsay, Orkney, is not demonstrably part of a cross-slab, but the carvings in low relief link it with those slabs.[14] At the bottom of the slab, as it now survives, are three warriors, one behind the other [2.5]. Each carries a shield and a spear, and has a sword hanging from a belt. The front figure clearly displays his higher status. His hairstyle is more elaborate, his spear is longer with a larger head, his shield is decorated[15] and his coat has a fringe at the bottom. This much would have been obvious to the viewer, especially if the sculpture was originally coloured. Yet there are less obvious suggestions of differences in status between the middle and final figures, though here it may only reflect superiority within a shared social group. Both look very similar. They share the same subdued hairstyle, but the

COMMUNITIES

73

middle figure has an elegant beard while the final figure is clean shaven. This is probably not to be interpreted as personal choice. The hairstyle of the front figure, who also has a beard, suggests that the treatment of hair on the face and head was used to denote status, or at least age and experience. This was certainly the case in other Early Medieval communities.[16] It was potentially subject to strict rules or conventions, although these may only apply to artistic depictions and may not be a reflection of everyday practice.

This is also seen in other images: on the stone from Benvie, Angus, for example, the upper rider has the same hairstyle as the front figure of the Birsay stone, while the lower rider has a simpler hairstyle comparable to those of the following figures at Birsay [2.6, 2.7].[17] Further, the final figure on the Birsay stone stands at a lower level than the first two figures. This is a conscious choice on the part of the sculptor, as nothing about the shape or surface of the stone has forced him to place the third figure at a lower level. This may be reading too much into small differences, but the treatment of the front figure suggests that the expression of rank was usually an understated affair differentiating certain individuals in small ways, while at the same time emphasising the membership of a wider community. We have no way of knowing whether such understatement was characteristic of all levels of society, but it seems unlikely. Instead it needs to be seen as a device to promote the coherence of the ruling group in the face of the images of it painted by the texts as fractured, aggressive and competitive.

A key consequence of this understated approach is that there are no obvious images of kings on the stones. It has been argued in specific cases that the mounted rider represents a king. A good example is the mounted figure on the cross at Dupplin, Perthshire.[18] But the figure has apparently a simple hairstyle, is not certainly equipped with sword or shield, and his horse does not have a saddle-cloth. He is not given most of the features we would expect a king or high-ranking noble to have. In most cases though, this simple distinction between mounted and unmounted figures, while doubtless reflecting rank, does not enable us to recognise kings. Many stones have multiple mounted figures. The reverse of Meigle 2, Perthshire, for instance, has five riders: a larger single figure is above a group of three riders followed by a single horseman [2.8]. There are distinctions here – the group of three riders appears to be

Figs 2.6 and 2.7 (opposite): Details of the stone from Benvie, Angus, showing the upper (left) and the lower (right) of the two horsemen.

Fig. 2.8 (below): A detail of the stone from Meigle, Perthshire, showing horse riders.

COMMUNITIES

75

without the saddle-cloths seen on the mounts of the other two figures – but none is exclusive to a single rider. Other stones show the same absence of a single figure distinguished by material culture attributes from all the others. Of course, this may have been achieved through the use of colour, but the transient nature of such distinctions, relative to the carved detail, must surely have been obvious even when the stones were new. Conceivably, it was felt inappropriate to figure other kings on monuments to Christ the King. But once again the imagery of the stones is different from that of the contemporary historical texts where the importance of kingship is a continuing thread.

Perhaps these differences between stones and texts just reflect the different audiences that each was serving. The texts were clearly available only to the literate few. These were restricted to the upper echelons of society, perhaps more the religious than the secular, and necessarily reflected their interests and concerns. The stones, on the other hand, seem likely to have been intended for much wider audiences. Much depends on how these large cross-slabs were used. There has been a range of suggestions, all involving a degree of speculation because we have no stone that is demonstrably in its original position. But each assumes that the cross-slabs would be accessible to most, if not all, members of the community. This makes them very different to manuscripts. The images drawn from everyday life on the stones had to resonate with the whole community's sense of reality. They had to be sufficiently convincing that they threw up no challenge to the wider, more important, multi-layered messages of the cross's iconography. The same requirements did not apply to manuscripts. Access to them was restricted to the best educated and most sophisticated sections of the community, the clergy and aristocracy. The context as well as the medium allowed illustrations which were much more imaginative in their allusions to contemporary communities. It is the wider range of the intended audience, and the public display this involved, that makes the stones so much more important as windows on the community that created them.

Among the images on the stones, two major themes emerge, resonating one with another. The first concerns the warrior and the importance of his attributes for defining status and power. The second reflects human and animal relationships. Usually this centres on activities that similarly relate to rank and authority, riding horses or hunting. Occasionally it involves domesticated animals, principally cattle, although they are not here apparently introduced as symbols of wealth.

In the portrayal of the warrior we see echoes of the prehistoric past as well as representations of the contemporary world. The standard equipment for an elite warrior – sword, spear and shield – seems to have been established in Britain by at least the 1st century BC.[19] Little seems to have changed by the 9th century AD, although our understanding of the intervening period is hampered by the rarity of warrior burials until the appearance of Anglo-Saxon burials.[20] Moreover, the burial evidence we have is almost wholly restricted to Yorkshire and areas further south. Yet the images from the stones show that the tradition was fully maintained in Early Medieval Scotland. Many figures are portrayed with sword, spear and shield, but other combinations, such as spear and shield or spear alone, also occur. These patterns mirror those seen in the Anglo-Saxon burials to the south.

Fig. 2.9 (above): One of the silver-gilt cones from St Ninian's Isle, Shetland.

Fig. 2.10 (below): The gold and garnet pyramid from Dalmeny, West Lothian.

Only part of this warrior equipment is reflected in the surviving material. Indeed the finds are so few in number that without the support of the images on the stones we might hesitate in interpreting their significance. A fragment of a sword blade from the early excavations at Dunadd, Argyll, does not have secure context but seems best regarded as of Early Medieval date. Otherwise, we have only three stray finds from Gorton, Moray [2.14], Harvieston, Clackmannan, and Torbeck Hill, Ecclefechan, Kirkcudbrightshire, all often regarded as Viking but plausibly earlier in date, and a fragment of a blade from Carronbridge, Dumfries, loosely associated with a silver-gilt penannular brooch.[21] But only through their rarity do these blades now speak to us of status and authority.

These qualities are more obviously seen in the silver-gilt pommel and chapes (the metal strengthening at the bottom of the scabbard) in the hoard from St Ninian's Isle, Shetland [2.11–13], or the pommel from Culbin Sands, Moray. Perhaps the highly decorated silver-gilt cones from St Ninian's Isle [2.9], the garnet and gold pyramid from Dalmeny in West Lothian [2.10], or the similar stud from Markle, East Lothian, are also to be seen as parts of highly decorated swords or their belts and scabbards. The separation of these decorative elements from the blade may represent more than the retention of the most valuable parts of damaged weapons where the blade has become scrap metal to be reworked in the forge. Rare literary evidence suggests that swords were closely associated with their users and were often handed down as heirlooms. Some acquired their own histories. Captured in battle, the destruction of swords by re-using the iron of their blades may have been one of the elements involved in the wider confirmation of victory.

COMMUNITIES

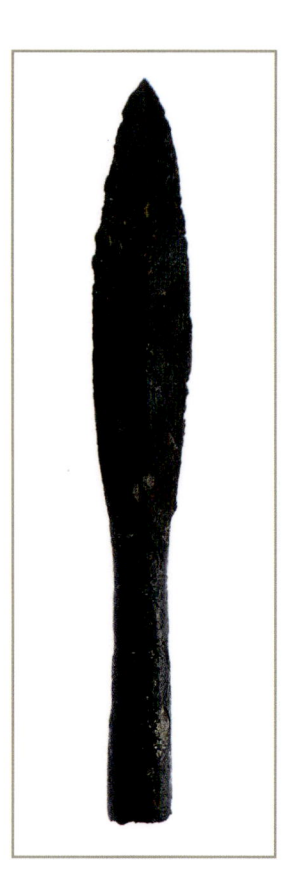

EARLY MEDIEVAL SCOTLAND

78

Fig. 2.11 (opposite, above left): The silver-gilt pommel from St Ninian's Isle, Shetland.

Figs 2.14 and 15 (opposite, above right): An iron sword from Gorton, Moray (2.14, left) and an iron spearhead from Buiston, Ayrshire (2.15, right).

Figs 2.12 and 2.13 (opposite, below): Silver-gilt chape (left) and silver chape (right) from St Ninian's Isle, Shetland.

Fig. 2.16 (right): A detail of the cross from Dupplin, Perthshire, showing infantrymen.

Despite the frequent appearance of spears on the stones, iron spearheads are not much more common than swords. Finds are known from Buiston in Ayrshire [2.15] to Scalloway in Shetland, but there are fewer than twenty examples overall. Forms are simple and may have been long-lived; dates for individual examples rely heavily on context. There is no satisfactory way of distinguishing between spears, lances and javelins in the surviving material. Indeed, it seems possible that the distinctions might not have been rigidly observed in the excitement of the fight or the hunt. The images on the stones show the same forms being displayed as weapons and used in hunting.

Shields, the third item of the warrior's equipment, are represented only by the depictions on the stones. No certain examples survive from Scotland. Two basic types are shown on the stones: circular and quadrangular. Circular shields are the most common and are invariably the type associated with mounted warriors, but it is not restricted to horse riders. Foot soldiers are shown using a circular shield on the Aberlemno battle scene already referred to, and the infantry carry them on the stone from Dull and on the Dupplin Cross [2.16], both from Perthshire.[22] The rectilinear shields – both square, rectangular and H-shaped – are represented and are much rarer. The shapes, however, echo those of later prehistory: for example, the shields of the defeated native warriors on the Roman distance slab from the Antonine Wall found at Bridgeness, West Lothian [2.17], or the leather-covered wooden shield from Clonoura townland, County Tipperary, Ireland.[23] They are

COMMUNITIES

Fig. 2.17 (left): A detail from the 2nd-century AD Roman distance slab from Bridgeness, West Lothian. This shows native warriors equipped with rectangular shields.

Fig. 2.18 (below): A detail of the stone from Kirriemuir, Angus, that shows a warrior with a square shield.

Fig. 2.19 (opposite, left): A fragment of a stone slab from Portmahomack, Easter Ross, that illustrates a cow licking its calf.

Fig. 2.20 (opposite, right): A detail of the stone from Scoonie, Fife, showing a hunting scene.

restricted to warriors on foot. Sometimes these images of individuals are not part of larger scenes, as on the stones from Eassie, Angus, and Kirriemuir 2 from Angus [2.18].[24] We have already seen on the Brough of Birsay stone, where all three individuals have square shields, that the decoration on the shield was one of the indicators of rank. From their rarity, we might go further and suggest that the presence of a rectangular or square shield of itself reflects the importance of the individual. Once again, we are brought back to the understated, but nevertheless evident, signs of differentiation of status even among the group that had power within the community, a reflection of their relative wealth.

That wealth is seen equally is the other major theme among the images on the stones: human and animal relationships. These images are not, by and large, concerned with agriculture, although there are some rare examples. The scene showing a cow tenderly licking a calf on the panel from Portmahomack, Easter Ross [2.19], or the cow wearing a bell around its neck led by a figure and followed by six further figures as though in procession on the stone at Fowlis Wester, Perthshire, appear to be isolated depictions appropriate to particular religious messages. Instead, the emphasis in the depictions is upon the importance of the horse and of hunting. We have already seen that the horse is central to some aspects of creating an image of the warrior. These are horses for riding rather than traction, although

EARLY MEDIEVAL SCOTLAND

a pair of horses is shown pulling the only image of a cart on the lost stone from Meigle, Perthshire.[25] But this unparalleled scene probably involved horses every bit as well looked after as those used by warriors, given their apparently plaited tails. As Leslie Alcock noted, the treatment of the animals on the sculptured stones without Christian motifs suggested close observation of live animals, including a horse on a stone from Inverurie, Aberdeenshire. He suggested that this naturalistic representation of horses was similarly reflected on some of the cross-slabs, but was abandoned by the group he termed 'the Benvie-Dupplin school of carvers'.[26] With this exception, the generally informed and sensitive treatment of the horses reinforces the sense of their importance.

Horses were, of course, a major element in the depictions of hunting that are such a notable feature in the decoration of the cross-slabs. Again, the symbolism involved in the choice of these images is less important for our immediate purpose than the requirement for a convincing portrayal of this aristocratic pursuit. It is crucial to realise that without the pictures on the cross-slabs, we would have very little sense of the nature and significance of hunting from the rest of the archaeological record. Three different forms of hunting are shown on the stones: the pursuit of deer by dogs and men armed in some instances with spears, individual hunters armed with a crossbow, and falconry. The depictions always show the hunt in progress rather than completed.

Of these three, deer hunting is by far the most common [2.20]. Normally, the scenes show armed men on horses, and sometimes on foot, along with dogs that are often harrying the deer. On a few occasions – for example, the cross at Mugdrum, Fife, or perhaps that of St Vigeans 1, Angus – only dogs and deer are shown, suggesting perhaps that hunting with dogs alone was also practised. These are images of aristocratic pursuits, pleasurable no doubt in their own right, but also to be seen as important training for military activities.[27] At the same time, they are not images that could be wholly reconstructed from the presence of

COMMUNITIES

EARLY MEDIEVAL SCOTLAND

Fig. 2.21 (opposite, above): A detail of a stone from St Vigeans, Angus, showing a man hunting a boar with a crossbow.

Fig. 2.22 (opposite, below): A detail of a slab from St Andrews, Fife, that shows a rider engaged in falconry with a hawk perched on his left arm.

Fig. 2.23 (below): An antler nut from a crossbow and iron crossbow bolts from Buiston, Ayrshire and Dunadd, Argyll.

antler and deer bone in archaeological bone assemblages. There are other ways of killing deer that might have been employed. In the Moss of Auquharney, Aberdeenshire, a wooden trap that was suitable for catching deer was discovered in 1921.[28] It has a calibrated radiocarbon date of AD 540–670.[29] These traps are widely distributed throughout Europe and found wherever waterlogged conditions have preserved wooden objects, suggesting that such traps were extensively used.[30] They were not used exclusively for deer, but a cross-slab from Clonmacnoise, County Offaly, Ireland, has an image of a stag with its foot apparently caught in a trap of this form.[31]

Another way of catching deer is shown on the stone from Shandwick, Easter Ross, where a single figure is using a crossbow to kill a deer. Just as in the case of swords, some have tried to use the representations of crossbow users as near photographic images,[32] instead of regarding them, like the other hunting images, as allusions to activities familiar to the viewer. The crossbow appears on very few stones, yet always, as far as we can tell, in the context of hunting rather than warfare. However, as Alcock noted, 'in moments of necessity, such a distinction vanishes'.[33] The most vivid image is on a stone from St Vigeans, Angus, where the hunter confronts a wild boar [2.21]. Examples of an antler crossbow nut that forms a key part of the trigger and crossbow bolts have been found at the early historic crannog at Buiston in Ayrshire and the royal centre at Dunadd, Argyll [2.23].[34]

The final form of hunting that we see depicted on the stones is falconry. Like the crossbow, images of falconry are rare, but given the range of fowling techniques it too is not an image we could have created with certainty from other archaeological remains. Stones at Elgin, Moray and Fowlis Wester in Perthshire, together with the sculptured slab from St Andrews, Fife [2.22], all show riders with hawks on their arms; an unmounted falconer appears on the cross at Bewcastle, Cumberland. Although these images provide the strongest evidence for falconry in Scotland, there is considerable evidence for the sport in Anglo-Saxon England and in Europe. Trained birds were often sent as gifts. A letter from Æthelbert II of Kent asked Boniface, then Archbishop of Mainz, to send him two falcons trained to catch cranes.[35] The bones of a goshawk found at Howe, Orkney, may represent just such a gift. Interestingly, bones of a juvenile crane, though not perhaps mature enough for flight, were also recovered.[36]

This brief survey is intended to be indicative of the potential that the sculptured stones have to provide important images of the community. These images can be considered in this way independent of the wider symbolic meanings that they may have had. Moreover, it has wholly

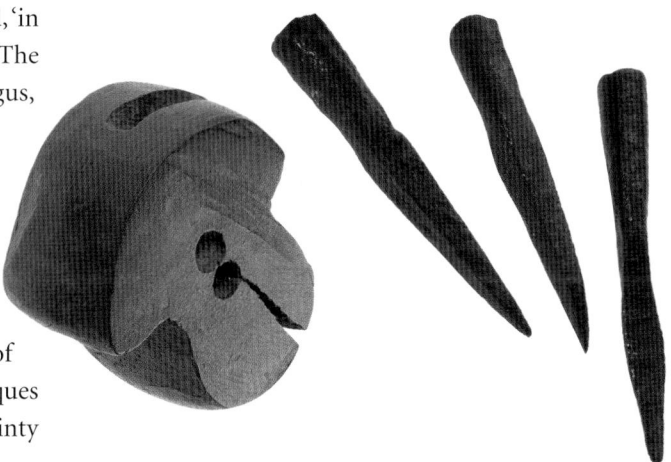

COMMUNITIES

ignored the large number of pictures on the stones that we now struggle to explain. Some are, as Isabel Henderson rightly observed, testaments to 'the existence of Pictish vernacular literary culture'.[37] To exploit fully the possibilities of using the stones in the way that I have been describing, we have to regard them as just another archaeological object. By developing critical interpretations of such things as use and locality, their capacity to inform our understanding of the community that created them will grow significantly.

COMMUNITIES OF PLACE

For many of us the word 'community' evokes a strong sense of place, the community that is formed of those who live near us and with whom we engage on a daily basis. That too seems likely to have been the case in Early Medieval times. We imagine that the social ties involving kinship, friendship and lordship defined for people their sense of community. Of these, kinship and friendship find no clear or easily recognised archaeological representation, but lordship is more ambiguously observed. There are sites, some of which can reasonably be identified in the historical record, that seem best interpreted as those of a lord. But the area over which that lord had control is less easily defined and we have very little evidence in most of Scotland for the dwellings of other, less aristocratic, members of the community. Moreover, lordship could be either secular or religious. The Early Medieval period sees the emergence of religious communities having separate lifestyles devoted to serving the Christian God. Perhaps there were similar communities in prehistory, but we have not recognised them in the same way in the archaeological record. What is clear is that such religious communities could not survive without the agreement and the support of the wider communities. A crucial expression of that support was the increasing appearance of Christian buildings as a feature of essentially secular places. Consequently, the artificial nature of the convenient division between secular and religious places adopted below has to be borne constantly in mind.

Secular places

Many of the central images of Early Medieval settlements are still contained within frames created by archaeologist Leslie Alcock. His major research programme of small-scale excavations on historically attested sites contributed a great deal of information, but it did so primarily in terms that align with the historical sources. In them, royal or aristocratic sites appear largely in the context of warfare. They are besieged or destroyed. The emphasis was on forts and 'all but one of the sites were examined principally by cross-rampart trenches'.[38] The sites were then investigated through their fortification, something that the historical evidence defines as their key role [2.24]. Underlying this approach is the mistaken, if firmly embedded, belief that rampart sequences define the occupation phases of a site.[39]

These fortified sites occupy the summits of hills and coastal promontories.[40] There are strong echoes here of parts of later prehistory, and indeed some sites did involve the re-use of localities previously occupied in prehistory.

Yet one of the striking features of Alcock's work was how little earlier material he recovered from the sites he investigated. Lane and Campbell's work at Dunadd was more extensive and did recover some evidence of early and middle Iron Age use of the hill.[41] But again the finds are limited and recognition is heavily dependent upon radiocarbon dates. Nevertheless, whether previously or newly occupied, the fortification of these sites as statements about authority and power was invoking symbols that had been well understood for more than a millennium. This authority and power was as much reflected in the ability to call on the necessary labour force, to acquire the large quantities of stone and timber to build the ramparts, and to deploy the required skills, as it was in their subsequent appearance. The enclosures so created were the principal means of marking off space for different activities, and they created clear barriers that set apart those inside from those outside.

The ramparts were constructed of stone, or stone and timber. No evidence of the latter has yet been found in Argyll, although it has been found at Castle Rock, Dumbarton, beside the Clyde. The best evidence for the use of timber comes from the excavations at the promontory fort at Portknockie, Aberdeenshire. Here the rampart was destroyed by fire. That resulted in the lowest courses of timbers being heavily carbonised, but retaining their original shape. Some of the timbers were re-used as they showed many mortice-holes, some of which were not used in the rampart structure. It seems that the wooden framework of the rampart was constructed first and then filled in with stone wall-face that left some of the timberwork exposed. How typical this might be is uncertain, but the same type of structure seems to have been used at the large promontory fort at Burghead, Moray.[42] The presence of timber enabled, on occasions, a particularly spectacular form of destruction known as vitrification. Setting the timbers on fire meant that as they burnt back into the body of the rampart, the resulting holes acted as flues allowing the temperature to be raised to the point where the stones themselves melted and fused together. Modern attempts to replicate these events have demonstrated just how difficult this is to achieve. But equally important it has shown what a major statement of power such destruction would have represented. Given the prominent position of these forts, the burning and indeed the incandescent glow, particularly at night, would have been an unmistakable declaration by the victors to the whole of the surrounding community.[43]

Our knowledge of life within the ramparts is, however, extremely limited. In large measure this reflects the restricted nature of most excavation work on these sites. Yet it is equally difficult to be confident that we can convincingly extrapolate from one site to many. It is clear that the plans of these fortified sites are extremely variable. Some, for instance, like Dunadd or Dundurn, Perthshire, [2.24] have central citadels with attached walls that form enclosures further down the hill. These are of a type that Robert Stevenson called 'nuclear forts', based primarily on his description of an example, now destroyed, at Dalmahoy, Midlothian.[44] It now seems unlikely that these are a single planned creation, but more likely that they represent a number of building episodes resulting in the final plan. Yet in neither case do they have any obvious resemblance to a fort like that at Clatchard Craig, Fife.[45] It resembled, before it was quarried away, a prehistoric hillfort with a concentric set of ramparts essentially following the con-

Fig. 2.24 (below):
An aerial photograph of the fort situated at Dundurn, Perthshire.

Fig. 2.25 (opposite):
An aerial photograph of the fort on the Mither Tap o' Bennachie, Aberdeenshire.

EARLY MEDIEVAL SCOTLAND

tours of the hill. These differences are not regional. Indeed, areas north of the Great Glen and in the islands of the north and west, have no fortified sites that might be considered the equivalent of those farther south. The variety in plan is mirrored by variations in size. For example, Burghead is more than nine times the size of Dunadd.[46] A few, like the fortification around the granite tor at the Mither Tap o' Bennachie in Aberdeenshire [2.25], or Dumyat, Stirlingshire, are at altitudes that ensure their wide visibility, but raise questions about the viability of year-round occupation.[47] Some of these differences may be explained by the idea of multiple uses for these sites. It seems generally agreed that the kings and nobles who caused these sites to be created had a peripatetic life. It was easier for them to move to and there consume the food renders that reflected their status, than it was to bring those renders to a central, permanently occupied place.[48] But it seems unreasonable to suppose that this movement led to temporarily abandoned sites across the land. Much more likely is that there was permanent occupation that ensured each site was ready to accommodate the king and his nobles when required.

It may also be that communities of craftsmen – like the late 7th-century metalworkers at Dunadd or the earlier group at Mote of Mark, Kirkcudbrightshire[49] – remained in one place rather than following the court around. If so, evidence of fine metalworking would cease to be indicative of all royal or noble sites.[50] This ignorance about how these sites functioned is mirrored by similar uncertainties about what replaced them when they went out of use, often in the 8th century. Much more excavation will be required before we can really start to analyse these issues in any depth.

In 1988 Leslie Alcock stated, 'The archaeological evidence itself demands the existence of peasant townships to produce the surplus on which kingship, fort-building, and high quality craftsmanship were founded'. But, he went on to observe:

... at present our knowledge of the monuments does not allow us to recognise settlements of this order, or to generalise about them with anything like the confidence which we feel when writing about royal or noble fortifications.[51]

The situation has not changed significantly in the intervening twenty years. Certainly there were then, and are now, other types of settlement, but it is unclear where they are to be placed in the anticipated hierarchy. Air photography has increased the number of potential sites, particularly in the fertile arable lands of eastern Scotland. Few though have been investigated, and the soil conditions in many areas prevent the recovery of the organic material, reflecting all the key activities, that might enable us to understand the workings of a typical farm.

What is clear is that there were significant changes in domestic architecture during the Early Medieval period. Rectilinear buildings replaced the traditional roundhouse. This change in shape was accompanied by a declining reliance on earth-fast elements, such as posts set into pits, as the principal means of ensuring the stability of the structures. Post pads and sill beams, lying directly on the ground or perhaps on very low dry-stone walls, are among the construction techniques that began to appear at this time. These are, of course, elements that are much more difficult to detect in the archaeological record than the earlier building techniques. It thus seems clear that Early Medieval Scotland saw the co-existence of round, cellular and rectilinear buildings. Regional variations in building types are influenced by location, climate and available building resources, but the move from circular to rectilinear appears a more fundamental change than those affected by local circumstances. The change is more observable in some areas than others and the ultimate triumph of rectilinear designs lies well beyond the 9th century. Yet while we can observe these changes, we have no convincing explanations for them.

Interpreting the status of the various building types we can identify in Early Medieval Scotland is far from straightforward. Crannogs or lake dwellings, for instance, are not an exclusive Early Medieval type, but it has long been clear that some were occupied at that time [2.26].[52] One of the first to produce clear evidence of Early Medieval occupation was Buiston, Ayrshire, excavated in 1880 and 1881.[53] Further excavations were undertaken in 1989 and 1990.[54] Buiston provides a case study of the difficulties involved in the interpretation of these sites. In 1993, without access to the recent excavation's data, Alcock accepted the existence of a large round or oval house in the 7th to 8th centuries AD with a floor area of some 200 square metres. He concluded:

While it is primarily the size [of the house] *that justifies the description 'noble' for this household, there are also high status finds.*[55]

Ten years later, with the new excavation data to hand, he abandoned the idea of a large house but maintained his original interpretation of the status of the site: 'Among the rubbish there were high status finds … [and] it is these finds which justify the description "noble" for this household.'[56] This rather suggests that crannogs as high status sites was a given that did not require consistent evidence to

Fig. 2.26 (opposite): A crannog on Loch Leathen, Argyll

support the interpretation. Similar ambiguities of definition characterise the excavator's views. She describes it as

> ... a wealthy farming community which is relatively self-sufficient in foodstuffs and crafts, making and repairing most of the equipment and clothes required by the community, but which produces enough of a surplus to acquire additional services, goods and manpower when needed.

This image of a self-sufficient community occasionally engaged in interactions with the wider world is then characterised as the milieu of 'nobles and princes'.[57] Nor can we suppose that models established at Buiston can be usefully applied to other crannogs. That at Loch Glashan, surrounded by moorland, cannot have the same agricultural base as Buiston. It is claimed that it might be associated with royalty. Yet 'the relatively small size of the crannog militates against its interpretation as a royal habitation site, so it may have served some other specialist function, such as a craftworking site'.[58] Among these variable interpretations, the desire to see crannogs as high-status sites provides the continuity. This view has been heavily influenced by work in Ireland where excavations at sites like Lagore or Ballinderry no. 2 have ensured the idea of the crannog as a high status site.[59] Yet even there it now seems that the assumed equation between high status and crannogs cannot always be substantiated.[60] Nor is a high status interpretation appropriately applied to late Bronze Age or Iron Age crannogs.[61] All of this suggests that viewing crannogs as the settlements of a particular group in society is likely to be mistaken.

Crannogs are, like other settlement types, regionally restricted. Early Medieval examples are known only in southwestern and western Scotland; Loch Glashan in Argyll is among the most northerly sites.[62] Further north and west there are no sites that, through their structures, can be considered high status sites in the same way as argued for sites further south. If the excavations at the Brough of Birsay, Orkney, had not included the site of a metalworking workshop, there would be little to make it a high status settlement. As we have seen, metalworking by itself appears to be an uncertain indicator of high status. Sites in the north and west show a significant reduction in size when compared to previous Iron Age structures, seemingly continuing and emphasising the earlier abandonment of monumentality.[63] The cellular buildings that we now find appear to be domestic, the home of a single family, although they are on occasion observed forming small communities as at Old Scatness, Shetland, or Pool, Sanday, Orkney.[64]

Yet even here the need to see these structures in status terms is not abandoned. The excavators of Old Scatness, wrote:

> *However even with this reduction of internal space the surviving wall heights at both Old Scatness and Jarlshof are impressive and arguably continue to provide status buildings.*[65]

Clearly then, we need to interpret Early Medieval settlement sites in terms of the archaeological data they have yielded. This will mean abandoning models constructed from the historical texts and seeking instead to reconcile archaeologically derived interpretations with the evidence provided by those texts.

Christianity: its communities and places

Apart from stone crosses in various forms, Christianity has left very few indisputable archaeological traces in the Early Medieval landscape. Of course, the continuing vitality of Christianity and our consequent understanding of its ideology enable us to interpret with some confidence many other objects in Christian terms. Thus, for example, the Monymusk reliquary can be seen as a reliquary (a container for relics of a saint), a ciborium (a container for the consecrated host) or a chrismatory (a container for small flasks holding anointing oils). Or, at a more sophisticated level, we can understand the bird heads on a brooch from Rogart, Sutherland, as refreshing themselves in the Fountain of Life and so reflecting mankind's desire for the reviving Water of Salvation through baptism [2.27].[66] But these interpretations gain their credibility from the known framework of established Christianity demonstrated through textual evidence. There is no overtly Christian symbolism on either piece that points us inevitably toward such interpretations. And the absence of such symbolism extends to most of the surviving objects from Early Medieval Scotland, except for the stone crosses.

Comparable problems affect the interpretation of Christian sites, particularly monasteries or major ecclesiastical sites. We know – for example, from texts – that Iona was the site of a monastery founded by St Columba in the 6th century, but apart from the later crosses no incontrovertibly Christian material has been recovered from the excavations there [2.28]. The same is true of the sites at Portmahomack, Easter Ross, Inchmarnock, Bute, or Hoddom

EARLY MEDIEVAL SCOTLAND

Fig. 2.27 (opposite): Birds' heads on the terminals of one of the penannular brooches from Rogart, Sutherland.

Fig. 2.28 (below): An aerial view of the island of Iona, Argyll.

COMMUNITIES

in Dumfriesshire. All may plausibly be interpreted as monastic sites, but none has provided evidence of Christian structures or material, other than sculptured stones. In particular, none has shown evidence of an Early Medieval church or baptistery.[67] Presumably at all these sites these key structures lie buried beneath later churches and graveyards. That seems to be the case at the Isle of May, Fife, where the vestiges of an Early Medieval church have been recovered from below the remains of a later priory. But even here the earliest church dates only to the 10th century and there is no equivalent structure associated with the presumptively Christian cemetery of the 5th–7th centuries.[68] Whithorn, Wigtownshire, alone has produced excavated evidence of an early church and its development.[69]

All of this seems, in part at least, to be reflecting the fact that a simple label, like 'monastery', may not be an adequate description for sites with long, although not necessarily continuous, occupation. These issues first arose in the interpretation of sites like Flixborough in Lincolnshire and Brandon in Suffolk.[70] At Flixborough the evidence for literacy, the presence of high quality imports and craft-working, together with the site of a possible church, led to initial interpretations that saw it as an undocumented monastic settlement. Subsequent analysis has not supported this view and has incidentally called into question the value of such finds in the recognition of monasteries. Moreover, the variation in lifestyles observable on a single site raises the real possibility that sites dating to before the end of the 9th century might have been both monastic and secular at different points in their occupation.

It is not in doubt that monastic centres had churches, luxury imports and craft-working, or that they will demonstrate evidence of literacy. But none of this seems to be exclusive to monastic sites. How then are we to recognise monasteries or major ecclesiastical sites in Scotland where the documentary evidence is much more limited than in England? The difficulties were admirably expressed by the excavator of Hoddom, who ended his report by asking, 'What kind of settlement was Hoddom: a secular site with a church or an ecclesiastical site with a farm?'[71] It is clear that neither imports nor craft-working can provide much of a guide. Churches might be better indicators, but as noted above we have not yet been very successful in locating early examples. Nevertheless, the sculptured panel from Burghead[72] [2.29] is best seen as a church fitting, albeit one that belonged to a church within an essentially secular place. Evidence of literacy, particularly in terms of quantity or quality, seems to offer a useful pointer. The sheer quantity of inscribed slates at Inchmarnock, Bute (see pages 6–7), or the evidence of parchment-making supported by a cross bearing an inscription in letters close to the scripts used in Insular manuscripts at Portmahomack, Easter Ross (see page 147), show the kind of material we might anticipate, though it seems unreasonable to expect it on every site.[73]

The one constant, in terms of finds, that is used to identify monasteries or major ecclesiastical sites, appears to be the presence of significant quantities of sculpture. Although never phrased as bluntly as that, and consequently never defining the quantity of sculpture required, it forms the underlying assumption when we seek to put groups of sculpture into some sort of context. Certainly, all sites that we can recognise by other criteria, literary or archaeological, appear to have collections of sculpture, some of it large and complex. Yet the function, as opposed

Fig. 2.29: A sculptured panel from Burghead, Moray.

COMMUNITIES

Fig. 2.30 (above): A stone arch from a church at Forteviot, Perthshire.

Fig. 2.31 (below): A stone architectural fragment from Meigle, Perthshire.

EARLY MEDIEVAL SCOTLAND

to the art, of such pieces is little discussed. Moreover, there is a significant disjuncture between the date of the sculpture and the supposed dates for conversion to Christianity based on written texts. The earliest Christianity in Scotland seems to have been largely without monuments, although we cannot rule out the possibility that wooden crosses fulfilled that role. Sadly, we know very little about the organisation and practice of the Early Church in Scotland. All of the identified ecclesiastical sites provide a very thin spread, suggesting that many saw a priest or a monk only on rare occasions after conversion.

This is an altogether more negative view of the archaeological evidence for Christianity than most would espouse. The absence of convincing remains of churches at major religious sites were earlier noted, but looking further there are some indications of their wider presence.[74] Our images of early churches are heavily influenced by Ireland and consequently we see them as small and often wooden or of dry-stone construction.[75] The timber and later stone-walled chapel at Ardwall, Kirkcudbrightshire, is typical of what is often envisaged.[76] Yet there are some pieces that suggest larger and more elaborate churches. Nechtan's well-known request to the Northumbrian abbot, Ceolfrith, for help with building a stone church is the only textual evidence that we have for the existence of larger churches, and the stone arch from Forteviot, Perthshire, might be our only fragment from the fabric of such a church [2.30].[77] There are other stone fragments, such as Meigle 22 [2.31], that appear to be architectural but are less certainly parts of a church.[78] They only become so if one believes that the sole buildings constructed of stone were churches. What appears to give the strongest support to the idea of large decorated churches are the pieces of stone sculpture that are best interpreted as the fittings for such churches. These take two forms. First, there are low decorated slabs and upright slotted posts that have conventionally been interpreted as shrines, but seem in many cases to be better seen as forming low screens to mark off areas of the church. And second, some of the large cross-slabs have features that suggest they were originally intended for the inside of churches rather than the open air.

Despite being usually described as shrines, the individual parts that survive from the most complete examples, like the St Andrews sarcophagus, make unconvincing components of a single decorative unit [2.32].[79] They do not fit well together, something that seems particularly surprising in what would have been important features in the church interior. A more convincing explanation would be that these are the surviving fragments of much larger decorative schemes enhancing screens dividing off parts of the church that have, on discovery, been forced together as parts of a more restricted scheme. Indeed, an upright slotted stone from Portmahomack does not match any of the proposed shrine forms, but would fit well as an element in a low decorative screen.[80] There are no obvious parallels for these shrines in areas to the south, whereas the evidence for internal screens seems present throughout Europe. But even if some of the fragments are indeed from a peculiarly Scottish form of shrine, it seems unlikely that such elaborate *stone* pieces would have been accommodated in small *wooden* churches.

A number of the large cross-slabs have features in their form that seem best interpreted as elements designed to tie them into walls or screens. These usually take the form of

EARLY MEDIEVAL SCOTLAND

Fig. 2.32 (opposite): The decorated stone 'sarcophagus' from St Andrews, Fife.

Fig. 2.33 (right): A detail of a large stone cross-slab from Meigle, Perthshire, showing one of the tenons on its sides and top.

projecting tenons, although the slots on the sides of the cross at Shandwick, Easter Ross, that now hold iron strips joining the two broken halves of the cross together, might also have originally served a similar role of enabling inclusion in a larger structure.

George and Isabel Henderson have drawn attention to the architectural quality of some of the cross-slabs, particularly the major monuments on the Tarbat peninsula in Easter Ross, that they regard as essentially contemporary productions.[81] In particular, they suggest that the Nigg cross-slab, because of its decorative intricacy, 'is admirably suited to stand in an Episcopal chapel' and that the Hilton of Cadboll cross-slab 'may have stood adjacent to or within a private chapel'.[82] Their arguments are developed from the artistic schemes of the cross-slabs, and not the physical evidence of the stones themselves. Nigg is elaborately decorated on every surface except one edge,[83] suggesting that it stood adjacent to a wall and was more likely to be inside a church than outside. Equally, Hilton originally had tenons projecting from either side of the slab, although they survive now only as vestigial remains.[84] Such tenons are found on both the sides and the tops of cross-slabs, such as Meigle 2, Perthshire [2.33], seen by the Hendersons as acting as the focus of a funerary chapel,[85] or on the top of the stone from Woodrae, Angus. While all of these could quite easily have formed elements in small chapels, it seems equally plausible to regard them as parts of screens in large churches that accommodated their decoration on both faces. In such situations the decoration on each face may have been intended for different audiences – the priests and the laity. Certainly, viewing these cross-slabs as part of an architectural interior creates the need for much larger churches than we presently have evidence for, although it seems reasonable to suppose that this evidence lies buried under more recent churches.

A question of towns

Most of us now take the urban environment as the background to our daily lives as a given. But it will be clear that this discussion of place has not mentioned towns at all. The earliest identifiable urban settlements in Scotland are usually regarded as those designated as burghs in the reign of King David I (1124–53).[86] It is difficult to see comparable settlements in Early Medieval Scotland where many, though not perhaps a majority, live through the pursuit of non-agricultural activities. Yet the publication of work at

Whithorn was provocatively subtitled 'the excavation of a monastic town'.[87] This was a concept introduced in Ireland to describe the major ecclesiastical centres where craft and other activities were carried on in conjunction with the religious life. These centres often involved, as we must suppose Whithorn did, an important role as a pilgrimage centre. Such centres may not have been towns in an economic sense, but they are likely to have been significant places with relatively-speaking large populations. A comparable site to Whithorn may well have been St Andrews.[88] Southeast Scotland, under Northumbrian control for much of this period, may have had settlements, like the one at Dunbar, East Lothian, that some might wish to characterise as towns. Without the textual records though, the excavated evidence would be difficult to interpret in those terms.[89] Access to the evidence for sites that we might wish to describe as towns is likely to be constrained by the existence of continuing settlement.

COMMUNITIES OF CRAFTSMEN

In many ways these are for us the key communities in Early Medieval Scotland. Most archaeological recognition of the period is achieved through their work and much of the continuing discussion articulates around their products. Yet our images of Early Medieval craftsmen – and it does seem likely that identifiable crafts were dominated by men in Early Medieval Scotland – are largely modelled on interpretations of metalworkers, their organisation and practices. Indeed, our discussion relies heavily on that evidence. There are, of course, connections between the various crafts. For instance, the shape of wooden crosses may well have influenced the form of stone crosses. Both may have used decorative motifs drawn from, and in imitation of, metalwork, but equally as much influence will have passed from the sculptors of crosses to the makers of metalwork. These interconnections are important in underpinning the idea of communities of craftsmen, but they should not lead us to suppose that the same model can adequately describe the working patterns of all Early Medieval craftsmen.

Nevertheless, this seems to be the situation that currently dominates our thinking. Sally Foster has provided an admirable summary of this view with the statement that 'specialised craftworkers, particularly fine-metalworkers, appear to have largely confined their activities to high-status sites where their food requirements were provided by clients, leaving them free to ply their trade'.[90] Unfortunately, there is the real danger of a circular argument in this position. The production of fine metalwork has been an important element in defining a particular site as high status. Yet subsequently we claim that such activity is confined to high-status sites. Essentially, this interpretation sees skilled craftsmen as under the direct control of ruling elites, both secular and religious. Their output then becomes dictated by, and directed towards, the maintenance of power by those elites. Through control of raw materials and managed distribution of key objects, including fine metalwork, the elites established relationships of power and obligation in the wider community.

This image of kings building and cementing power through gift-giving owes much to the discoveries at Dunadd, Argyll.[91] There an area known as Site 3 has been

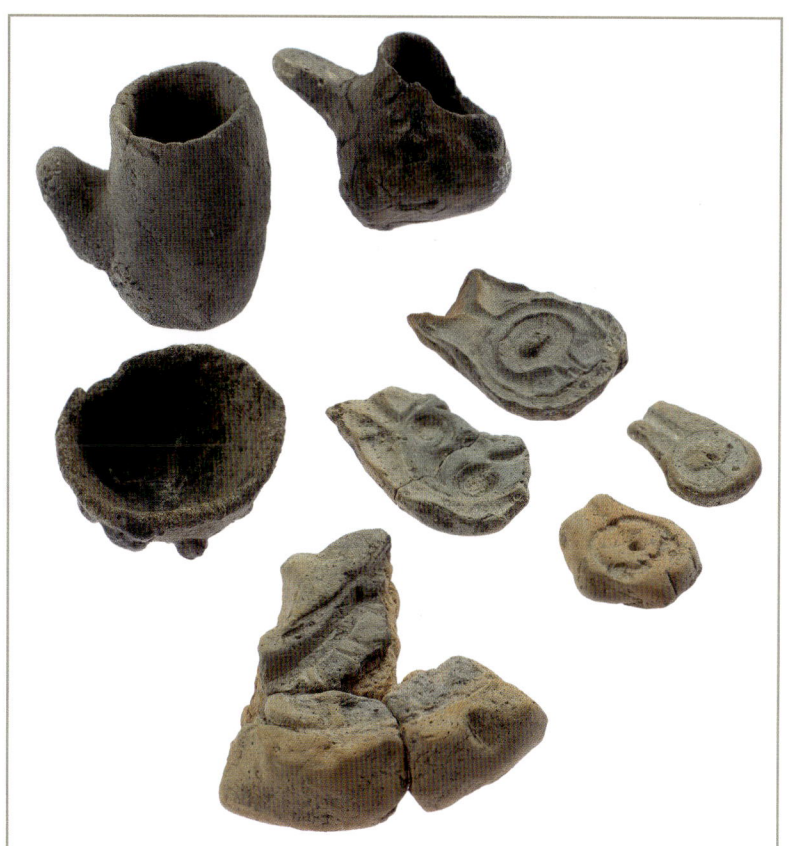

Fig. 2.34: Clay moulds (see close-up below) and crucibles from Dunadd, Argyll.

interpreted as a specialist metalworking area. Though only partially excavated, it is clear that deep deposits, a metre or more thick, existed across the area. The radiocarbon dates and the art historical analysis of the types of object being manufactured both suggest a rather restricted period of use from the mid- to late 7th century. The debris that is indicative of metalworking included moulds, crucibles, ingot moulds and semi-manufactured rods [2.34]. Other metal objects, such as pins or buckles, might reflect production, but equally might have been collected with a view to recycling their metal content. It certainly seems that some of the richer objects, such as the gold and garnet stud, or the stamped bronze foil of a type commonly found on Anglo-Saxon drinking horns, cups or buckets, were the result of stripping down elaborate objects for re-use.

Analysis of the crucibles shows that gold, silver and copper alloy were all being used. The main products – judging by the surviving moulds where the shape of the object can be recognised – were brooches and pins. It may be that these predominate because, as small and relatively simple objects, they are easily recognised, whereas the mould fragments from larger, more elaborate pieces, such as reliquaries or book mounts, are much more difficult to interpret. Even so, many of the brooch types represented by the moulds have never been found anywhere in Scotland. These small objects are the ones seen as central to the idea of gifts from the king to his subjects with the intention of building unity and obligation. Of course, there are larger objects, including brooches of the size and style of the Hunterston brooch, that were presumably intended for royal and aristocratic use or as gifts to major monasteries.

Among the same deposits, evidence of iron-working

COMMUNITIES

was also recovered.[92] Because the temperatures needed to melt iron could not be achieved at this period, objects could only be made by hammering the heated metal into the required form. This necessarily produces different residues in the archaeological record from those reflecting the casting of gold, silver or bronze objects. At Dunadd, smithing slags and hearth bottoms were the principal evidence of iron-working. No evidence for iron-smelting, that is the extraction of the metal from the ore, was found.

The excavators claimed that 'other crafts such as jet, wood, bone, stone and leather working may also have taken place in the same area'.[93] No evidence, however, is produced to support this statement. Equally fugitive was the evidence for structures on the site in which craft-work could have been undertaken: 'The flimsy nature of the physical remains on Site 3 suggests that the working areas were not within substantial buildings but a series of temporary shelters constructed of stone and organic material such as turf'.[94] Yet Humphrey Case has rightly drawn attention to the need for 'efficient architecture' for craftsmen undertaking delicate work. Such architecture has to ensure that craftsmen can work on stable surfaces in dust-free conditions with good light and still air.[95] Admittedly, he was discussing the making of gold objects some two thousand years earlier in the Early Bronze Age, but these requirements would have been equally important for those creating pieces like the Hunterston brooch. It does raise the question as to whether Site 3 was indeed an area for crafts, or just an area where the waste from craft-work was dumped.

Whatever the status of Site 3, it seems clear from the evidence there that the occupants of Dunadd, an assumed royal site, included craftsmen within their midst. But was this community of craftsmen just serving the needs of the king and his immediate entourage and household, rather than providing objects for an extended regime of gift-giving? The former may be thought to provide a better fit with the evidence than the latter.

Within the close vicinity of Dunadd are three sites that appear to be Early Medieval in date, but with evidence of non-ferrous metalworking. Yet this is not metalworking on the large scale seen at Dunadd. Instead, it seems to represent only a single episode. At Ardifuar and at Loch Glashan there was only a single crucible recovered at each site, whereas at Bruach an Drumein there were fragments from what appeared to be three different crucibles and a single fragment of a mould.[96] Analysis of one of the crucibles from Bruach an Drumein as well as the crucible from Loch Glashan showed that they had been used to work silver. These suggestions of occasional metalworking using precious metals do not appear to fit easily with royal control of production and gift-giving.

It can be argued that this is evidence of royal metalworkers from Dunadd working at important local sites, but this does not explain why the smith was sent rather than the finished product. One possible answer lies with the status of the metalworkers. It has been well demonstrated that they were seen in pre-literate societies as being powerful because of their special knowledge that was reflected in their ability to transform one material into another. The presence then of metalworkers at a site might have enhanced the significance of the object they made as a royal gift.[97] Overall, the powers of the craftsman, the value of the raw materials and fineness of the finished object

Figs 2.35 (pages 101–103): Details of the terminals of the silver-gilt brooches from St Ninian's Isle, Shetland.

might all be needed to provide sufficient reflection of the king's powers.

Clearly though, this is not an interpretation that can be applied to all craft-workers. Many crafts use straightforward techniques that do not imbue their practitioners with the aura of magician often attached to metalworkers. Equally, it does not provide an adequate model for explaining the evidence for metalworking from the Atlantic north and west. Here the widespread use of stone architecture has left us with many archaeological sites. But within the Early Medieval period it is difficult to identify sites where architecture has been used to reflect the high status of their occupants. Indeed, it has been argued that in this area the expression of status became focused on personal ornaments at the expense of elaborate architecture in the Early Medieval period.[98] The ornaments, predominantly pins and brooches, were still seen in this interpretation as the products of gift-giving with the intention of building power and obligation. Viewing the objects this way rather ignores the widespread evidence for limited episodes of metalworking on sites across Atlantic Scotland.[99] Some of this suggests extensive shared styles rather than far-travelled gifts.

The silver hoard from St Ninian's Isle, Shetland, contains brooches with a number of variations in the designs of the terminals [FIGS 2.35].[100] It has been generally assumed that these brooches, along with the other items in the hoard, were made in a workshop in Shetland.[101] Yet moulds for brooches using the same designs have been found at Brough of Birsay, Orkney, and at Cnoc a' Comhdhalach, North Uist, in the Western Isles. Cnoc a' Comhdhalach is an undefended and inconspicuous settlement. The mould

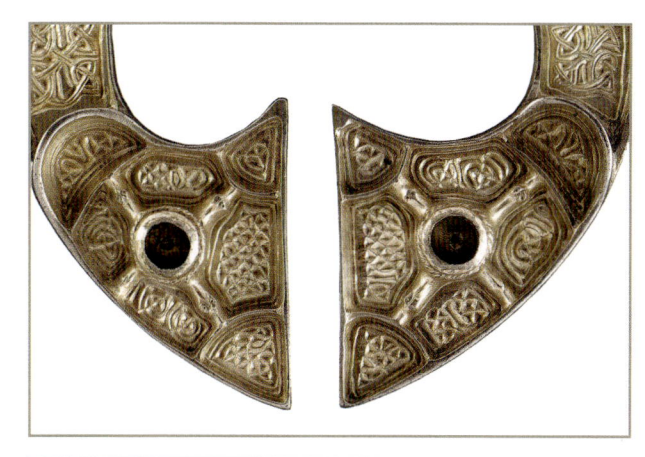

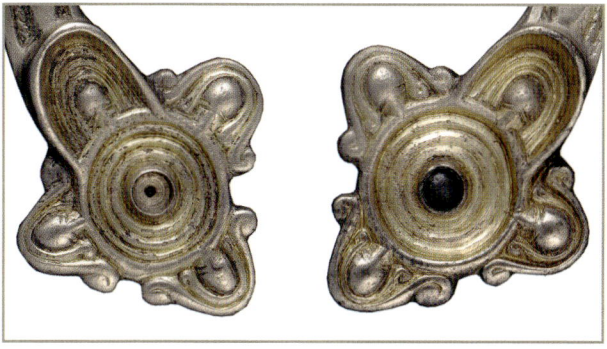

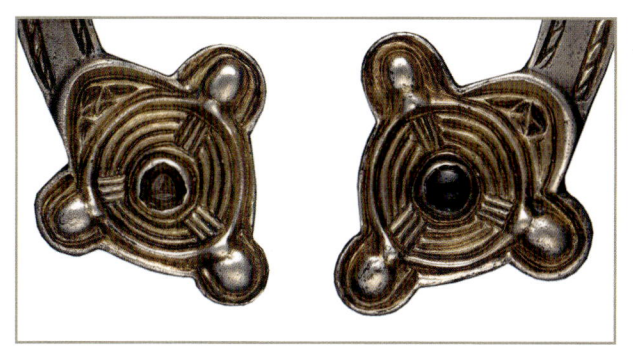

COMMUNITIES

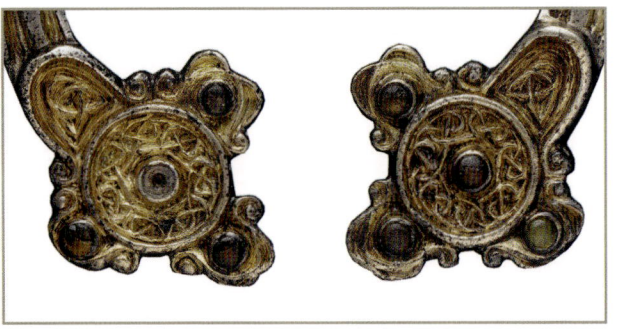

may represent an isolated episode of metalworking in what was already an abandoned structure.[102] In contrast, the Brough of Birsay has produced considerable evidence for a metalworking area comparable to that discovered at Dunadd.[103] As with Dunadd, the evidence at the Brough of Birsay is in the form of metalworking debris such as moulds or crucibles. There too, no meaningful structures can be associated with the workshop. Indeed, unlike Dunadd, the Brough of Birsay is not even distinguished by major fortifications. What makes it special is its location on a tidal islet off the west cost of Mainland, Orkney. It appears to be as close as we come to a high status site in the Atlantic north and west.

Yet here, as at Dunadd, metalworking seems to have taken place for only a short time in what was an extended period of occupancy at both sites. At Brough of Birsay it took place during the second half of the 8th century – whereas at Dunadd it was a century earlier. An even more short-lived workshop in a previously abandoned settlement has been excavated at Eilean Olabhat, North Uist.[104] Here metalworking debris, comparable in content to that from the Brough of Birsay, was recovered. Evidence of both bronze- and silver-working was present, but the range of objects being made was restricted to pins and other small decorative pieces. There was no evidence that brooches were being made. Although the workshop produced a substantial quantity of debris, the excavator commented that it may only 'represent the activity of a few days, weeks or months at the end of the building's life'. This brief period of activity was then presented as suggesting two possible models. The first involved an itinerant smith serving a range of clients throughout the Western Isles. The second

EARLY MEDIEVAL SCOTLAND

102

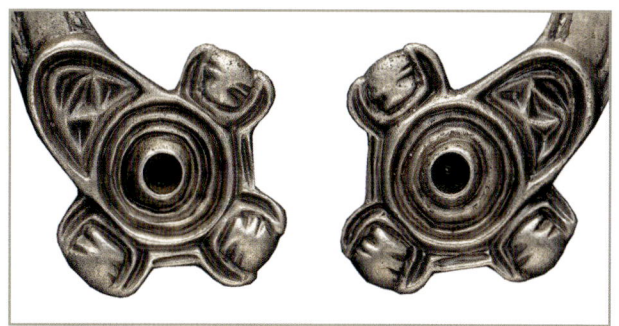

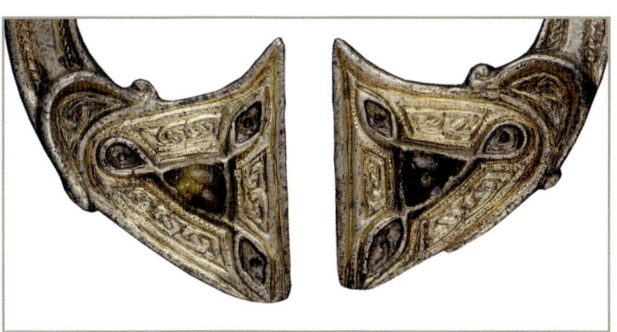

saw it as the 'gift' of skilled craftsmen, rather than finished objects from an aristocratic patron to his followers to cement the bonds of obligation. Neither model is easily reconciled with the comment that 'the metalworking debris does not seem to co-exist with any significant settlement activity on the promontory, far less with the sort of high status occupation usually thought to be the appropriate context for the production of fine metalwork'.[105]

What this excursus into the making of fine metalwork in Early Medieval Scotland demonstrates is the paucity of our models for explaining the archaeological evidence. A key difficulty may be our willingness to treat all evidence for craft activity as of equal value and intimately connected. We have already seen that the amount of non-ferrous metalworking at Dunadd is of a different order and scale from that indicated by three crucible fragments and a piece of a mould from Bruach an Drumein. Perhaps it is a mistake to see them as part of a unitary craft system, rather than being linked only through access to some of the same craft skills. That, of course, raises issues about how these skills might be acquired and equally, once acquired, what freedoms the craftsman had to exercise them. It seems reasonable, however, to suggest that the most skilled metalworkers may well have been an integral part of royal and aristocratic households, perhaps at times producing items for use in gift-giving. This would not preclude changing patterns through time, so that on some occasions there was a workshop producing items for gift-giving while at others the craftsman himself was loaned. At the same time, less skilled metalworkers might have operated in a different, more peripatetic structure that nevertheless ensured their regular, if intermittent, appearance at various localities.

COMMUNITIES

EARLY MEDIEVAL SCOTLAND

Fig. 2.36 (opposite): A stone tombstone for the children of the Master of Works at Drumlanrig in the churchyard at Durisdeer, Dumfriesshire.

Fig. 2.37: A simple stone tombstone in Old Rosyth churchyard, Fife.

Fig. 2.38: This stone mould is from Ardifuar, Argyll.

This would have provided wider access to fine metalwork, but in items that were limited in both quantity and quality.

This distinction between the finest metalworkers and others practising the same craft might be expected to apply to a wide range of crafts; nor need the division be a simple binary one between the best and the rest. There could easily have been several recognised skill levels, with the lowest concerned with providing a settlement's basic needs for tools and the maintenance of them in good repair. As a reflection of the skill ranges involved, we can use the analogy of the early modern tombstones in lowland Scotland, all of them carved by local masons. Some, like that in the churchyard at Durisdeer carved by the Master of Works at Drumlanrig, Dumfriesshire, one of the residences of the Duke of Buccleuch, were very fine indeed [2.36]. But at the other end of the scale, many can hardly provide more than a pair of initials and a date [2.37]. We can get an idea of this reflected in archaeological material in Joseph Anderson's comments on a stone mould from Ardifuar [2.38]. Anderson was writing in 1905, but with considerable awareness and experience of crafts as practised in the 19th century. He noted:

This mould does not seem to be capable of being used as a closed mould with another half fitted over it; and as the middle parts of the cavities are worn quite smooth, it may have been a mould for shaping malleable-iron things, like the stone moulds for crusies [open iron oil lamps] *that were till quite recently used in most country smithies.*[106]

COMMUNITIES

Figs 2.39–43 (opposite and following page): Photographs taken of Adrian McCurdy during the various stages of making the wooden throne. Figure 2.43 shows the finished throne with its stone foot-stool.

This is the world of local blacksmiths making and repairing tools and fittings, a world far distant from the craftsmen working in precious metals to make a large and highly elaborate brooch.

Fine metalworking dominates our images of crafts for two main reasons. It has produced some of our finest objects of the period and it results in large quantities of debris, mainly moulds and crucibles, which survive easily in the archaeological record. Comparable situations are not found in other widely practised crafts. What is remarkable is how few tools are found on excavated sites, even for fine metalworking. For example, where are the tongs needed to hold all those crucibles full of molten metal? Rare finds are known from Ireland, but there are no certain Early Medieval examples from Scotland.[107] Moreover, even where evidence of craft activities survives, as at Buiston, their interpretation is far from straightforward. Buiston is a crannog built in the Roman period, but with occupation in the Early Medieval period. Many of the iron tools could well be Roman, but with high levels of functional efficiency the forms may well have continued into the Early Medieval period. Unfortunately, the publication of the site has to conclude that 'the majority of artefacts from Buiston are chronologically undiagnostic'.[108]

An important way out of this difficulty lies with good excavation of reliable contexts. A good example of this has been the recognition of a *parchmenerie* (an area for making parchment) at the early monastic site at Portmahomack, Easter Ross. Excavation there showed that a small number of relatively simple artefact types – a curved iron knife, rubbers made of pumice, sharpened cattle metapodials (bones from the feet) and small pebbles – together with a rectangular stone-lined pit, could be plausibly interpreted as an area for the manufacture of parchment.[109] The interpretation drew support from other material from the site and from the effective use of information from modern craftsmen engaged in the manufacture of parchment. Using the comments and products of modern craftworkers employing essentially the same skills as we have ephemeral evidence for in Early Medieval Scotland, is an important method of enlarging our appreciation and understanding of crafts at that period.

Using replication

The Glenmorangie Research Project on Early Medieval Scotland has been exploring ways of improving our understanding of both craftsmen and their products. This aim is allied to an equally important wish to be able to see the objects as they might have looked when they were new. We have been working with modern craftsmen to make versions of objects that we have only limited information about. Some initial remarks will help to show how these approaches can greatly increase our understanding of the role of craftsmen in Early Medieval Scotland. To date we have commissioned a wooden throne and two different book satchels.

The wooden throne was made by Adrian McCurdy, a furniture-maker based in the Scottish Borders [2.39–2.43]. Thrones are important expressions of power throughout Early Medieval Europe and the Mediterranean, derived originally from the Roman world. But while they are universal symbols, their form varies from place to place.

COMMUNITIES

107

Fig. 2.44: A detail of the stone from Fowlis Wester, Perthshire, showing the image of the throne on which the new throne was based.

EARLY MEDIEVAL SCOTLAND

108

Very little evidence for early thrones now survives and our knowledge of thrones in Scotland is largely derived from images on sculptured stones.[110] Among these, some of the best depictions are provided by the stone from Fowlis Wester, Perthshire.[111] The new throne was modelled on this image [2.44]. Of course, what we see on the stones was not intended to be a blueprint for creating a new throne. To do so requires a good deal of interpretation, largely on the part of the craftsman. There is no way to determine whether the depicted thrones were made of stone or wood. Indeed, it seems likely that they were made in both materials. Fragments of comparable thrones are known in stone from Monkwearmouth, Tyne & Wear, and Lastingham, Yorkshire, and in gilded wood from Dublin.[112] Our choice was to make the new throne in wood.

The throne on the stone from Fowlis Wester clearly shows that the arm and front leg are carved as a single curved piece. Initially, none of us involved in the project believed that obtaining suitable pieces of curved oak to make these parts would be at all difficult. That proved a very foolish assumption. Eventually, Adrian acquired the pieces locally, cut from trees blown down in gales. It made clear, even in these days of timber merchants, the importance of local knowledge. Moreover, in using these substantial pieces of wood in their green state we accepted the possibility, subsequently realised, that these sections of the throne might be subject to cracking. Since it seems unlikely that cracking would have been acceptable in Early Medieval times, we have to suppose that the thrones would have been made wholly of seasoned timber with all the extra difficulties in working that this would have entailed. What this most emphasised was the need for the wood-worker to be permanently based in the same place. Only in these circumstances would he be able to build up the required knowledge of his available woodland that ensured he knew where to find pieces of the right shape for each new task.

A second feature of the image on the Fowlis Wester stone is the way that the figures on the thrones seem hardly to be sitting in them at all. They seem to perch on them. Yet when it came to locating the seat in the frame of the throne, it was clear that only by setting it in the thickness of the arms could the seat have the necessary strength to support an adult. When sat in, it confirmed the accuracy of the Fowlis Wester depictions. Many have subsequently commented that it looks an uncomfortable seat. This is not at all the case when used with a footstool. The seat does not allow you to slouch, but instead requires you to sit upright, exactly the posture expected of a king or senior religious figure. As you rise from the throne you are, through the footstool, standing above the assembled subjects.

All pictures of these thrones show them with footstools. We all felt that a wooden footstool was impractical, as it would soon become worn with use. Such a shabby appearance would be inconsistent with the images of power and authority that such thrones were intended to convey. So we decided to make it of stone. This necessarily involved decisions about the height of the footstool. Through this we realised that to be most effective the footstool needs to be made to suit an individual. Put simply, a footstool designed for an individual 1.65 metres tall would make someone with a height of 1.90 metres look ridiculous, and the reverse would be equally true. Given the real possibility that a throne would continue in use over a long period of time, confirming as it were the legitimacy of its occupant's rule, the individuality of each occupant would be marked with the necessary creation of a new footstool tailored to his height.

The second commission involved the creation of two book satchels. These were made by Ian Dunlop of Soda-Kitch [2.46–49]. In a world where books were handwritten, their numbers were low and each book was very precious. Without large numbers of books there would be no need for bookshelves. But it was still important to protect the book from casual damage. This was achieved with a book satchel that allowed the book to be carried around, and when the book was not in use it could be hung in its satchel on a hook in the wall.

Sources for the new book satchels were part archaeological, part literary. One was based on leather fragments found at Loch Glashan, Argyll, that have been interpreted as the remains of a book satchel.[113] The second was an interpretation of the description of the making of a book satchel found in *Hisperica famina,* the 7th-century Irish text.[114] There are images of clerics wearing book satchels on two cross-slabs from Bressay and Papil [2.45] in Shetland, but these add nothing in the way of detail.[115] The central issues here concerned the contribution that craftsmen can bring to our understanding of surviving material.

The Loch Glashan fragments suggested a satchel large enough to contain a major manuscript, something the size of the *Book of Kells*. Their condition had precluded identification of the type of skin used, and examination of the pieces suggested that the published reconstruction was incorrect. Our version, incorporating the changes we believed necessary, was made of roe deer skin.

In marked contrast to the plainness of this bag, the

Fig. 2.45 (opposite): A detail of the stone from Papil, Shetland, showing clerics wearing book satchels.

Figs 2.46–2.49 (below): Ian Dunlop making the leather book satchels. The finished satchels (2.49, below, right) were displayed with a replica of the *Book of Kells*.

COMMUNITIES

111

one created from the description in the *Hisperica famina* is smaller but more elaborate. The language of the poetry is very obscure and consequently filled with ambiguities, but it does refer to gleaming white skin; our interpretation is in white sheepskin. It seems a more conscious attempt to signal the importance of the book inside than the workaday feel of the Loch Glashan satchel. Given the size, and therefore importance, of the manuscript the Loch Glashan satchel could accommodate, the restraint in the design of the satchel is striking. There is a real doubt as to whether it is indeed a book satchel as opposed to a bag for the hunt or other everyday activities.

Making these satchels raised other questions about leather-working in Early Medieval Scotland. Did it, for instance, involve the leather-workers in all aspects from initial preparation and tanning of the skin to the making of final products? Or might it not have been similar to glass, where the making of the raw material is undertaken separately from the creation of the finished objects? At Buiston there was clear evidence for leather-working, but none that indicated the production of the basic raw material.[116] The latter admittedly involves rather unpleasant processes. The location of this activity might then be situated some distance from the crannog, but equally the activity may have taken place at a different site altogether.

These briefly described examples show the value of involving working craftspeople with the archaeological record. From this will emerge a richer understanding of this aspect of Early Medieval Scotland, not only in terms of the environments in which individual crafts needed to be undertaken, but also in an improved understanding of what objects looked like when they were brand new.

COMMUNITIES OF THE WIDER WORLD

In the surviving texts we find the largest communities identified by names like the Picts or the Britons, albeit named principally by outsiders. For each of these larger communities in what we would now call Scotland, the others were part of their wider world. And of course, in the wider world beyond their immediate neighbours, there were many larger and richer communities. Yet integrating these historical names and the archaeological evidence is not straight-forward because the surviving material culture shows high levels of shared ideas and beliefs.

The Hunterston brooch, found in Ayrshire, provides a good example of the varied inputs that contribute to the final form of some objects [see Figs 1.19 and 1.20]. The hoop of the brooch is a continuous, unbroken circle, an annular form largely associated with Ireland. Yet moulds for making such a brooch have been discovered at Dunadd, Argyll.[117] The gold panels set into the brooch seem to have been made by a craftsman trained in, or very familiar with, techniques used in Anglo-Saxon workshops to the south.[118] The amber for the insets comes from the Baltic, either through trade with Scandinavia or as fragments collected on the beaches of eastern Britain. No ethnically-based term can usefully be applied to the brooch. It seems the status and power expressed by brooches such as these far outweighed for the owner the need to use them to indicate group identity.

This willingness to use common styles and techniques when creating objects seems to have been prevalent among all the historical groups making up northern Britain. But these designs and craft skills were not the only things that were shared. Foremost among the things that over time came to be part of every community was Christianity. It is a religion with a strong historical component and that history would have had important effects on all the communities that adopted it. Their view of the world must have been greatly expanded, because the events of the Bible were enacted in the eastern Mediterranean or, in the case of some parts of the Old Testament, in areas even further east. Moreover, the growing appreciation of martyrs and saints that had particular places associated with them would have brought expanding European geographies to place alongside those generated by biblical texts. It is not clear whether the material that arrived in Scotland during earlier centuries through contact with the Roman Empire had attached to it a sense of the place where the object was made. Since the Empire had a developed economy with established merchants handling a wide range of goods, it seems possible that those passing the material north across the frontier may themselves have had no clear knowledge of its origins. That it was exotic and rare may have been more than sufficient for the recipients in Scotland. But the key texts of Christianity required an appreciation, however distorted, of the geography of Europe and the eastern Mediterranean.

Some may have travelled from Scotland to the Mediterranean world, although we have no texts to confirm this. Some were certainly aware of places there in some detail, although they never visited. Adomnán, abbot of Iona, wrote a description of the Holy Places. The source of his information he describes thus:

Arculf was a holy bishop, a Gaul by race. He had experience of various faraway places, and his report about them was true and in every way satisfactory. He stayed for nine months in the city of Jerusalem, and used to go round all the holy places on daily visits. All the experiences described below he carefully rehearsed to me, Adomnán, and I first took down his trustworthy and reliable accounts on tablets. This I have now written out on parchment in the form of a short essay.[119]

While few would have made it to the Holy Land, the number travelling to Rome seems likely to have been greater. We know from contemporary writers like Bede that some, such as Benedict Biscop, abbot of the monastery at Monkwearmouth and Jarrow in the second half of the 7th century, made not one but five journeys to Rome. As well as stories about what he had seen, he also brought back manuscripts, paintings and other material to adorn his monastery.[120] It seems likely then that individuals from Scottish monasteries trod a similar path, meeting along the way Scottish and Irish monks in Continental monasteries. They would certainly have known of people who had made the journey. The difficulty is in recognising such events in the archaeological record. For example, a 6th-century wooden box with a sliding lid illustrating scenes from the life of Christ, now in the Vatican, contains stones and wood fragments from the Holy Land [2.50–51].[121] None of these relics would be recognisable as such in the archaeological record once they were separated from their containing wooden box. Yet they reflect a widespread human concern with acquiring mementoes or souvenirs of travels undertaken. From the 12th century onwards, these needs in pilgrims were often satisfied by pewter or lead badges produced at the main pilgrimage sites. Before that date, pilgrims appear to have had to improvise. Interpreting now what may have survived of their efforts is not straightforward.

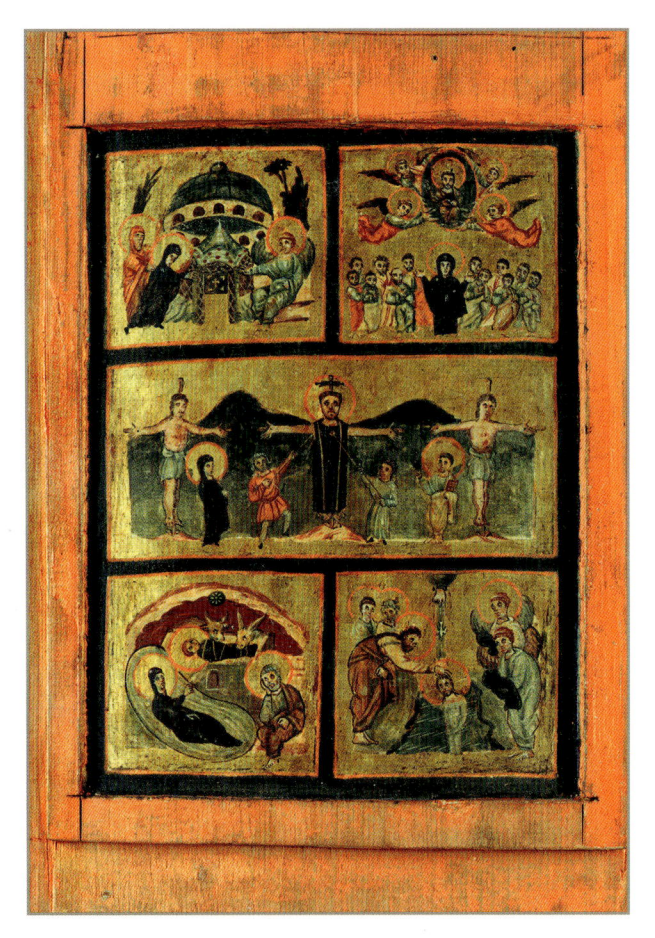

A good example of such mementoes may be a pottery fragment from Iona that comes from a bowl of African Red Slipware.[122] This type of pottery was made in North Africa in the area of Carthage from the 2nd to the 7th century, but it was imported into Atlantic Britain only in the second quarter of the 6th century. Apart from a small number of similar fragments recovered at Whithorn, Wigtownshire, this type of pottery is found only in south-west England and south Wales.[123] Import of this type of pottery into Britain seems to have ceased before the monastery at Iona was founded, so its presence there is unlikely to reflect trading activity. Other material, however, is more problematic.

More than a dozen Byzantine coins have been found in Scotland, most of which were minted in the Early Medieval centuries.[124] Some indeed have superficially suggestive contexts: a worn bronze coin of Constans, AD 641–68, minted at Carthage, was found on the probable site of a tithe barn at Aberdour in Fife, owned by the monastery of Inchcolm, while a similarly worn bronze coin of Tiberius II, AD 574–82, minted at Nicomedia, was found among the ruins of St Fillan's Church, Kilmacolm in Renfrewshire.[125] Interestingly, Nicomedia, the modern Izmit in Turkey, was a major Christian centre with many martyrs, but whether this was a factor in the acquisition of this particular coin cannot be demonstrated. Although these Byzantine coins have often been accepted as ancient losses, this acceptance has not been accompanied by an explanation of who might

Fig. 2.50–2.51 (opposite): A 6th-century wooden box with a painted lid and containing fragments of stone and wood from the Holy Land.

have brought them here.[126] Others have rejected all British finds as ancient losses, except for the gold *solidus* from Wilton, Norfolk, because none has been found during any excavations.[127] The gold coin from Wilton was set as the centrepiece of a gold and garnet cross from the 7th century.[128] Yet it was not found during excavations, although it is undoubtedly an Early Medieval arrival in Britain. Its incorporation with its own cross-decorated face outwards within a more elaborate cross encourages the view that it had more importance than being just a rare foreign gold coin. Certainly, it shows that coins were not considered inappropriate components of religious pieces. Indeed, the regular use of Christian symbols on these coins perhaps helps to explain why some were brought back to Scotland. The idea then that such coins are pilgrimage souvenirs provides a reasonable suggestion for some, if not all, of the Scottish examples.

The same interpretation might apply to a number of the late 4th- and 5th-century Roman coins found in Scotland. These have generally been regarded as modern losses because they are predominantly from eastern Mediterranean mints. Consequently, they display a markedly different patterning in terms of the mints where they were made when compared to coins of the same date found on known Roman sites.[129] Yet if some were arriving as mementoes of pilgrimages in the 6th or even 7th century, their worn condition and their production in eastern mints is exactly what one might expect.

Small fragments of decorative material, presumably from churches, provide a final example of possible pilgrimage contact with the Mediterranean world. The first group involves glass *tesserae*, the small individual pieces that collectively make up a mosaic. A number of sites have produced these: one from Dunadd, the only *tessera* from Scotland with inlaid gold leaf; thirteen from Whithorn, though not all from early contexts; one from the Brough of Birsay in Orkney; and a possible example from Mote of Mark. These *tesserae* were imported in large quantities into Scandinavia from the 8th century for use as jewellery inlays or to be melted down to make beads. Only the piece from Dunadd and one from Whithorn seem certainly early enough to have arrived as Mediterranean imports, perhaps with pilgrims, rather than via Scandinavia.[130]

The second group involves pieces of green (less commonly red), porphyry also known as *verde antico*. Quarried in Laconia, Greece, it was used by the Romans to decorate walls and floors of important buildings. Large quantities were re-used in the post-Roman period to enhance religious buildings, particularly in Rome, and it is through this new association that the material seems to have entered Scotland and Ireland as pilgrimage souvenirs. Most finds come from contexts dating from the 11th or 12th century, though these need not, if they were relics of a particular holy place, be indicative of the date of their arrival in the north. One find from the Brough of Birsay suggests that pieces may have been arriving at an earlier date [2.52]. It was recovered from deposits of the so-called 'Pictish Horizon' dating to the 8th century. Mrs Curle, who published the finds from the site, accepted it as being of that date, but the excavator is quoted elsewhere as saying that the deposits from which it came were 'not sealed'.[131] So the piece can only be regarded as possibly imported in the Early Medieval period.

None of these objects is overtly religious in either its material or form in the way that later pilgrim badges

COMMUNITIES

115

Fig. 2.52: A fragment of green porphyry (*verde antico*) found at the Brough of Birsay, Orkney.

Figs 2.53 and 2.54 (opposite): Reconstructions of DSPA (left) and E ware (right) pottery vessels from Dunadd, Argyll.

and signs are, and for that reason it can be no more than a suggestion that they represent pilgrimage to the Mediterranean. Equally it needs to be stressed that pilgrimage could involve much shorter journeys, for all countries seem to have developed sites that attracted pilgrims. For sites in Scotland the evidence is effectively restricted to the High Medieval period, but it is not unreasonable to suppose that some began receiving pilgrims in the Early Medieval period. Bede's remarks, for instance, about St Ninian's church at Whithorn 'where his body rests, together with those of many other saints', give a strong hint of such a site.[132] But at this level it is much more difficult to know how we might distinguish pilgrimage souvenirs from other forms of contact between communities.

Even with areas as distant as the Mediterranean or Continental Europe, we must not suppose that the only contacts were of a religious nature. The fragments from pottery bowls made of African Red Slipware from Whithorn have been noted above. The site has also produced pieces of Late Roman amphora from the eastern Mediterranean. One has an incised cross that is filled with red paint, and another a red-painted mark of the kind used by traders to signify contents or ownership. As well as this pottery, fragments from eight glass bowls, five of which had wheel-cut scrolls and inscriptions, were also found at Whithorn. These too came from the Mediterranean. In addition, single sherds of Late Roman amphora have been found at Mote of Mark, Kirkcudbrightshire, Dumbarton Rock and now at Rhynie, Aberdeenshire. None of this may have involved direct contact with Mediterranean traders in the first half of the 6th century, coming instead from contacts with south-west England, but the range and quantity of material from Whithorn does suggest this as a real possibility.

If uncertainty surrounds the idea of merchants from the Mediterranean reaching Scotland, there can be no doubt of trade with Europe, particularly France, in the late 6th and 7th centuries. Adomnán describes an incident when Columba prophesied to Luigbe, one of his monks, the destruction of an Italian city, saying 'before this year ends you will hear news of this from Gallic sailors arriving here from Gaul [essentially modern France]'. This was subsequently proved to be true, Adomnán tells us, when some months later Columba and Luigbe, while visiting 'the capital of the country', questioned sailors from Gaul who confirmed the events Columba had prophesied. Our concern here is not, of course, with Columba's prophesy or indeed the events in the Italian city, except to note the continuing interest in the events and places of the Mediterranean. It is instead to note the presence of Gallic sailors and traders in the area that we now know as Argyll in the late 6th century. We have already seen that Adomnán's contacts with Gaul were not restricted to knowledge of sailors or traders. Nothing in his description of Columba and Luigbe's experience suggests that the presence of ships from Gaul was at all exceptional.

The archaeological evidence for this trade is, like that for the earlier Mediterranean contacts, largely provided by pottery and glass. Many more sites though are now receiving some material. This need not mean that there was direct communication between all the sites and the incoming traders. And while the Mediterranean material is only sufficient to suggest occasional contact, there now seems to have been regular trade between Atlantic Scotland

and France from the late 6th century to the end of the 7th century. This trade did not involve material coming over land through England, but was the result of traders using the Atlantic seaways. There has been much discussion about the nature of this trade. Some have wanted to see it as a form of coastal tramping. In this model voyages have an unpredictable quality, being dictated by the cargoes and clients encountered in successive ports.[133] Ewan Campbell has called this the '*Para Handy*' model. He rejects it in favour of trade at regular known intervals involving merchants from western France.[134] Irregular coastal tramping would, he believes, result in a wider range of products being visible in the archaeological record. Merchants and their customers, however, would require a stable pattern of contacts. This would enable both sides to assemble the materials that form their side of the trade in the sure knowledge that the effort would not be wasted. Moreover, it seems likely that the sailors would wish to avoid the uncertainties associated with sailing relatively small boats in autumn or winter.[135] All of this forms a more convincing model than coastal tramping.

The archaeological record in Scotland is, of course, only providing a one-sided view of the transactions that made up this trade for a period perhaps as long as 150 years. What was being given in return is entirely a matter for speculation, as no objects of British or Irish origin have been found in western France. The most commonly suggested items include slaves, leather, furs, sealskins, eiderdown and freshwater pearls.[136] Even if evidence were found of such items, there would be no clear way to determine their place of origin. While we are unable to describe what went from Scotland in this trade, it is equally important to recognise that what arrived from western France was not restricted to just pottery and glass.

Two types of pottery are involved. The earliest, tableware, is now known as DSPA [2.53] (*Dérivées sigillées paléochrétiennes* Atlantic group). The forms suggest that it was valued as a luxury item in its own right. It is found in Scotland only at Dunadd, Whithorn and Mote of Mark.[137] The other type retains its original title 'E ware' [2.54] because its source has not yet been precisely identified.[138] The period of the greatest number of imports appears to have been the early 7th century, but overall it ranges in date from the late 6th century until the late 7th century. Unlike DSPA, E ware is found widely in Scotland with twenty sites having produced fragments so far.[139] It seems unlikely that this wide distribution, ranging from Craig Phadrig above Inverness and Dun Ardtreck on Skye in the north to

COMMUNITIES

Whithorn and Mote of Mark in the south-west, is to be explained by direct contacts with merchants from Gaul. Instead the contact would have been restricted to representatives from the royal sites like Dunadd, enabling the king to control access to the Continental imports. Small quantities of these imports would then be distributed to royal kin or clients in return for renders of surplus produce, mainly but not exclusively from agriculture. Gifts further afield to sites in the north and east, without direct access to Gaulish merchants, might represent claims to political hegemony over those areas, but could just as easily reflect diplomatic gifts between equals.[140]

The variety in form that we see among E ware raises the question of the range of material being imported. While bowls, beakers and jugs could have been important as feasting equipment in a world without other pottery, the contents of the storage jars will have been much more valuable than the containers. Analysis of some fragments from Dunadd and Buiston, Ayrshire, has confirmed the presence of dyer's madder (*Rubia tinctorum*) that produces a bright red colour in fabrics. This has to be a Continental import, as the plant was not grown in Britain until the late Saxon times. Another colouring agent that probably arrived through this trading system is yellow orpiment (arsenic sulphide) used in illuminating manuscripts. The nearest sources at this period were in the Mediterranean at Vesuvius in Italy and in Asia Minor. Fragments have been found at Dunadd and the Sculptor's Cave, Covesea, on the Moray coast.[141] A wider range of dyes and colorants seems a likely component in this Continental trade. Other items that were imported through this trade included herbs. Fruits of coriander (*Coriandrum sativum*) and dill (*Anethum graveolens*) – neither of which are native species – have been recovered from Buiston and Whithorn. Other possibilities include honey, spices, dried fruits such as olives, raisins or figs, and nuts. All of this would have provided the evocative tastes, smells and colours of exotic places. Campbell, however, believes that the important elements in this trade were salt and wine.[142]

While the E ware suggests a range of materials being imported, it seems that the glass, which forms an equally important part of the archaeological record, was brought as a luxury item. The fragments seem to be largely those of beakers that are strikingly similar in form and decoration. The glass from which they are made is of very high quality with thicknesses ranging from only 0.2 to 1 millimetre. None of this suggests that they were intended as containers for other substances. Adomnán describes in one of the episodes recounting St Columba's conflict with King Bridei's wizard, Briochan, how Columba foretold that an angel would break a glass cup in Briochan's hand as he was about to drink from it.[143] Although the overall event is miraculous, the glass cup is incidental to the narrative as a whole. The only reason for its introduction seems to be to emphasise Briochan's high rank in his community. We may reasonably suppose that the glass beakers brought from France were intended to do the same thing for members of the communities with access to them. The significance of these drinking vessels is emphasised by Ewan Campbell's identification of glass cone beakers that are only found at Whithorn and which he believes were probably made there, most likely by a Continental glass-blower.[144]

It is important to stress these contacts with the Mediterranean and Continental Europe to avoid thinking that all relations with these areas were mediated through neighbours to the south, the Anglo-Saxons, or the south-west, Ireland. There are, of course, a small number of items in the Scottish archaeological record that are not easily fitted into the trading patterns described above. For example, there is a fragment of mica from the fill of a post hole that was part of the early church at Whithorn.[145] The condition of the piece suggests that it had been well looked after and its size indicated that Spain was a likely source. Items such as this might well have arrived via Irish or, less likely in this case, Anglo-Saxon hands.

Communities in Ireland or in Anglo-Saxon England were the nearest neighbours to the communities that are our concern here. Indeed, the Anglo-Saxon kingdom of Northumbria included south-east Scotland as far north as the Firth of Forth, and the Irish are portrayed as the founders and occupiers of the western kingdom of Dál Riata centred on Argyll. Yet their proximity does not make relations with them any easier to define, other than in the conventional terms of the conflicts that populate the historical sources. Instead we are faced with ambiguities and contradictions.

Relations between Ireland and Scotland are particularly difficult to describe. That they were close seems inescapable, for they are separated only by the North Channel. Northern Ireland is visible from most of south-west Scotland and many of the islands. Yet variable levels of evidence and the attitudes they have engendered bedevil our understanding of the interplay between the two areas. Ireland, unlike Scotland, has an extensive collection of Early Medieval texts, and the period is a particularly important one in Irish history. The effect of this is that much of the archaeology of Atlantic Britain and Ireland is viewed through an Irish prism. Virtually all decorated metalwork from this area is still labelled Irish as a matter of course. Not until the publication in 1973 of David Wilson's work on the brooches from the St Ninian's Isle hoard was there a recognised brooch type believed to have been made only or largely in Scotland.[146] It may well be that the view that virtually all the metalwork is Irish in origin is correct, but the detailed analysis that would support such a view is unavailable. Indeed most of the major metalwork pieces from across the area still await modern scholarly publication. When it takes place, as it has for the Hunterston brooch, the picture becomes, as we have seen, rather more complex.[147]

The historical texts tell us that the kingdom of Dál Riata centred on Argyll was created by settlement from northern Ireland. Yet the archaeological record there contains little that could be regarded as quintessentially Irish.[148] Objects of this type thus far recovered – such as the glass armlet fragment from Fraoch Eilean, Loch Awe, Argyll [2.55] – could just as easily be explained through trade as migration.[149] Equally problematic is the absence in Argyll of major Irish settlement types like the ringfort.[150] Instead, the royal capital at Dunadd has a physical layout very reminiscent of sites further east like Dalmahoy, Midlothian, or Dundurn, Perthshire.[151] In marked contrast, much of the area's sculpture – like that at Iona, a monastery founded by the Irishman Columba – shows close, but not exclusive, links with Ireland.

Similar issues surround relations with the Anglo-Saxon world to the south.[152] Again, sculpture gives an indication of close connections, but it is almost alone as a

Fig. 2.55: A fragment of an Irish glass armlet from Fraoch Eilean, Argyll.

Fig. 2.56: A silver horn mount from Burghead, Moray.

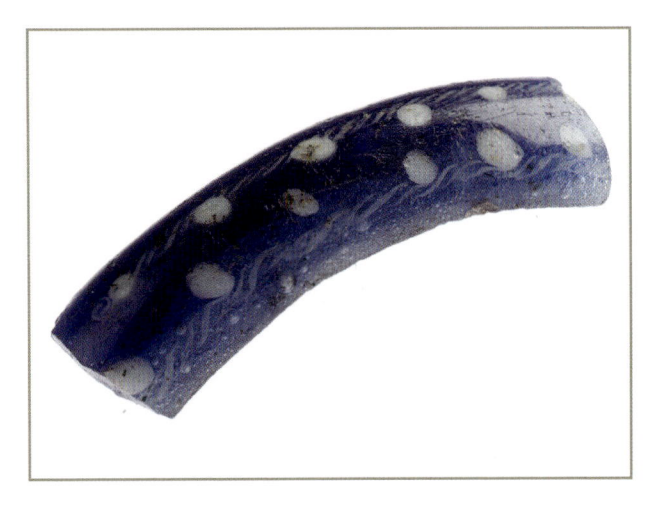

marker of Northumbrian control of south-east Scotland. The emerging spread of 'strap-ends', largely in areas south of the Forth, may be indicative of comparable connections, but the wider geographical area involved makes interpretations more problematic. The evidence from Dunbar, an historically attested Anglo-Saxon settlement in East Lothian, is full of ambiguities and uncertainties.[153] The scatter of decorated metalwork in south-east Scotland, often involving gold and garnets, comes from uninformative contexts, and their meaning is consequently open to several interpretations. A piece of comparable quality was found at Dunadd in a state that suggests it is the last fragment of a larger piece broken down and reworked.[154] This metalwork might be no more than diplomatic gifts. Certainly this would provide the best explanation of other rare pieces from elsewhere in Scotland, like the silver blast-horn mount from Burghead, Moray [2.56] or the sword equipment in the St Ninian's Isle hoard (although the latter are not universally accepted as Anglo-Saxon).[155]

That the same pieces from the St Ninian's Isle hoard can simultaneously be labelled as Mercian – the Anglo-Saxon kingdom centred on the Midlands of England – as well as Pictish by equally eminent scholars, highlights the problems associated with interpreting relations between communities through such material. Our approaches to connections between communities cannot be based on preconceptions rooted in style attributions that are ethnically based. It is interesting to note that discussion of the trade with the Mediterranean and Continental Europe does not involve the use of ethnic labelling of material culture. Of course, any discussion around communities of the wider world has to be framed by the realisation that for most members of Early Medieval communities the wider world was described by the distance one could travel in a day by land or sea, supplemented only by views of distant lands across the sea or from a hilltop.

EARLY MEDIEVAL SCOTLAND

COMMUNITIES OF MEMORY

In the final years of the 4th century AD, St Augustine suggested that 'the present of past things is the memory'.[156] He recognised, as we do now, that the creation, maintenance and manipulation of memory are important means for ensuring and enabling the social reproduction of communities. Normally texts would be key elements in observing these processes, although this is not the case in Early Medieval Scotland where documents are scarce. But the handling of memory can also be seen in aspects of material culture; objects can be powerful triggers for memories. Here we look briefly at four areas where this occurs: undressed stones with carved symbols, the curation and use of decorated metalwork, burials, and finally the re-use of Roman material.

Undressed stones with symbols

Many archaeologists use the shorthand term 'Class I stones' to describe these stones. The term was first coined by J Romilly Allen in 1890 and remains much employed today. It describes unmodified boulders on which symbols are incised or pecked. Normally these symbols are restricted to just two, but in some cases this pair of symbols may be accompanied by symbols representing a mirror and comb; sometimes the mirror occurs unaccompanied by a comb. Because many of these stones were subsequently re-used in building work, they often appear now to be more regular in shape than would likely have been the case originally. A good example of this is the stone from St Peter's Church on South Ronaldsay, Orkney, that was found forming the sill of a window in the church [2.57].[157] The regularity that resulted from this secondary use has been achieved at the expense of removing part of the symbols.

At first sight these stones appear to have little to do with memory. They are the first stone sculpture to be placed in the landscapes north of the Forth-Clyde isthmus for almost two millennia. They were a striking and new phenomenon. In these circumstances it is not clear where the required stone-carving skills were acquired. Yet the form of many of them shared that of much earlier prehistoric monuments, the standing stones and stone circles. Although no doubt often ruined, these were still a very visible part of the Early Medieval landscape. So the contemporary explanations of their meaning, however mistaken they might have been, would nonetheless have formed part of the prevailing social memory. Indeed, some symbols were carved on standing stones or stones that had once formed part of stone circles and avenues.[158] In rare cases, like the stone at Edderton, Ross-shire [2.58],[159] or Craw Stane at Rhynie, Aberdeenshire,[160] the standing stones seem to have been left in their original positions. But more usually, as for example at Brandsbutt, Aberdeenshire, we cannot tell whether the newly-decorated stone [2.59] remained part of the earlier stone circle or was repositioned into a new location that still enabled it to maintain a dialogue with the older monument and its perceived meanings.[161] In either situation this was a conscious linking of old and new in the Early Medieval milieu of memory.

Yet beyond this evocation and use of earlier monuments, these stones have been seen to have a more direct link with memory. The symbols, and therefore the stones

Fig. 2.57 (left): A sculptured stone from St Peter's Church, South Ronaldsay, Orkney.

Fig. 2.58 (below): A prehistoric standing stone subsequently decorated with symbols at Edderton, Ross-shire.

Fig. 2.59 (below, left): A sculptured stone from Brandsbutt, Aberdeenshire.

EARLY MEDIEVAL SCOTLAND

122

Fig. 2.60 (right, above): A sculptured stone from Firth, Orkney, that has the same symbols as the stone from St Peter's Church (Fig. 2.57, opposite).

Fig. 2.61 (below): A stone from Kirkmadrine, Wigtownshire, that commemorates two priests (or more likely bishops), Viventius and Mauorius.

themselves, have been usually interpreted as commemorative, perhaps even reflecting names of some kind.[162] What has not been convincingly explained is what caused the need for this new, highly structured and complex form of commemoration. This view inevitably requires the symbols to be seen as some form of text. Perhaps then, we should see them as forming the equivalent of multiple sets of the same text, or as a related set of texts preserved in different manuscripts. In such circumstances we might have to envisage regional groups where, rather as in the case of dialects, their form and meaning might reflect different nuanced messages. This might help enlarge our perspectives in considering, for example, why the symbol combination of crescent and V-rod, and rectangle [2.57, 60], occurs in Shetland (Breck of Hillwell), Orkney (Firth and St Peter's Church), Sutherland (Clynekirkton 1, 2) and Aberdeenshire (Old Deer).[163] Rosamond McKitterick, in a rather different context, suggested that we should not be overly concerned with identifying the original text of a history, but rather accept that all texts of a history are the key text for some community or other.[164] We might usefully adopt a similar view towards the symbols instead of looking at them in typological sequences and consequently seeking *ur*-symbols (the original symbols from which all variants developed).[165] They might all be engaging with the same past, but with local perspectives and variable skill-bases determining the final outcome.

The idea that these stones might be commemorative derives from the suggestion that they are the equivalent of the inscribed stones found elsewhere in Atlantic Britain and Ireland. These stones have simple Latin or ogham inscriptions, often using a formula that translates as 'Here lies …

COMMUNITIES

[the name of the individual]' [2.61].[166] The difficulty with this idea is that very few, only around a dozen, of these Latin stones survive in southern Scotland and none occurs north of the Forth.[167] It is certainly unsatisfactory to suppose that rarity in the surviving group necessarily betokens rarity in the original group. But these stones were created in a Christian milieu and so should not have provoked exceptional levels of destruction in later periods. Indeed their creation as overtly Christian monuments makes them strange role models for people in eastern Scotland who were still apparently pagan at the time. Very few of the Class I stones now stand in what might be their original position and this adds to the problems surrounding the reasons for their creation. But none has yet been found marking a burial. So if they are commemorative, it seems likely that they functioned as memorials not tombstones.

An alternative view, not acceptable to everybody, is that the Class I stones are erected as an explicit renouncement of the purpose of Christian missionary activity emanating from Iona and other western monasteries, and from the Church in southern Scotland. This interpretation sees the stones and their symbols as the active expression of a range of social memories and beliefs, some of them possibly very long-lived, harnessed together in defence of the established order. It removes the need to see the symbol set as created simultaneously. Such an event is certainly not hard to imagine, but is difficult to explain in terms of what might have prompted it. The rejection of Christianity, on the other hand, allows us to envisage the bringing into play, perhaps *back* into play, symbols that had been created centuries before. This does not preclude the development of new symbols in this crisis to augment those already in existence; but it does mean that other objects with comparable symbols are not necessarily the same date as the Class I stones. In this interpretation, the stones are then harnessing the power of the symbols, both old and new, and allying them with forms that allude to those of stones associated with earlier prehistoric ritual. In so doing, the communities that erected them called into play a wide range of social memories in a vain attempt to halt the spread of Christianity.

The curation and use of decorated metalwork

Many objects of all periods can be associated with memory, but in Early Medieval Scotland the close links between memory and objects are best explored through the surviving decorated metalwork. These links involve a number of different features. No single object exhibits them all.

The most straightforward of these aspects is where objects are carefully looked after over a number of generations, becoming in the process heirlooms. This is not always easily demonstrated in the case of individual pieces, but there are examples where careful curation over extended periods can be clearly established. Although the very fine Hunterston brooch was made around AD 700, scratched on the back are later 10th-century runes saying 'Máel Brigte owns this brooch'.[168] These runes do not, of course, tell us when the brooch was buried, only that it was at least 250 years old and probably much older when that happened.

An alternative approach to the preservation of heirlooms was the deliberate creation of objects with archaic forms. While this cannot be shown with certainty among

Fig. 2.62: The crosier of St Fillan.

the Scottish metalwork, there are pieces from elsewhere in the Early Medieval world that show that for some this was an eagerly adopted approach. For example, a reliquary of the True Cross, the Enamelled Cross of Pope Paschal I, has decoration that deliberately copies enamels of an earlier period. Paschal, who was Pope from AD 817–24, commissioned a range of material that copied earlier styles, most notably mosaics in some basilicas modelled on those of early examples at Ravenna and Rome.[169]

Finally, and perhaps most common of all, there was the deliberate incorporation of fragments from older objects in those being newly created. This seems to have been particularly something that occurred when religious objects were being created.[170] Some of the mounts on the Monymusk reliquary may have come from another object. The new mounts were then made to reflect the overall appearance of the earlier pieces, although we have no real understanding of the time difference between the two sets.

All of these processes promoted the creation of stories that are the very encapsulation of memory. We can best see the processes, especially those suggested for the Monymusk reliquary, among Early Medieval objects that continue to be venerated as relics into the High Medieval period. The crosier of St Fillan is a good illustration of this. St Fillan is believed to have been alive in the early 8th century AD.[171] His crosier, a simple wooden crook, was embellished on a number of occasions from the late 11th or early 12th century until the 15th century [2.62]. Twelfth-century filigree from the earlier of these embellishments was re-used as part of the later schemes.[172] The earlier of these decorative plans only survived, although modified, because it was completely encased by the later ornament. It seems likely then that the original wooden crook, if indeed it dates from the time of St Fillan, was adorned with earlier decoration that has not survived.

But the use of metalwork as objects of memory was not restricted to relics and reliquaries. Aspects of the practices can be seen on presumptively secular metalwork. Good examples are to be found among the hoard of objects buried on St Ninian's Isle in Shetland that was discovered in 1958. It was buried in a wooden box under the floor of what may have been an early church. The occasion for its burial has usually been assumed to be the Viking raids of the early 9th century. The hoard has three groups of silver or silver-gilt objects: bowls and table implements, fittings for weapons, and brooches. It also contained part of the jaw of a mature porpoise (see Fig. 1.51). The material has been interpreted as the treasure of a local lord and his family, although there now seems to be a growing consensus that

COMMUNITIES

Figs 2.63–2.74 (opposite and following page): All the silver-gilt brooches from the St Ninian's Isle hoard, Shetland.

its apparently secular objects formed part of a church treasury. Neither interpretation is without its difficulties, but both allow the presence of objects of memory.

Quite a number of the pieces can be so regarded, although with varying levels of credibility. At the most straightforward level it has always been recognised that all of the objects were not made at the same time. Even the earliest date for the burial of the hoard, the early 9th century, would mean that the hanging bowl was more than a century old. Other objects among the weapon fittings and the brooches might also be heirlooms that, perhaps through multiple lives, witnessed the accumulation and discarding of associated stories in their development as memory objects, even though we lack sufficient chronological precision to be sure.

Among the weapon fittings are two chapes, mounts for the bottom of a scabbard that stop the sword blade ripping through the base when it is sheathed (see pages 26 and 78). One is silver and one silver-gilt, but both share the same overall U-shape that ends with animal heads in relief. Yet there is a marked difference in their condition. One is in an excellent state. It looks unused with all the glass mounts for the animals' eyes still in place. It has no role in the present discussion. The other, in contrast, shows evidence of considerable wear. Only one complete and one broken glass mount now survive. It has a Latin inscription on both faces that is believed to form a single continuous statement. On the front face it says 'INNOMINEDS', i.e. 'in nomine d[ei] s[ummi]', translating as 'in the name of God the highest'. On the other side the inscription reads as 'RESADFILIS- PUSSCIO'. The interpretation of this is less straightforward, but it seems to be 'res ad fili sp[irit]us s[an]c[t]io', 'property of the son of the holy spirit'. While the wear on the back is consistent with its use as a chape rubbing against the leg of the warrior, the wear on the front face is far less easily explained. Here the panel containing the inscription is flanked by projections formed by four spheres with a central sphere on top. Another projection of exactly the same form is placed in the centre of the inscription. These three projections should have protected the inscription when the piece was in use as a chape. Instead, the inscription is the most worn part of the front face on what is generally a well worn object. We know that in other Early Medieval parts of Europe certain swords acquired considerable prestige and were handed down through the generations. The use of silver-gilt here suggests that it was the property of a very important man. Perhaps this chape came from the scabbard of a sword with its own history, or, given the religious nature of the inscription, was even a memento or a relic of a sword used by a holy man or saint, a veritable defender of the faith.

The brooches present rather different aspects [Figs 2.63–2.74]. Eleven of them are very similar in overall design and size. Their hoops range in diameter from 65 millimetres to 77 millimetres, although the diameter of seven of them is either 70 or 71 millimetres. All are worn – some

EARLY MEDIEVAL SCOTLAND

126

COMMUNITIES

EARLY MEDIEVAL SCOTLAND

extremely so – and all are missing glass mounts. Thirty-eight of the glass settings are missing out of an original sixty-six and several appear to be replacements. This level of loss is not to be explained by poor workmanship involving the creation of inadequate mounts. One brooch retains eight of its original ten glass settings, even though it is so worn that most of the gilding is now missing. In addition to the long use suggested by the absence of many glass settings, two of the brooches have replacement pins, one other has a pin that is either a replacement or has been re-gilded, and one brooch was used with a broken pin. The overall impression is of a group of brooches ranging in condition from worn to extremely well worn.

Their preservation as a group raises interesting issues. If, as appears probable, the size of the brooch was related to the status of the individual wearing it, it seems unlikely that eleven brooches of the same size would be in simultaneous use by members of a single family. A more reasonable explanation is that some of the brooches were intended to replace others that were becoming too worn to satisfy all the functions required of a brooch. The question then arises – why were they all kept? After all, this was a period in which the recycling of obsolete, damaged or unfashionable jewellery was certainly undertaken. Their preservation is more readily understood if they were gifts through time to a church treasury. But before that happened they were subjected to considerable wear. Each through that wear acquired, no doubt, a range of memories peculiar to it. Indeed, those memories may have been the reason why the brooches became part of a church treasury and which ensured an important new life for worn and damaged pieces.

Burials

Burial provides closure. It initiates the creation of a complex set of memories involving both person and place, and these memories develop through time. While this would currently be the normative position, the importance of the burial and its associated memories does not seem to have been a consistently-held view through prehistory and early history. Nevertheless, the Early Medieval period does see a serious increase in the number of formal burials after a long period when such burials are notably scarce. Even so, many aspects of Early Medieval burial are indistinguishable from burials of the preceding Iron Age, although the presence of grave goods and the use of multiple or partial burials in the earlier period are not replicated in later burials. The increase seen in Early Medieval burials is not spread consistently across Scotland. The main concentration lies in the lands around the estuaries of the Forth and Tay, together with the area in between. It has recently been suggested that this distribution is 'an artefact of visibility', although the supporting evidence for this claim is as yet unpublished.[173]

It has been usual to regard Early Medieval burial as Early Christian burial and the two terms have been regarded as synonymous. Indeed there has been a long-held view that long-cist burials are the earliest evidence we have for the appearance of Christianity in Scotland. Though it is reasonable to suppose that many of these graves contain Christians, it cannot be assumed that they are. This has become clearer as more and more reliable radiocarbon dates are made available. The largest set of dates presently available is from the cemetery at Thornybank, Midlothian.

Fig. 2.75: Long-cist burial at Lochhead Quarry, Auchterforfar, Angus.

Here a suite of thirty dates has produced calibrated dates that range from AD 230–430 to AD 670–880.[174] Clearly the earliest dates would make it unlikely that those graves contained Christians. In this context it is interesting to note that those involved in burying the hoard of Roman silver at nearby Traprain Law, East Lothian, seem to have treated the objects with Christian symbols with as little respect as was accorded the pieces decorated with pagan motifs.

The most common form of grave is the long cist [2.75]. Examples have been found across the whole of Scotland. The cist forms effectively a stone coffin and the individuals are laid full-length on their back. It is very unusual for the body to be accompanied by grave goods. The excavations at the cemetery at Hallow Hill, St Andrews, Fife, while showing a number of variations, did produce a construction sequence. After the grave had been dug, the west end stone, together with the north-west side slab, were placed in position first. The south-west side slab was next, and thereafter the side slabs were put in place working eastwards. The east end stone was inserted last. Sometimes the basal slabs were positioned first, but equally commonly they were laid in after the side slabs were in position. The best base slabs were reserved for the west end of the cist. Some of the cists were filled with soil soon after burial. The covering slabs were laid with the central stone first, extending from there out to the ends of the cist.[175] There is some incidental evidence to suggest that special care was taken in the selection of the slabs. Yellow, red and white sandstone was used in the cists at Hallow Hill, and yellow, red and grey sandstone at Thornybank.[176] Unfortunately, in neither case do the reports allow us to understand if there were patterns in this use of colour. At Hallow Hill Cist 69, the stone used for the east end slab may have been selected because it showed a fossil plant.[177]

Although long cists are the dominant form in the cemeteries of south and east Scotland, there are other forms of graves. There are dug graves with and without wooden linings or log coffins. At Whithorn it was suggested that long cists of stone, wood, or stone and wood combined (called by the excavator 'lintel graves'), were replaced in a later phase by log coffins.[178] This sequence, based on stratigraphy, is not mirrored in the cemeteries elsewhere that rely on radiocarbon dates to sequence the burials. From Angus northwards to the Moray Firth, we find a different type of burial form involving square barrows. These were previously believed to be restricted to this area, but they have recently been recognised in Dumfriesshire, suggesting that they might have been as widespread as long cists.[179]

EARLY MEDIEVAL SCOTLAND

Fig. 2.76 (left): The cemetery at Redcastle, Angus, that contained square and round barrows as well as unmarked graves.

Fig. 2.77 (below): A grave marker from Iona. This small sculptured stone bears a cross symbol.

Square barrows also occur in cemeteries and, where extensively excavated as at Redcastle, Lunan Bay, Angus, they occur alongside other burial forms such as round barrows and unenclosed graves [2.76].[180] We have no evidence to explain what determines the choice of burial form, except that it does not appear to reflect gender.

Apart from the barrows that may be a form of special grave, virtually none of these burials is individually marked, although the organised nature of most cemeteries with very little intercutting between graves suggests that their positions remained known in subsequent generations. This is our most direct evidence linking burials and memory. A small number of graves at Whithorn do seem to have been marked by posts or stones, but even here these are exceptional within a large number of excavated graves.[181] Certainly there are sculptured stones, usually small in size and bearing only a cross, that can reasonably be described as grave markers, but we seldom find them attached to graves [2.77].[182] We have seen already that the available evidence does not support the claim that the undressed stones with symbols are tombstones. So what makes some graves special is often the fact that they are marked. At Thornybank, for instance, two graves out of a hundred were surrounded by unbroken ditched enclosures that seem to have held wooden superstructures, and a third grave was marked at the four corners by a post-hole, again suggesting a free-standing wooden superstructure or perhaps a wooden fence around the grave. While two of these had graves large enough for an adult, one was sufficient only for a young child.[183] There is no reason to suppose that these burials were the focus around which the cemetery grew up, although such a role might be argued for Cist 54 at Hallow Hill with grave goods including a Roman seal-box.[184]

Some of these graves occur in large cemeteries that appear to have no enclosure around. Some cemeteries are positioned within existing prehistoric monuments, for example the dug graves at Camp Hill, Trohoughton, Dumfriesshire, and the cemetery at Montfode, Ardrossan, North

COMMUNITIES

131

Ayrshire.[185] At the latter site, some of the graves overlay the encircling ditch. As well as the absence of an enclosure, there is also no evidence that these cemeteries grew up around a church. Instead they seem to have been local community graveyards enabling burial with one's kin. These cemeteries appear to fall out of use in the 8th and 9th centuries as burial becomes linked to graveyards around churches. David Petts has argued that this might coincide with changes in Christian beliefs and attitudes to death, particularly the emergence of purgatory as an intermediate place on the way to salvation.[186] The requirement for aid from the living to enable the dead to escape from purgatory brought burials and memory together in new forms.

The continuing presence of Rome

It is hard to know how the communities of Scotland viewed Rome in the aftermath of the collapse of the Western Empire. To judge from the texts, they had seen the Empire as a place to be attacked and plundered, or alternatively a place that offered bribes and gifts not to take part in such things. Perhaps for the leaders it lived on most vividly in their silver metalwork fashioned from reworked Roman silver. The large hoard of late Roman silver from Traprain Law, East Lothian [2.78], the fragment of a Roman silver spoon in the Early Medieval hoard from Norrie's Law, Fife, or the hoards of silver *denarii* (Roman coins equivalent to a day's pay for a soldier in the imperial army) found across Scotland, are the archaeological expressions of this.[187]

While this appears to have been the dominant view,

Fig. 2.78 (opposite): Some of the treasure of Roman silver found at Traprain Law, East Lothian.

Fig. 2.79 (below): A Late Roman silver brooch from Carn Liath, Sutherland.

there are a few hints that some found aspects of Rome still symbolically powerful and appropriately expressed in silver objects. One such piece is a late Roman brooch, decorated apparently with the double-disc symbol seen also on the sculptured stones discussed earlier in this section, which was found at Carn Liath, Sutherland [2.79].[188] Another may be the pair of silver circlets with twisted hoops and expanded terminals from the Norrie's Law hoard that some have seen as imitating Roman military insignia.[189]

We see this continuing commitment to matters Roman most strongly in the south of Scotland, the areas most likely to have been in contact with communities within the Empire. The earliest Christian monuments, the inscribed stones of the 5th and 6th century, are largely funerary memorials, but they are equally concerned with secular power. They are erected by elites using both the language, Latin, and the religion of the Empire, to assert their power. It has been convincingly argued that the earliest of these monuments, the 5th-century Latinus stone at Whithorn, was set up by a group that was still familiar with spoken Latin [2.80].[190]

Because these southern Scottish communities were Christian, they already have two of the key things that conversion to Christianity would bring to the rest of Scotland – literacy and the use of Latin. With no tradition, however, of either in these areas of southern Scotland, their use in a Christian milieu will have made little impact on the daily round.[191] Both are, of course, intimately involved with the Roman world. Through time, Rome becomes increasingly acknowledged as *the* centre of Christianity in western Europe. So conversion to Christianity in the areas north of the Forth-Clyde isthmus inevitably brought Rome into a wholly new perspective. No longer the enemy or the other, Rome now became a place of guidance with values and styles to be aspired to. This must have required some adjustments in memory structures to accommodate the new reality.

This is most clearly reflected in an incident described by Bede. In *c*.713 or 714, Nechtan, 'king of the Picts', asked Ceolfrith, abbot of the Anglo-Saxon monastery at Monkwearmouth and Jarrow, 'for builders to be sent to build a church of stone in their country after the Roman fashion, promising that it should be dedicated in honour of the blessed chief of the apostles'.[192] This was part of a much wider commitment on Nechtan's part to promote and adhere to the practices of the Roman Church. Some have chosen to see this church as providing a startling contrast in an area dominated by timber-building techniques.[193]

COMMUNITIES

Fig. 2.80 (left): A stone from Whithorn commemorating Latinus, the grandson/descendant of Barrouadus, and his five-year-old daughter.

Fig. 2.81 (opposite): The excavated wall-face of the rampart of the vitrified fort at Castle Law in Abernethy, Perthshire.

But this seems mistaken. There were long-established traditions of stone building stretching back into prehistory. Even where timber construction was important, a skilled stone-working tradition is evident, as we see, for example, in the timber-laced stone rampart of the vitrified fort at Castle Law, Abernethy, Perthshire [2.81].[194] A stone building would not have been sufficient to make the necessary impact. Nechtan was clearly seeking masons who could build using dressed stone and mortar. One wonders whether it was similar thinking that caused the cross-slabs to be created using dressed stone, in which case they too are evoking memories of Rome.

Even before this request from Nechtan, dressed stone from Roman sites seems to have been special. A small number of long-cist burials in the cemeteries at Lasswade and Thornybank in Midlothian were constructed using re-used Roman stones. At Thornybank the pieces were from an arch of a bathhouse, and one of the cists produced a calibrated radiocarbon date of AD 390–550.[195] In neither case were these stones available in the immediate vicinity. Cynthia Hahn has drawn attention to the importance attached to the re-use of Roman dressed stones, or even entire vaults built of that material, in honouring saints in the Early Medieval world.[196] It is clearly impossible to map such ideas directly onto the graves at Lasswade and at Thornybank, but it is not unreasonable to wonder if the use of Roman stones here marks the graves of noted Christian individuals. But the re-use of Roman masonry is not to be linked exclusively with a Christian setting. The hillforts at Ruberslaw in Roxburghshire, and Inchtuthil in Perthshire, have dressed slabs incorporated into their ramparts.[197] Both appear to be opportunistic use of stone on the site. Inchtuthil was the site of a Roman fortress and Ruberslaw may have had an earlier Roman building on it, probably a signal station but perhaps a temple. It is less easy to explain the presence of such stones, including one with a figure of Pegasus in relief, in the souterrain (i.e. underground chamber) at Crichton Mains, Midlothian.[198] There are about thirty stones scattered throughout the structure. They may have been brought from a distance, but there remains the possibility of an undiscovered Roman fort in the area. Perhaps the most remarkable example of Roman building material is the presence of a tile fragment on the Isle of May, Fife.[199] The nearest Roman forts – the most likely source – are around fifty kilometres away, but the reason for its presence, if it is not a pilgrimage souvenir, might be that it arrived accidentally as part of ballast dumped on the island.[200]

EARLY MEDIEVAL SCOTLAND

Maintaining the memory of Rome, and its ways, was not restricted to collecting the physical remains of a Roman past. It also included attempts to use contemporary material to evoke that Roman past, rather as Nechtan intended with his church of dressed masonry. Ewan Campbell has suggested that the Mediterranean glass bowls, many with decoration, found at Whithorn were intended as tableware calculated to display the wealth of their owners, while at the same time creating memories of a Roman lifestyle. The same impression is created by some of the later imports from France. The DPSA *mortaria* found at Dunadd and Mote of Mark were designed to produce purées of vegetables and fruit, reflecting a Roman style in food production. The glass vessels that accompanied this pottery are largely absent from Argyll, concentrating instead in areas to the south.[201] These too were intended for use at the table, perhaps seeking to make imagined links with Roman practices. They seem to concentrate in that area of southern Scotland where the early inscribed stones suggest elites using allusions to Rome to bolster their political positions.

* * *

There are, of course, many aspects of communities that have not been covered at all in these four sections of place, craft, the wider world and memory. Many more have been accorded just a passing allusion that only hints at what they might contribute in a more extensive discussion. The aim here has merely been to suggest the wealth of information we have at our disposal. Communities will be central to our understanding of Early Medieval Scotland and they can be discussed without resort to simple ethnic labelling. Without the distraction of ethnicity, communities represent our easiest pathways into the Early Medieval world.

NOTES

1. Henrik Ibsen, *The Master Builder*, trans. by Ellis-Fermer (1958).
2. Moar and Stewart 1944.
3. *Adomnán of Iona: Life of St Columba*, trans. by Sharpe (1995), 181–84.
4. Härke 1989; Bone 1989.
5. See, for example, Laing's comparison of swords on Aberlemno 2 with Anglo-Saxon swords (2001, 246, fig. 22.5). Neither provides a close match with the other, although everything here depends on how a close a match is required to satisfy the interpreter of its validity. Some are more easily satisfied than others.
6. For example, Cruickshank 1985; 1999; Ritchie 1989, 22–27; Aitchison 2003, 145–46.
7. For example, Fraser 2002a; Aitchison 2003.
8. This straightforward distinction is maintained even in Alcock's more nuanced interpretation of the stone (2003, 172–75).
9. Tweddle 1992.
10. Woolf 2006.
11. For example, Aitchison 2003, 145 reads it from bottom to top; Alcock 2003, 173 reads it from top to bottom.
12. Allen and Anderson 1903b, plate 156.
13. Henderson and Henderson 2004, 135.
14. Curle 1982, 13–14, 97–100.
15. Or more decorated if one rejects Aitchison's interpretation of the circles and square on the other two shields as representing a metal shield boss attached to the shield by pairs of rivets (2003, 61).
16. Dutton 2004, 3–42.
17. Allen and Anderson 1903b, 248, fig. 260B.
18. Alcock 1998, 522; Aitchison 2003, 76.
19. The evidence is conveniently summarised in Sealey 2007, 32–40.
20. For a list of prehistoric burials, see Hunter 2005, 64–66. For Anglo-Saxon graves, see Härke 1989.
21. For Dunadd, see Christison, et al. 1905, 318; Craw 1930, 116 and 118, fig. 5.36. For Gorton, see Grieg 1940, 159 and 158, fig. 74. For Torbeck Hill, see Grieg 1940, 13–14 and 16, fig. 2. For Harvieston, see Laing 2000, 89 and 92, fig 7. For Carronbridge, see Owen and Welander 1995.
22. For Aberlemno, see Fraser 2008, 47, illus. 51.2. For Dull, see Allen and Anderson 1903b, fig. 329. For Dupplin, see Alcock and Alcock 1992, 240–41, illus. 13–14.
23. For Iron Age shields, see Ritchie 1969. For Bridgeness, see Keppie 1979, 10, plate 1. For Clonoura, see Rhynne 1962, 152 and plate XVII.
24. For Eassie, see Fraser 2008, 53, illus. 58. For Kirriemuir, see Fraser 2008, 57, illus. 65.2.
25. For Portmahomack, see Carver 2008, 101, fig. 5.5. For Fowlis Wester, see Fraser 2008, 123, illus. 182. For Meigle, see Stuart 1856–67, plate LXXVI.
26. Alcock 1998.
27. Cummins 2001, 4.
28. Reid 1922.
29. Sheridan 2005, 21: 1440±45 BP (OxA-6052).
30. Berg 1951.
31. Reid 1922, 286, fig. 2.
32. Macaulay 1996.
33. Alcock 1995, 77.
34. MacGregor 1976. For Buiston, see Alcock 2003, 168, illus. 51.4–5; Lane and Campbell 2000, 160–62, illus. 4.71.881.
35. Huff 1998, 7.
36. Bramwell 1994, 155–56.
37. Henderson 2005, 78.
38. Alcock et al. 1986, 258.
39. Clarke 2001.
40. Urquhart Castle is, of course, a loch-side promontory: see Alcock and Alcock 1992, 242–67.
41. Lane and Campbell 2000, 87–90.
42. Ralston 2004, 27–29.
43. Ralston 1986.
44. Stevenson 1949.
45. Close-Brooks 1986.

46 See, for example, the comparative plans in Driscoll 2010, 265, fig. 7.6.
47 Ralston 2004, 12–13.
48 Foster 1998a.
49 Laing and Longley 2006.
50 Compare Alcock 1988.
51 *Ibid.*, 37.
52 Crone 1993, 246–49.
53 Munro 1882, 190–239. Munro seems to have taken charge of the finds and through that written up the work, but he does not seem to have been in charge of the excavations.
54 Crone 2000.
55 Alcock 1993a, 30.
56 Alcock 2003, 269.
57 Crone 2000, 166.
58 Crone and Campbell 2005, 122.
59 For Lagore, see Hencken 1950. For Ballinderry no. 2, see Hencken 1942.
60 Boyle 2004.
61 Cavers 2010, 1.
62 *Ibid.* 32, fig 4.5.
63 Sharples 2003.
64 For Old Scatness, see Dockrill et al 2010, 27–75. For Pool, see Hunter 2007, 97–109, 111–16.
65 Dockrill et al 2010, 69–70.
66 Henderson and Henderson 2004, 102.
67 Yeoman (2009, 233) argues that the fragment of early walling that Carver (2004, 9, fig. 6) interpreted as part of an 8th-century church might be better dated to the 10th century.
68 James and Yeoman 2008.
69 Hill 1997, 139–62.
70 For Flixborough, see Loveluck 2001, 120–21; Loveluck 2007, 144–47. For Brandon, see Carr et al. 1988.
71 Lowe 2006, 190.
72 Henderson 1998, 109–10.
73 For Inchmarnock, see Forsyth and Tedeschi 2008. For Portmahomack, see Carver and Spall 2004 and Higgitt 1982.

74 Sally Foster (in press) is providing a wide-ranging review of the evidence for Scottish churches that is not duplicated here.
75 Irish churches are comprehensively reviewed in Ó Carragáin 2010.
76 Thomas 1967.
77 Colgrave and Mynors 1969, 532–33; Alcock and Alcock 1992, 223–26.
78 Ritchie 1995, 5.
79 Foster 1998b. We intend to develop these criticisms of the shrine interpretation in a forthcoming article.
80 Carver 2008, 100, fig. 5.4, no. TR 27.
81 Henderson and Henderson 2004, 181.
82 *Ibid.*
83 Henderson 2001, 141.
84 Henderson 2008b, 78–79, illus. 4.5.1–4, where the tenons are shown as very shallow.
85 Henderson and Henderson 2004, 201.
86 Spearman 1988, 96–97.
87 Hill 1997.
88 Hall 1995.
89 See Perry 2000.
90 Foster 2004, 62.
91 Lane and Campbell 2000, 238–39.
92 McDonnell in Lane and Campbell 2000, 218–20.
93 Lane and Campbell 2000, 220.
94 *Ibid.*
95 Case 2003, 189, footnote 22.
96 For Ardifuar, see Christison et al. 1905, 269. For Loch Glashan, see Crone and Campbell 2005, 63–64. For Bruach an Drumein, see Heald and Hunter in Abernethy 2009, 42–43.
97 Discussed more fully in Heald 2010.
98 Sharples 2003.
99 This is most recently listed in Heald 2010.
100 These are most easily compared in Clarke 2008.
101 For example, Henderson and Henderson 2004, 113.
102 Campbell and Heald 2007.
103 Curle 1982.

104 Armit et al. 2008.
105 *Ibid.*, 99.
106 Christison et al. 1905, 267–68.
107 Youngs 1989, 211–12.
108 Crone 2000, 151.
109 Carver and Spall 2004.
110 For a wide-ranging review of thrones, see Charles-Gaffiot 2011.
111 Waddell 1932.
112 For Monkwearmouth, see Cramp 2006, 171, AS 11 and 172, fig. 28.2.3 AS 11. For Lastingham, see Lang 1991, 172–73, illus. 614, 617. For Dublin, see Lang 1988, 53–54, plate V.
113 Crone and Campbell 2005, 83–84.
114 Herren 1974, 104–107.
115 Allen and Anderson 1903b, 7, fig. 4 and 12, fig. 7.
116 Crone 2000, 156.
117 Lane and Campbell 2000, 118–19, 115, illus. 4.19 and 116, illus. 4.20.
118 Stevenson 1974.
119 Wilkinson 2002, 167.
120 Farmer (ed.) 1988, 188–90.
121 Bagnoli et al. (eds) 2011, 36–37.
122 Campbell 2007, 26.
123 *Ibid.*, 18, fig. 8.
124 For Byzantine coins in Britain, see Abdy and Williams 2006, and Moorhead 2009.
125 Robertson 1983, 412 and 415.
126 Robertson, 1971, 137 and Robertson 1983, 430.
127 See Casey 1984, 295, where he wrongly attributes the coin to the brooch from Ixworth.
128 Webster and Backhouse 1991, 27–28.
129 See Casey 1984, where he quotes but then denies the more measured statements of Robertson.
130 Campbell 2007, 78.
131 For the Birsay find, see Curle 1982, 46 and 120. More general discussions are Lynn 1984 where the Birsay excavator, Radford, is quoted, and Cormack 1989.
132 Colgrave and Mynors 1969, 222–23.
133 Wooding 1996.
134 Campbell 1996, 79.
135 Campbell 2007, 137.
136 Alcock 2003, 91; Campbell 2007, 137.
137 Campbell 2007, 27–32.
138 *Ibid.*, 47–49.
139 *Ibid.*, 116.
140 *Ibid.*, 114.
141 *Ibid.*, 80; Benton 1931, 201 and 199, fig. 19.11.
142 Campbell 2007, 79–81.
143 *Adomnán of Iona: Life of St Columba*, trans. by Sharpe (1995), 181.
144 Campbell 2007, 69–72.
145 Hill 1997, 469.
146 Small, Thomas and Wilson 1973, 81–105.
147 For Hunterston, see Stevenson 1974.
148 Campbell 2001.
149 For the armlet, see 'Donations and Purchases for the Museum, 1976–77', *Proceedings of the Society of Antiquaries of Scotland* 108, 385.
150 For ringforts, see Stout 2000.
151 See Stevenson 1949.
152 The completion of Alice Blackwell's major study on this material will undoubtedly clarify many aspects: Blackwell (in press).
153 Blackwell 2010.
154 Lane and Campbell 2000, 150–51.
155 For Burghead, see Graham-Campbell 1973. For St Ninian's Isle, see Webster 2001, 56, but this is challenged in Henderson and Henderson 2004, 113.
156 *St Augustine's Confessions*, trans. by Pine-Coffin 1961, 269.
157 Allen and Anderson 1903a, 3–4.
158 A possible list is provided in Clarke 2007, 38–39.
159 *Ibid.*, 36, fig. 10.
160 Gondek and Noble 2011, 283.
161 For Brandsbutt, see Coles 1901, 229–30.
162 Thomas 1963 and 1984; Samson 1992; Forsyth 1997 and 1998.

163 Conveniently illustrated in Fraser 2008.
164 McKitterick 2004, 36.
165 Stevenson 1955, 101–106; Alcock 1996.
166 The best documented of these stones are in Wales (see Nash-Williams 1950; Redknap and Lewis 2007; Edwards 2007).
167 Admirably surveyed in Forsyth 2005.
168 Barnes and Page 2006, 217–21.
169 Bagnoli et al. (eds) 2011, 81.
170 *Ibid., passim*.
171 Farmer 2004, 194–95.
172 Glenn 2003, 106–14.
173 Hatherley 2009, 209.
174 Rees 2002, 342–43.
175 Proudfoot 1996, 403–06.
176 *Ibid.*, 403; Rees 2002, 328–29.
177 Proudfoot 1996, 403.
178 Hill 1997, 70.
179 Cowley 1996.
180 Alexander 2005.
181 Hill 1997, 114.
182 Henderson 1987.
183 Rees 2002, 335–39.
184 Proudfoot 1996, 413–14 and 419, illus. 21.
185 Simpson and Scott-Elliot 1963; Hatherley 2009.
186 Petts 2002, 44–45.
187 For Traprain, see Curle 1923. For Norrie's Law, see Youngs 1989, 26–27. For coin hoards, see Holmes 2006.
188 Ritchie 1989, 51.
189 Laing 1994, 24–25.
190 Forsyth 2009, 33.
191 See Geary 2009, 267, where his remarks about Ireland could equally well be applied to most of Scotland.
192 Colgrave and Mynors 1969, 532–33.
193 For example, Smith 2005, 288.
194 Christison and Anderson 1899, plate I.
195 For Lasswade, see Henshall 1956 for the cemetery and Henshall 1966 for the Roman stones. For Thornybank, see Rees 2002, 328–29.
196 Hahn 1997, 1082.
197 For Ruberslaw, see Curle 1905, 225. For Inchtuthil, see RCAHMS 1994, 92.
198 Rosehill 1870, 108; Edwards 1925, 94–95.
199 Hunter 2008.
200 I owe this suggestion to Colin Wallace.
201 Campbell 2007, 72, 27, 135.

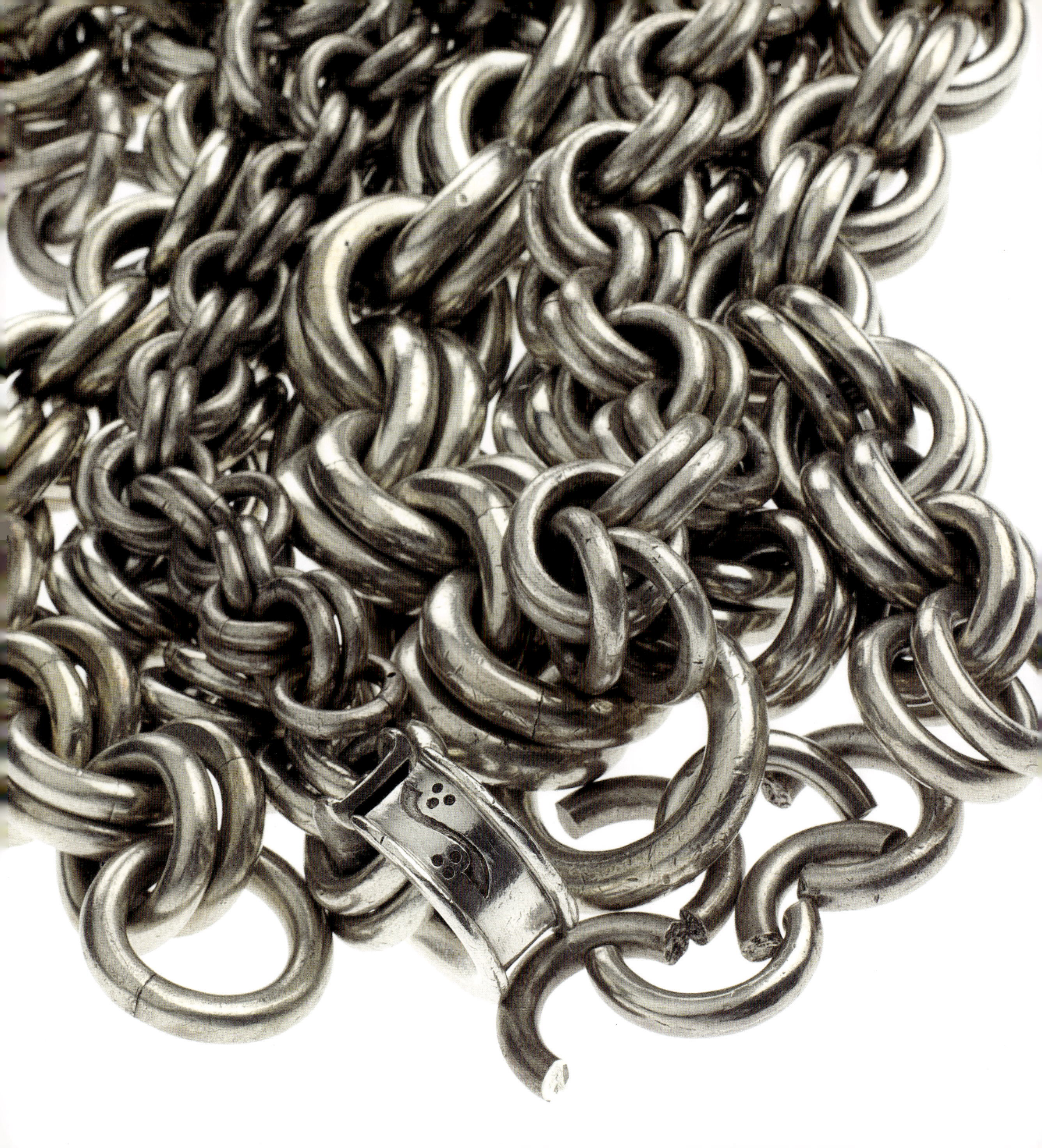

CHAPTER THREE
Ideas and Ideologies

Martin Goldberg

*Inspiration can be found in a pile of junk.
Sometimes you can put it together with a
good imagination and invent something.*[1]

✶

Attributed to Thomas Edison,
late 19th century

Individuals are full of ideas, but how do they communicate these ideas to others? How do communities of people share common ideas, values and beliefs?

Ideas are related to ideologies, but they are not the same thing. Ideology was initially conceived in the 18th century as a 'science of ideas', a way of knowing about ideas and a way of interpreting them.[2] Since then, ideologies have developed a broader meaning as particular ways of thinking and acting that make ideas known, that make them real. Religion and politics are among the most frequently discussed ideologies and it is relatively easy to understand how the ideas involved have direct impact on peoples' lives and the ways they think and act.[3] Such ideologies are based on common values and goals, beliefs about life, death, the world and a person's place within it, and ideas about how society should work and be organised. Ideologies can be expressions of both individual authority and group identity. They bind people together, separate them from others, and give them reasons to act together. Ideas and ideologies are shared within and between groups of people, as well as between individuals, including leaders, and their wider community.

Ideas can become ideologies when they are put into practice. Ideology can be understood in two ways: as the way people in the past expressed what they thought; and through interpretation of the surviving material evidence, ideology, 'a science of ideas', can also be our way into understanding those ideas. One of the central questions to ask within this chapter of the book is how we go about interpreting ideas and ideologies from surviving material culture. Ideas and ideologies can tell us some of the most intriguing stories about how objects have been used and interpreted, both in the past and now.

Fig. 3.1 (opposite): A mass of massive silver chains, a type of artefact unique to Early Medieval Scotland.

FROM BIG BEN TO CHRISTIAN HAND-BELLS

Objects can embody ideas and ideologies. A modern example – the Big Ben bell in London – can help to illustrate this. Big Ben is part of the palace of Westminster, the United Kingdom's seat of government. The bell was originally intended to be named after the ruling monarch at the time, Queen Victoria. Through this association with a particularly powerful person, we can see nationalist ideological motivations that stretch back to the object's creation. However, the bell has since picked up the more colloquial name of 'Big Ben'. Naming suggests a personality – for those who hear it, the bell is more than just an object, even though most never see it. Through the sound of its chime in particular, and its wider ideological role, the bell has become a part of people's lives.

Big Ben was originally just the bell, but in modern perception the name has transferred to include the clock tower that houses the bell. It has also become associated with wider notions of place as a pervasive media image used to represent Parliament, London and even the nation. The tower is recognised as one of the most iconic images of the United Kingdom for an international audience and it is thus important in the construction of modern national identity.

Big Ben's role in keeping time has become a part of our everyday lives and our national consciousness. This role is used in perpetuating certain ideologies, some with nationalist overtones. Every day the chime of Big Ben features at the beginning of the 'ITN News at 10' and the 'Six o'clock News' on BBC Radio 4, where the people of Britain are informed about current political and social events.

These roles date back to the moments of stress and fear during the Second World War when Big Ben's chimes acted as a focus for the nation during important news announcements on the radio. At times of joy or sadness, the chimes of Big Ben annually mark important events – the countdown to the New Year festivities and the minute's silence during the ceremonies of Remembrance Day. Nationalist ideologies are reinforced at war memorials all over the country as the chime of Big Ben's bell marks the appropriate moment to remember those who died in war.

Big Ben continues to fulfil this vital role of marking time with analogue technology that is fast becoming obsolete in our modern digital age. It is something from the past that still functions in the present, despite its antiquated technology. The bell's modern value relates to several factors – its age, the place it belongs, what it represents or symbolises, and its practical role in the keeping of time.

We can use this analogy to explore some of the material remains of Scotland's earliest Christian communities – hand-bells.[4] These hand-held bells are far smaller than Big Ben. Some are made from bronze, but most are made from iron that has been brazed – that is, coated with bronze.

There are certain points of contact between these ancient bells and the modern example of Big Ben. Early Christian hand-bells are associated with places, people and communities, as well as the ideologies that bind these together. Just like Big Ben, the ideological role of hand-bells relates to how they would have functioned in practice. The scientist Ivan Pavlov famously proved that the action of ringing a bell affects the thoughts of those who hear it; and organised repetition through time can produce certain responses.[5] Thus Early Christian bells would have functioned

Fig. 3.2: The range of sizes of hand-bell can be seen in these examples from Knowe of Burrian, North Ronaldsay (left), and from Kingoldrum, Angus (right).

Fig. 3.3: The bell-shrine handle from Inchaffray, Perthshire.

in similar ways to Big Ben: making appropriate moments resonate, calling attention, or structuring work and worship during daily and wider time cycles. Hand-bells would have sounded a variety of signals to the Christian community: the call for certain prayer-times, specific moments during ceremonies, heralding announcements, creating a clamour at times of danger, or the slow peal marking death.

As we explored in chapter one (see page 54), we very rarely get a sense of sound, mood, lighting and timing from the material record, but all of these elements impact on the perception and reception of ideologies, especially during formal or ceremonial events. Hand-bells were part of the ritual repertoire of Early Christianity, and as such allow us to imagine one of the sounds from the past and how that chime was meaningful at certain times.

Most of these Early Christian bells no longer ring. The brazed iron bells are now corroded, rusted shadows of the objects they once were [Fig. 3.2]. But they have been preserved and curated so that they survive today. Their present fragile condition and preservation over the centuries is testament to the ideological importance of these objects.

The distribution of these bells has been linked to the missionary activity of the Columban Church as it spread the new religion through Early Medieval Scotland.[6] Later tradition often associated bells with particular missionary saints, and the objects became venerated as relics, and in some cases enshrined and treasured at certain churches [3.3]. Elaboration with precious metals and symbols often ended the original function of the bell, and involved the objects in new practices of worship.

The sound of hand-bells signalled important moments for the Christian community. In monasteries, life, work

IDEAS AND IDEOLOGIES

and prayer revolved around the daily canonical hours and the liturgical year. The sound of a hand-bell would have accompanied or initiated some of these actions. But the chimes would also have been carried beyond the church building. The agricultural production of the wider economic communities operated on annual and seasonal cycles that slowly became Christianised through various strategies of controlling and defining time. Through the Medieval period the Christian calendar structured the basic functions of government such as tax and rent collection.[7] Older festivals that had marked key points in the agricultural cycle became saints' days,[8] although they may have retained vestiges of previous significance as dates for seasonal markets, courts and assemblies. These events would have been marked in some way: by ceremonies, festivities and pilgrimage to locally or regionally significant assembly places.[9]

The hand-bell leads us into a much broader discussion about the regulation of time as a strategy for perpetuating ideologies. Time was important, structuring life in such a way that the ideological goals of the powerful became part of the natural order of things. Calculations for the central Christian feast of Easter was one of the main subjects of an important meeting of powerful British churchmen and kings at the Synod of Whitby in AD 664 and provided one of the most commented upon divisions between the Columban and Roman Churches. Hand-bells and more obviously decorated Christian objects – such as monumental stone crosses – are easily connected with ideology because of their religious associations. However, it is how the objects functioned in practice that reveals more about the associated ideas and ideologies embedded within people's lives.

INTERPRETING THE INTANGIBLE FROM THE TANGIBLE

Ideologies are not just about the exercise of power, political control, religious authority and economic exploitation.[10] The crux of the matter is that ideologies are materialised through action.

Once ideas are acted upon, the effects of those actions leave their material traces and that evidence is then open to interpretation. This is by no means straightforward, but it is of central concern in understanding how Early Medieval people put their ideas into practice. Ideas might seem like intangible products of the mind, but people in the past put great effort into communicating ideologies, making their ideas real and tangible through material culture.[11] As archaeologists we face the challenge of interpreting meaning, motivation and people's actions in the past from that tangible material. How do we go about doing that?

Any interpretation will be shadowed by the fact that in attempting to understand the past, people apply their own biases.[12] This is often inadvertent, but easily done when generalising or relying on modern notions of common sense that might not have been appropriate to past peoples. However, with careful reasoning and by taking into account as many additional factors as possible – for instance, social, political and economic contexts, or find circumstances – we can reconstruct the events that led to the archaeological survival and present condition of any material culture.

Archaeologists refer to this as 'putting things in context'. Contextual archaeology works best from the results of modern excavations, when multiple points of support for interpretation provide a web of supporting evidence. This is like building the strongest case possible during a trial, when the results of a criminal investigation are presented to the court. Any archaeological interpretation will be judged by the quality of information amassed and used to recreate context and circumstances – that is, the lives and times that the surviving objects were part of.

SYMBOLS IN CONTEXT: A TALE OF TWO BONES

Two examples of the same type of material, found in different circumstances, will demonstrate the higher levels of interpretation and information that can be gained from objects with good contextual information. Both types are objects made from the small bones of the feet of cattle.

When discovered during excavation, the presence of small cattle bones might represent the butchery of these important economic resources and the everyday activity of food production. Even these can receive an ideological interpretation. Cattle often represent a basic unit of wealth in non-monetary economies like Early Medieval Scotland. Comparing amounts and types of cattle bones across a range of sites hints at the wealth and status of the inhabitants, although it is not as simple as more bones equals more wealth. The age and gender of the animals can tell us whether they were being used primarily for dairy or meat production. And closer analysis of the type of cattle bones, and the butchery marks on them, can suggest what cuts of meat were being consumed on site, whether they represent cheap cuts, or whether they were being butchered for export to higher status sites. Some wealthy sites, for example, may have had no cattle bones because inhabitants were consuming prime cuts of meat that had been butchered off the bone elsewhere. However, the following two examples take us beyond cattle as a symbol of wealth and status to wider ideological implications.

The hoofed feet of cattle are of limited meat value and were often left attached to the carcass to provide handles for stretching out the skin. Sharpened cattle metapodials were found together, arranged in rows, during recent excavations at the monastery of Portmahomack, Easter Ross.[13] They were associated with deposits inside a building which also produced a range of tools that could be used for leather-working. Neighbouring structures produced evidence for a range of crafts including glass-working and the smithing of metals. This wealth of information has allowed excavators to present a detailed interpretation of the crafts being employed at the monastery and to speculate about the types of material being made, even though the finished products have not survived. This includes components found on ecclesiastical metalwork, such as the Irish hoards discovered at Ardagh and Derrynaflan [3.4].[14] Unfortunately, such objects have not survived in Scotland, but the evidence from Portmahomack suggests that similar items were being produced there.

The sharpened metapodial bones associated with a range of other leather-working tools, on a monastic site with a variety of complex crafts, suggested to excavators the art of vellum production.[15] Through this extended process of interpretation, the humble cattle bones become proxy evidence for the production of manuscripts, another important class of objects that rarely survive from Early Medieval Scotland. Literacy and new forms of art, such as stone sculpture, were among the most innovative and powerful ideological tools being used by Christians in Scotland.

One fragment of sculpture from Portmahomack [3.6] had suggested a familiarity with written manuscripts even before the recent excavation. It has relief carving of a type of script (insular majuscules) more commonly used in manuscripts such as the Lindisfarne Gospels [3.7].[16] Allied with the excavation evidence interpreted as vellum production, this has led to the suggestion that similarly beautiful manuscripts were being produced at Portmahomack.[17]

Cattle phalanges from the Broch of Burrian, Orkney, also take interpretation beyond butchery waste. Several have been decorated with carved symbols; one in particular has recognisable Pictish symbols incised on both sides [3.5].[18]

Methods of recording finds from early excavations, like the Broch of Burrian, often prove difficult to interpret. The 19th-century excavators only recorded information from the site in two broad layers. They certainly lacked the benefit of all the scientific techniques that have been developed to gain information from modern archaeological excavation. The dearth of contextual information will always make the task of interpreting old finds infinitely more difficult. However, the presence of a small hand-bell, an ogham-inscribed cross-slab, cross-inscribed pebbles and the inscribed bones suggest an early Christian community at the site.[19] But this North Ronaldsay community was very different to the monastery at Portmahomack. Even with the varying quality of the information, it emphasises that very different expressions of Christianity were possible in northern Britain.

Despite the limited information from the excavation, the Burrian phalanges themselves can provide further clues. The bone has been radiocarbon dated to between AD 570 and 655 (with 95 per cent probability). And as the symbols were most likely to have been carved on fresh bone, so, by association, the use of the symbols could be roughly dated to this period.[20]

In this case, and many others, without the benefits

EARLY MEDIEVAL SCOTLAND

Fig. 3.4 (opposite, left): The Derrynaflan paten (opposite, left) and chalice (opposite, middle), fine ecclesiastical metalwork from Ireland.

Fig. 3.5 (opposite, right): A cattle phalange incised with Pictish symbols from the Knowe of Burrian, North Ronaldsay.

Fig. 3.6 (below, left): Relief carved letters on a sculpture fragment from Portmahomack.

Fig. 3.7 (below, right): *The Lindisfarne Gospels*, folio 27r.

IDEAS AND IDEOLOGIES

147

of wider and multi-layered contextual interpretation, we must rely on the object itself to provide whatever information we can glean from it. The symbolism inscribed on the Burrian phalange, and other examples of Pictish symbols, remains difficult to interpret and the associated ideologies are no more clearly revealed. We know that there are powerful ideas involved, but we require more information about how the symbols were used and what this meant in practice.

A WEALTH OF SYMBOLISM AND THE SYMBOLISM OF WEALTH

Traditional narratives of Early Medieval Scotland have often focused on religious, political and social institutions such as church and state, or powerful individuals such as kings and saints. Silver jewellery and stone crosses provide the main types of material evidence used to illustrate these ideologies. Silver was the main material for symbolising portable wealth in Early Medieval Scotland, while stone monuments display a wealth of symbolism. The patronage and display of art and the accumulation of wealth are obvious ideological signals that we can still easily understand in today's world.[21] However, relying on this most obvious of material creates the danger of simplifying historical situations too much, or only documenting the dominant political position.[22]

The tendency to focus on the fabulous, the valuable or the most mysterious objects has meant that discussions of power, politics and religion are often considered too simplistically. Relying on vague notions of powerful objects – such as the massive silver chains or the enigma of the Pictish symbol-stones [3.1, 3.9] – is a way of crudely characterising the evidence while skirting around the issues involved. This runs the risk of both generalising and mystifying the very real practices of politics and beliefs. These ideas and ideologies were so important to people in the past that they expended great effort and resources to try to communicate them to future generations.[23] Art and symbolism, silver and stone, are unavoidable in this discussion of ideas and ideologies, but we must try to integrate them with other evidence and, where possible, pursue richer interpretations.

Instead of the potent symbolism of a carved stone cross, or an elaborate silver object, a simpler example on an apparently mundane object might prove useful. A stone quern from the Dál Riata power centre of Dunadd, Argyll [3.8], is inscribed with a simple, small cross. Querns were used for the processing of a staple food, grinding cereal grains into flour. However, the addition of a symbol makes this quern different to similar but undecorated querns and adds to its interpretation.

Querns were important objects in past societies, and they are one of the most common finds from later prehistoric sites. They have at times been treated in unusual ways: some are buried unused, while others have been deliberately and aggressively broken up. Prehistoric beliefs are notoriously difficult to reconstruct, but this unusual treatment has been suggested as evidence for prehistoric fertility rites, with the quern perhaps acting as a symbol for the agricultural cycle. The quern's everyday use in transforming agricultural produce into edible flour may have been linked to ideas beyond these practicalities, extending

Fig. 3.8 (left): A rotary quern from Dunadd, Argyll, incised with the symbol of the cross.

Fig. 3.9 (below): A symbol-stone from Invereen, Inverness-shire.

into deeper underlying beliefs about life, death and regeneration.[24]

Bearing all these characteristics in mind, it does not require a great stretch of the imagination to suggest that this quern [3.8], with its Christian symbol, makes an explicit ideological connection to a particular type of bread – the Eucharistic bread. Perhaps this quern was reserved for the production of flour for the bread used during the Eucharist, the bread that was central to Christian rites. Dunadd is not an ecclesiastical site, but a heavily fortified hilltop interpreted as a high status, secular power centre. However, its population was Christian, as reflected in other finds – such as a pebble inscribed with a Latin phrase, and orpiment, a pigment used in the Early Medieval period to decorate illuminated manuscripts.[25]

This quern is made of an unusual glittering and dappled schistose stone imported to Dunadd, and the material and inscribed cross suggest that it may not be an item of everyday use. The style of the cross on the quern links it to similar crosses found across Argyll, and focuses on the major monastery of Iona.[26] Was the quern a gift from an Ionan cleric to a king of Dál Riata?

IDEAS AND IDEOLOGIES

Fig. 3.10: A section of the cross-shaft of the Ruthwell cross showing the fine relief-carving and the inscriptions on the border.

THE CROSS IN ACTION

Symbolism provides an obvious starting point for ideological analysis. Symbols serve to draw attention to an object, but how the object functioned in practice is equally important for interpretation. While material symbols may represent fundamental ideas, we must be cautious, as both art and symbolism are open to manipulation (subversion), borrowing (adoption), changes in meaning (adaptation), multiple meanings (ambiguity), and even contradictory interpretations (ambivalence). The Christian cross is perhaps one of the least ambivalent symbols, but there is often more that can be said than simply pointing out that it is the primary symbol of Christianity. As with the cross-inscribed quern, the symbol of the cross can act as the gateway into considering the complex and interrelated repertoire of practices that make up the Christian religion.[27]

The cross as the primary symbol of Christianity was glorified in Britain and Ireland by the production of a range of such objects carved in stone. But there is one major problem – few stones are clearly in their original context and therefore very little is known about how these monuments functioned in practice. Beyond the rich symbolism and the great investment of time and labour in producing stone monuments, what actions continued to swirl around these objects after carving was complete?[28]

The Ruthwell cross [3.10] from Dumfriesshire 'has the most extensive iconographic programme extant from any sculptural monument in early 8th century Europe'.[29] Needless to say it has generated a huge body of scholarship. The richly decorated cross-shaft benefits from runic inscriptions and Latin titles that allow links to be made between liturgical drama, contemporary Anglo-Saxon poetry and the biblical scenes depicted in the rich iconography.[30] This combination of epigraphic, literary and artistic evidence allows the ideas behind the iconography of the Ruthwell cross to be interpreted in great detail and integrated with the Christian practices that would have continued to focus around the monument. Among these are processions at particular times of the liturgical year, with special reference to the central feast of Easter, but also more frequent rituals such as Communion.[31] The iconography can even indicate the songs and psalms sung and chanted during worship.[32]

Literacy is a particularly potent method for recording certain ideas and ideologies and the skill was used with increasing frequency by people in Early Medieval Scotland. The five languages that Bede tells us were spoken in northern Britain (Latin, Brythonic, Gaelic, English and Pictish)

Fig. 3.11: Ogham and symbol-script on the same stone from Ackergill, Caithness.

could be communicated by nearly as many scripts (Roman letters, runes, ogham, and Pictish symbol script). As with Ruthwell, sometimes two scripts could appear on the same monument: for example the Ackergill symbol-stone [3.11].

Contemporary texts can give insights into the ideas associated with particular symbols. Christianity has this advantage over the pagan religions of the prehistoric past: we know so much more because contemporary and earlier Christian documents survive, and Christianity continues today as part of a lived tradition of beliefs. The other extreme is represented by our lack of knowledge of what the enigmatic Pictish symbols mean. The Picts left no historical documents that might help us to translate the symbols, and neither did contemporary commentators in Ireland and the Anglo-Saxon kingdoms. This has undoubtedly limited their study and leads to endless speculation. But the Picts did create stone monuments to rival the Ruthwell cross. The Picts are particularly associated with elaborately carved Christian cross-slabs that display a wealth of symbolism including their own set of unique symbols.

HILTON OF CADBOLL

One of the most elaborate Pictish cross-slabs, first erected at the chapel of Hilton of Cadboll, Easter Ross, has been moved and re-erected many times, and now provides a striking centrepiece for the archaeology collection in the Early People gallery at the National Museum of Scotland [3.12–3.15]. Only one original face survives intact: the cross-bearing face was systematically chipped away and replaced with an inscription in the 17th century. Despite this, its rich iconography seems almost pregnant with symbolism, ripe for ideological analysis.[33]

For example, universal Christian symbolism (in the form of the lost cross) appears with very local symbolism in the form of the Pictish symbols at the top of the surviving face. The triskele spiral panel at the bottom of the stone is in essence a new reworking of what was already an old motif. It is juxtaposed with the scene of a deer hunt above. Depicting people was in itself a relatively new innovation when Hilton of Cadboll was carved and the hunt scene may represent an image of contemporary elite society. The vine-scroll border that encompasses these designs is a Christian Eucharistic symbol that was popular in the eastern Mediterranean. Its presence implies long-distance connections, but the animals which live amongst its leaves and eats its berries are an expression of the local Pictish love of fantastic beasts. Old and new, near and far, these diverse designs are masterfully combined on the Hilton of Cadboll cross-slab.

If – and we have no evidence that they did – visitors from the Mediterranean heart of Christendom had travelled to the Fearn peninsula, they would have recognised the inhabited vine-scroll as a familiar Eucharistic symbol. The

IDEAS AND IDEOLOGIES

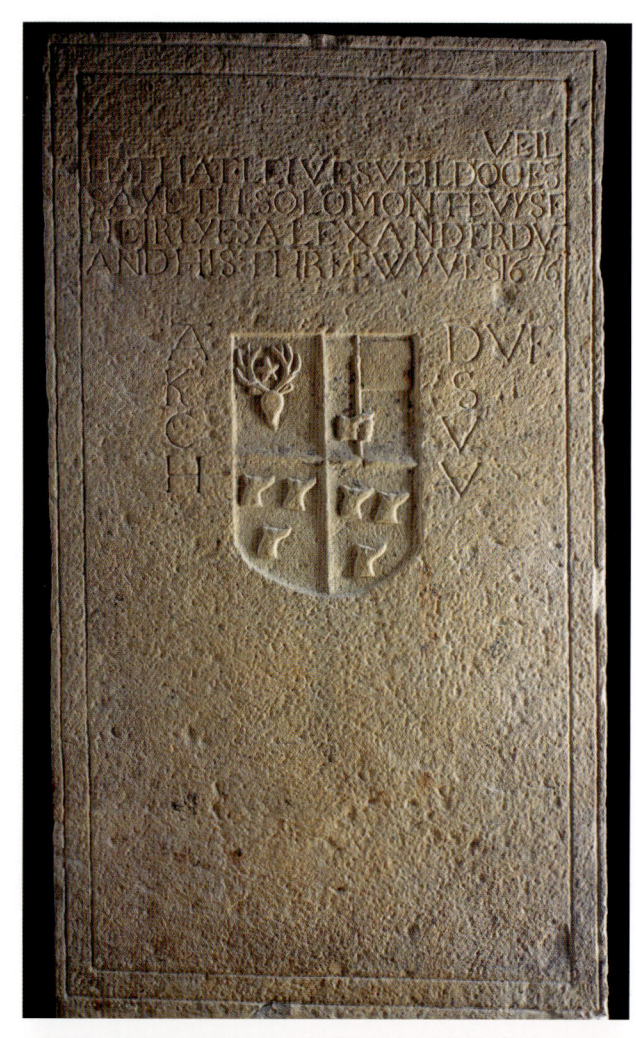

EARLY MEDIEVAL SCOTLAND

152

Fig. 3.12 (opposite, left): The back of the Hilton of Cadboll cross-slab. It was broken in 1674, leaving the lower portion in the ground. This was rediscovered in 2001.

Fig. 3.13 (opposite, right): The cross on the Hilton of Cadboll cross-slab was chipped off to make a 17th-century gravestone. The only surviving portion of the cross is shown below.

Figs 3.14 and 3.15 (below): Two jigsaws, composed from the thousands of fragments from the cross of the Hilton of Cadboll cross-slab recovered during modern excavations.

motif was also popular in Christian Northumbria, but ultimately originates from the eastern Mediterranean and pre-Christian wine-drinking cults of Dionysus/Bacchus. Vine-scroll ornament was adopted into early Christian art because Jesus had likened himself to the vine in John 15: 1–17, and the wine used at the Last Supper became symbolic of Christ's blood, central to the celebration of the Eucharist. On the Fearn peninsula the inhabited vine-scroll had received a distinctively local interpretation, filled with fantastic beasts also of distant inspiration, but recurrently popular in Pictish Christian art.

The cross of the Hilton of Cadboll cross-slab was chipped off in the Late Medieval period, but many fragments [3.14–3.15] were recovered in the recent excavations that also rediscovered the broken base of the monument.[34] The lost cross would have been universally recognised by a visitor from anywhere in Christendom, even if it was decorated in a barbaric fashion distinctive to Britain and Ireland. Art historians refer to this art style as Insular art, not because it was inward looking (quite the contrary), but because in the broader context of Early Medieval Europe it was distinctive to the islands of the far west – Ireland, and the north and west of the British Isles. Some of the finest examples adorned Christian liturgical objects, metalwork, monumental crosses and illuminated manuscripts from the mid-7th century AD.

During the Early Medieval period, the adoption of new technologies such as literacy, stone-carving and various jewellery crafts, allied with the influence of Classical, Anglo-Saxon and Continental art styles, brought a creative fusion and renewed vigour to the expression of traditional motifs. There was frequent cross-referencing between portable and static art, stone, metal and manuscript. This fusion used to be called Hiberno-Saxon art, reflecting the scholarly bias towards the more plentiful historical sources for Ireland and England, but is now less ethnically defined as Insular art.

The triskele panel on the Hilton of Cadboll cross-slab

IDEAS AND IDEOLOGIES

153

is symmetrically composed of multiple inter-locking trumpet spirals which originate as a pre-Christian motif, but like vine-scroll had been renewed with new Christian meaning. Triskele, trumpet spirals, key patterns (frets) and vegetal scrolls became part of the wide repertoire of Insular art and prominently featured in the decoration of manuscripts, stone crosses and metalwork. In contrast the Pictish symbols are a local form of communication with a distinct use in northern and eastern Scotland. However, the Insular art-style was also used to elaborate some of the Pictish symbols on cross-slabs, as can be seen on the symbols at the top of the Hilton of Cadboll stone.[35]

The central panel depicting a hunting scene is also seen as a distinctive secular feature of Pictish art [2.1, 3.12]. It has previously been interpreted as a snapshot from contemporary life and the pursuits of the elite who are presumed to have commissioned this sculpture.[36] This central panel contains a key to getting beyond reading symbolism to consider how this richly symbolic cross-slab, and others like it, might have functioned in practice.

PICTISH *ADVENTUS*

The only thing we can be sure about the role of cross-slabs is that they were the focus of devotion. They project eternal messages as part of a belief system still relevant today. Clues hidden in the central panel of the Hilton of Cadboll cross-slab, and on other similar monuments with rider imagery, allow us to narrow our focus onto the Easter vigil, the ceremonies of the night before the most important feast of the Resurrection on Easter Sunday. From dusk on Saturday, Christian communities gather to celebrate the Lord's triumph over death and welcome new members of their community through the rite of Baptism. The Easter vigil used to be the only time of year when Baptism occurred. Given the importance of Easter, it is perhaps not surprising that we might find reference to these central events of the Christian calendar in Early Medieval iconography.

The Hilton of Cadboll stone, and other cross-slabs that show narrative hunting scenes, feature two main motifs. Let us refer to them as 'the majestic rider' and 'the harried deer'. The fully developed hunt scene depicts deer being chased and harried by hounds, normally as the lowest register or line of action within the scene. Above this may be several other registers with both armed and unarmed riders. There is normally one rider who is distinguished from the other riders in some way, whether through central, apex or lead positioning, or being depicted slightly larger, or sometimes through subtle differences in clothing and hairstyle. These motifs reference the Easter vigil and a range of inter-connected ideas and practices.

Psalm 42 was sung on the Easter vigil in preparation for the rite of Baptism of new Christians. This psalm likens the deer to the soul thirsting for the waters of salvation. St Augustine's exegesis of Psalm 42 likened the deer to the catechumen awaiting Baptism. The method of hunting depicted on the Hilton cross-slab shows hounds being used to harry the deer until it was exhausted. The hounds would then be called off and the thirsty deer would immediately seek the nearest water source where the hunters awaited their quarry. Pictish hunt scenes focus on the harried deer and this is the moment of the hunt which Psalm 42 describes perfectly with reference to Baptism.

Fig. 3.16: A Roman sarcophagus from Arles depicting a variety of hunting scenes.

The two main motifs of 'the majestic rider' and 'the harried deer' were adapted from Roman models: the first was the imperial iconography that depicted the emperor as a majestic rider; the second being the hunt scenes that were popular on Late Antique sarcophagi.[37] Rather than just being sources of artistic inspiration, there is a common underlying theme to both – the ceremony of the *Adventus*, which structured those momentous occasions of a lord's arrival, the anticipation of his entrance into a place, and reception by his subjects.[38] The concepts associated with *Adventus* bring us closer to the ideological practices that surrounded Pictish monuments. In the ancient world, these important events were commemorated through the iconography of public art – coins, medals, monuments and rhetorical literature.

The majestic rider is one of the most common motifs used to depict an *Adventus* in imperial iconography. Equestrian victory over real and mythical beasts signified both political victory and the emperor transcendent in all his god-like majesty, his *Apotheosis*. The majestic rider need not be purely secular or religious, but can simultaneously depict both a practical, contemporary political message, as well as timeless, religious and mythical themes.

The Roman gentleman's return home from the hunt, depicted on Late Antique sarcophagi [3.16], represents the diffusion of imperial *Adventus* models and adaptation for the higher ranks of Roman society. As with our Pictish examples, the sarcophagi were not just showing ideals of aristocratic life, but rather had an underlying message as 'an eschatological dream' of the soul's afterlife.[39] Eschatology is the branch of religious doctrine that is concerned with the fate of the human soul in relation to eternal questions about death, salvation, judgement, and heaven and hell. These concepts remain central to Christian doctrine. Thus it seems reasonable to deduce that both the majestic rider and the hunt scenes can evoke eternal themes through apparently realistic, secular and even mundane depictions.

IDEAS AND IDEOLOGIES

Fig. 3.17: The back of the Meigle 1 cross-slab with the action emanating from the oblique cup-marked facet at the bottom corner.

ANGELS AT MEIGLE

Nearly half of all Pictish cross-slabs have a majestic rider on them (30 out of 62 examples). The most developed narrative scenes, like the Hilton of Cadboll stone, have tended to disguise the variety of imagery employed. For instance, two cross-slabs (Meigle 1 and 2: Figs 3.17 and 2.8) have often been labelled as 'hunt' scenes, although no quarry is represented.

On the back of Meigle 1 are five riders in two registers, with the lines of action unusually moving diagonally upward, ascending from lower right to upper left. The point where the action originates from is an oblique undressed facet at the lower right corner of the back of the slab where prehistoric cup-mark carvings are still visible, preserved on the undressed original surface of the stone. Leading the lower register is a rider who, though worn, is differentiated from the others by riding sideways or athwart the steed like the main Hilton rider.[40] In front of this rider is a winged being, an angel, acting as a precursor.[41] Behind the main rider is a leaping quadruped usually interpreted as a hound, but bearing little resemblance to the long lean hounds of Hilton of Cadboll. If this is a hound, it is the only indication of the chase; otherwise the scene appears more like a procession emanating from the older carved surface with its Bronze Age cup-marks (although the ferocious-looking beast next to the oblique facet may give this a more hellish and sinister reading).

Meigle 2 [2.8] can be interpreted as a later and elaborated version of Meigle 1 as they share key features of five riders and an angel precursor. The main difference is that Meigle 2 has more developed Christian iconography and no

EARLY MEDIEVAL SCOTLAND

Pictish symbols. The majestic rider and angel precursor have displaced the Pictish symbols of Meigle 1 and taken up the prominent position in the apex of the stone. The majestic rider is also distinguished from the other four riders by size (larger) and appearance (longer hair, grander garment). Like his companions, the Meigle 2 majestic rider is depicted in profile, riding astride, not athwart like the main rider on Meigle 1 or Hilton. The angel hovers above two standing hounds in front, motionless, suggestive of the chase and yet hardly qualifying as one.

We can point with some confidence to specific biblical passages that the rider with angel precursor refers to – Matthew 11:10, Mark 1:2 and Luke 7:27. These ultimately refer to the Old Testament messianic prophecy Malachi 3:1, 'Behold I send my angel before thy face, who shall prepare thy way before thee'.[42] These New Testament passages based on the prophecy of Malachi refer to John the Baptist as the precursor to Christ, anticipating Jesus's mission, performing the first Christian Baptism and acting as the herald announcing the arrival of the messianic king.

Every year, the Easter celebrations begin on Palm Sunday commemorating Jesus's Entry into Jerusalem, the archetypal Christian *Adventus* where Christ (the anointed one) was received in kingly fashion as the messianic son of David. The acclamation Christ received on his Entry into Jerusalem was, 'Hosanna son of David – blessed is he who comes in the name of the Lord'.[43] This *Benedictus* (Latin for 'blessed') was sung as an antiphon to greet the arrival of popes, kings and emperors during the Middle Ages, and likewise *Ecce mitto angelum meum* – 'Behold I send my angel before thy face'.[44] These passages were also used in the Christian liturgy as readings on successive weeks in the run-up to Christmas, during the period that is appropriately named Advent.

The *Adventus*, as depicted in Christian iconography, took two main forms: the literal representation of Jesus's entry into Jerusalem, as described in the New Testament; and the more symbolic or eschatological representation using an angel precursor preceding a mounted figure, as it appears at Meigle.[45] In Early Christian art the rider with an angel precursor was adapted from Roman imperial imagery where a triumphant emperor was often preceded by a winged victory.[46] Roman imperial and Hellenistic royal models of *Adventus* were also adapted to represent Jesus's Entry into Jerusalem. In the Western Empire, Jesus was more often depicted riding astride his steed like his imperial predecessors, whereas in the Eastern Empire he was more likely to be depicted riding side-saddle or athwart a donkey in a more literal interpretation of the New Testament [3.18].[47] The Entry into Jerusalem was also a popular choice of scene on Late Antique sarcophagi.[48]

On Meigle 1 the angel as precursor is a clear indicator of an eschatological *Adventus*, but riding sideways/sitting frontally also evokes Jesus's Entry into Jerusalem. This conflation on Meigle 1 serves to emphasise doubly the *Adventus* themes central to the iconography.

There is a much clearer figure of a rider, sitting athwart a steed – the celebrated 'Lady' or 'Pictish Princess' on the Hilton of Cadboll cross-slab [2.1]. The acclaiming trumpeters behind the Hilton rider would also support the identification of an *Adventus*, but in light of the previous discussion the gender assumption can be questioned.

Riding sideways does not necessarily denote a female in Christian art: Jesus's Entry into Jerusalem is one of the

Fig. 3.18: The scene showing Jesus's Entry into Jerusalem from the wooden lintel of the doorway to the al-Muallaqa church in Cairo. Compare this icon with the majestic rider on the broadly contemporary Hilton of Cadboll cross-slab.

most prominent models for riding athwart a steed. Once this possibility is entertained, the apparent femininity of the main Hilton rider can be explained in other ways. The mirror and comb certainly do not have to be gender signifiers and are only considered female through modern chauvinistic reasoning that would also consider long hair feminine.[49] Early Christian and especially eastern Mediterranean depictions of Jesus quite often display him as youthful, fleshy-faced, often with an emphasis on robes and flowing locks derived from earlier Classical models.[50] Similar treatment of the hair and garments of Jesus can be seen on broadly contemporary Christian *Adventus* art, such as the wooden carved lintel from the al-Muallaqa church in Cairo [3.18]. The lintel is dated by inscription to AD 735.

The city gate behind Jesus is thought to be a realistic depiction of the al-Muallaqa city gate where the church was sited, and the lintel itself would have been over the doorway of that church. This layering of *Adventus* and entry associations provide insights into positioning of monuments and the role of iconography in directing and reflecting the actions that surround it.

There are lessons here for how we might consider the role of some Pictish cross-slabs as *Adventus* monuments. The Hilton of Cadboll cross-slab, erected close to the best beach landing site on the east coast of the Fearn peninsula, might have marked an entry point onto the territory of the northern end of the peninsula, focused on the monastery at Portmahomack. Meigle 1 may have performed a similar function somewhere in the local landscape of Angus, but the tenons on Meigle 2, and the better preservation of deep relief carving, imply that this large slab was incorporated in a structural framework, perhaps a rood or a chancel screen within a church.[51] Or it may have filled the central arch in a triple arcade at another transitional point within a religious building, perhaps in the entrance to a church with two matching arched doorways either side.

DAVID AND THE HARROWING OF HELL

Some of the more elaborate hunt scenes in Pictish sculpture are associated with the Old Testament hero, David. He is most frequently depicted wrestling and pulling apart the maw (i.e. jaws) of a lion that has threatened his flock

Fig. 3.19 (above): David pulling apart the jaws of a lion from the St Andrews sarcophagus.

Fig. 3.20 (below): David the Psalmist from the Dupplin cross.

[3.19]. On this basis the majestic rider has been interpreted as David,[52] but this is a conflation that ignores how the Old Testament was used as a precursor and parallel for later Christian developments.

David is commonly interpreted as a kingship reference, which would chime with the *Adventus* theme. But the image of the rending has a more specific Christian meaning as a type of representation used to evoke the episode that is known as the Harrowing of Hell. In between his crucifixion on Good Friday and his Resurrection on Easter Sunday, Jesus threw open the gates of the underworld to free noble pre-Christian souls, including Old Testament figures such as Adam and of course David.

The Harrowing of Hell was also considered an *Adventus* and one that was celebrated as part of the Easter vigil through the singing of Psalm 24. The apocryphal Gospel of Nicodemus, the main source for the Harrowing episode, has David acclaiming Christ's descent into the underworld using *Adventus* terminology adapted from Psalm 24. The Harrowing of Hell was a popular subject in sermons circulating from the 6th century AD, which adapt the rhetorical language used in Roman imperial *Adventus* acclamations.[53] One sermon, attributed to Eusabius Alexandrinus, describes how David as Psalmist musically acclaimed Christ upon entering the underworld: 'First David struck his cythar [zither] and said, "Come, let us exult in the Lord because our king fighting for us was victorious"'[54] [3.20]. This imperialist language is supported by reference to the '*signum*', the cross placed in hell as a sign of victory, in the manner of a Roman battle standard.

IDEAS AND IDEOLOGIES

SINGING THE CROSS-SLAB

As we have seen, the two main motifs of 'majestic rider' and 'harried deer' evoke an *Adventus* and Baptism respectively. Appropriately, both motifs have their origins in older *Adventus* art. These were skilfully adapted for use on Pictish cross-slabs, layering *Adventus* references within single realistic scenes. The harried deer which refers to Psalm 42, and the important rite of Baptism, leads us to consider a different type of entry – giving admission into the Christian community. This complements the *Adventus* themes of the Harrowing and both these practical and timeless messages were celebrated during the Easter vigil.

Dipping the Easter candle into the baptismal water consecrated it and was interpreted as a metaphor for the Harrowing, the descent into the underworld, and the Ascension of Christ reflecting Baptism and the emergence of newly-saved Christian souls.[55] As noted with the Ruthwell cross, it is rare that interpretation of Pictish sculpture gets to this level of detail. But here we can suggest at least one specific annual feast in the Christian calendar when the Hilton of Cadboll cross-slab, and others like it, could have regularly become a focus for devotion and ceremony.

The web of practical and conceptual connections interpreted from the majestic rider and harried deer allows an insight into the important moments when people became Christian during the pivotal ceremonies of the Easter vigil. Archaeology finds it difficult to reconstruct the full sensory impact of such a ceremony (chapter one, pp 54–55). However, through its rich symbolism the cold stone of Hilton of Cadboll still evoked some of the actions that surrounded it – the flickering flame of the Easter candle, the water of Baptism trickling down the skin, the exotic taste of the Eucharistic wine, the singing of psalms in a foreign tongue.

A single image can provoke several different stories, but this is the story that the harried deer and the majestic rider tells me. To many others it will continue to tell a story of a Pictish princess. It is possible that in the Early Medieval period this image may have communicated all these messages, and likely others, to its viewers. A lot more ideas can be imagined than simply warriors hunting. This may be what the uninitiated would have seen, but there was a deeper underlying message for those who had eyes to see and ears to hear. Christ had advocated teaching the mysteries of the faith through everyday images, word-pictures called parables. The image of the hunt was, presumably, familiar to everyone in Pictish society, but its layered Christian meanings would have been appreciated on different levels depending on the education and knowledge of the viewer. A similar range of ideas and ideological practices have been deduced from the iconography of the Ruthwell cross, supported by the runic inscription and related devotional literature.[56] Perhaps the Pictish symbols on the Hilton of Cadboll cross-slab would provide similar support if only we could decipher them.

The potency of the symbolism and iconography of the Hilton of Cadboll cross-slab is still obvious today, but it is more meaningful when related to people's lives and actions. The slab has also served as a device to introduce some of the main themes that will be pursued through the rest of this chapter on ideologies: Christianity as a central theme, connections with the wider world and the past, and how the constant renewal and local adaptation of these make Early Medieval Scotland distinctive.

Fig. 3.21: The double-disc and Z-rod (top) with the crescent and V-rod (bottom) on the Hilton of Cadboll cross-slab.

PICTISH SYMBOLS

One of the most distinctive aspects of Early Medieval Scotland is the Pictish symbols. What can these symbols, now indecipherable, tell us about ideas and ideologies? How did sculpture with symbols work in practice? What did the symbols add to objects?

Let us return to Hilton of Cadboll briefly. The symbols on this cross-slab are not in a separate panel [3.21]. The top square panel contains only the crescent and V-rod and two interlace-filled roundels, which Allen and Anderson (1903) included as symbols, but which others have not.[57] The other symbols are outside this panel. The double-disc and Z-rod[58] is above and adjacent to the crescent and V-rod, so that they appear to be paired, which is the usual format for symbols. But the double-disc and Z-rod is in the top border where the vine-scroll terminates. The mirror and comb symbols are much smaller and are placed in the central panel next to the majestic rider. Despite the clearly demarcated panels and border, the symbols on Hilton of Cadboll are interacting across separate panels and tying together the whole top half of the composition[59] – this is another unusual feature of this cross-slab.

The basic terminology for classifying the symbols is over a hundred years old.[60] The Class I Pictish symbol-stones are rough-hewn or undressed stones decorated with incised symbols, but without any overt Christian iconography. These symbol-stones are best understood against the wider background of other British and Irish inscribed monuments using Latin and ogham scripts. Class II Pictish cross-slabs (such as the Hilton of Cadboll) are dressed stone slabs, carved in relief, where the main symbol is the Christian cross, but on which Pictish symbols are also used.

On Class I stones the most popular pairing of symbols is the double-disc and Z-rod with the crescent and V-rod. The pair are not always organised in the same way, with sometimes one, sometimes the other, in prime position at the top, and occasionally with the addition of a mirror and comb. These variations are likely to disguise differences in meaning. At Rhynie and Tillytarmont there are clusters of Class I stones, and two stones at each location bear this symbol pair. At Rhynie there is an association with a high-status enclosure,[61] and at Tillytarmont there were reports of burials. There are no Class I pairings of double-disc and Z-rod with crescent and V-rod from southern Pictland (that is, south of the Mounth where the Grampians almost reach right to the North Sea shore). There are two western outliers on Skye, at Tore and at Fiskavaig [3.22].

This most popular symbol pairing of double-disc and Z-rod with crescent and V-rod stood the test of time, appearing with some of the finest Christian iconography

IDEAS AND IDEOLOGIES

Fig. 3.22: The double-disc and Z-rod (top) with the crescent and V-rod (bottom) on the Fiskavaig symbol-stone.

on Class II cross-slabs. On these impressive Christian monuments, the symbols are usually large, prominently placed and elaborated with the same kinds of intricate decoration that feature on the accompanying cross. The pairing of symbols makes a bold statement writ large at the top of five tall Class II cross-slabs. On all but one of these five grand monuments, the paired symbols are placed above the hunting scene [see FIGS 3.12, 3.23, 3.24] or an *Adventus* style procession [Cossans: 3.25].[62]

The exception is the cross-slab from Rosemarkie, which is a similar form of tall slab, but which lacks figurative art and has multiple repetition of the crescent and V-rod symbol. However, the recurrent link between specific iconography, large format of slab and this symbol pair certainly hints at related meaning and function. Use and meaning might vary from region to region.[63] The only southern examples of this most common symbol pairing are on the two large Class II cross-slabs in Angus: at Aberlemno 3 and the St Orland's stone at Cossans. On both, the symbol order is the opposite of the two northern examples.

An awareness of the size of symbols and variations in the placement on the cross-slab could contribute to an increased understanding of the function of the Pictish symbols, if not the meaning. The large monuments of the Fearn peninsula at Nigg, Shandwick and Hilton of Cadboll are among the most striking examples of Class II cross-slabs. They would have been matched by equally impressive monuments that can be glimpsed among the collection of fragments excavated from the recently discovered Pictish monastery at nearby Portmahomack. At that monastery they were undoubtedly producing high-quality sculpture, and it seems likely that the same school of masons produced the other large cross-slabs on the peninsula. However, what sets the many sculptural fragments at Portmahomack apart from the cross-slabs at Hilton of Cadboll, Nigg and Shandwick is the conspicuous lack of symbols. The only symbols from Portmahomack appear, unusually, on the narrow face of a fragmentary cross-slab, which has a very similar vine-scroll border to that on Hilton of Cadboll [3.26]. The treatment of the symbols is identical to the relief-carved Latin inscription on the Portmahomack sculpture fragment [3.6]; as is the positioning on the narrow side of the cross-slab, much like other inscriptions such as the Drosten inscription from St Vigeans 1. This use of Pictish symbols supports the idea that they are also a form of script.

So why was there so little need for the traditional Pictish symbol script at this 'Pictish' monastery? Is it

EARLY MEDIEVAL SCOTLAND

Fig. 3.23 (left): The Aberlemno 3 (roadside) cross-slab shares many parallels in design with the Hilton of Cadboll cross-slab including the fanfare behind the majestic rider and the choice of Pictish symbols.

Fig. 3.24 (below): The Elgin cross-slab has the same symbols as on Hilton of Cadboll, but with its own distinctively composed hunt scene including the harried deer, and a majestic rider with a hawk on his arm.

IDEAS AND IDEOLOGIES

because it was a Columban/Irish-orientated foundation?[64] And yet the monuments placed well beyond the monastery, such as the Hilton of Cadboll stone, display the symbol script prominently. Hilton and Shandwick are just inland from the best beach landing sites on the Fearn peninsula and the cross-slabs may have been erected at points where visitors to the peninsula could have been received. Hilton of Cadboll might have marked the transition between outside world and monastic territory,[65] and at this point it was appropriate for the Pictish symbols to be proclaimed large at the top of the slab, not on a small side panel. The near absence of symbols from Portmahomack suggests either that this message was not necessary within the monastery precinct, or that it was conveyed through other means; whereas would seem that the Hilton of Cadboll, Shandwick and Nigg cross-slabs were communicating a particular message to visitors from wider surrounding communities in a form that was best understood using the traditional medium of the symbols.

This observation of different social arenas for symbol use on the Fearn peninsula can be glimpsed elsewhere. Symbol use is also rare at some other key Christian establishments in northern Pictland. Among the large collection at Rosemarkie there is only one example – the tall cross-slab with the curious repetition of crescent and V-rod with

EARLY MEDIEVAL SCOTLAND

164

Fig. 3.25: St Orlands stone, Cossans – the unusual dressed cavity has the same dimensions and shape as the carved riders. Was the majestic rider a precious metal insert?

Fig. 3.26: The only cross-slab from Tarbat to bear symbol script – not visible, but on its narrow edge – also shares a very similar vine scroll border with the Hilton of Cadboll cross-slab.

double-disc and Z-rod. At Drainie/Kineddar there is one Class I fragment and one cross-slab with mirror and comb symbols. There are very few Class II cross-slabs in Aberdeenshire, where we know Early Christian communities were established.[66] At the important Early Christian site of St Andrews, as in most of eastern Fife, there are no Pictish symbols.[67] The symbol script was certainly compatible with Christianity, but there is obviously some complexity in its use in relation to different Christian communities within northern Britain.

These different attitudes to scripts and literacy hint at the relationships between different communities, different types of knowledge, the variable fortunes of the Columban monastic mission and its relation to other forms of church organisation in northern Britain. Better chronological understanding of the full corpus of Early Christian stone sculpture would also help, but remains difficult. Scone and Dunkeld become prominent in the historical record in the late 9th and 10th centuries and have no sculpture with symbols. Does this suggest the traditional script of Pictland was losing its ideological importance by this time, or is it just at these places? Why, for example, are there no symbols at the 'Pictish' palace of Forteviot or on the Dupplin cross, which can be dated to *circa* AD 820? These observations of the uses of the symbols as a script warn us that the distribution of the symbols represents more than the extent of Pictish ethnicity. The popularity of displaying this form of script on cross-slabs also relates to their role in communicating between different communities, within the cultural melting-pot of Early Medieval Scotland.

COMPLEX MESSAGES

Some of the Aberdeenshire Class II cross-slabs are unusual because of their relatively undressed form and their use of incised symbols instead of relief-carving. These characteristics are more associated with Class I monuments and it suggests a close relationship with the symbol-stones so popular elsewhere in Aberdeenshire. A recent survey of Donside by the Royal Commission on the Ancient and Historic Monuments of Scotland chose the area partly because of the notable cluster of Pictish symbol stones.[68] All four sites that produced Class II cross-slabs in the area have at least one ogham inscription, and often more, in the vicinity.[69] The slab from Dyce has an ogham inscription on it. This implicates the symbol script with other forms of literacy and an interface with Christian guardianship of these skills. Were these Christian monuments deliberately trying to look traditional in form and appropriating the local script to support conversion?

Class I symbol-stones have a standardised format of a single pair of symbols, with occasionally the addition of a mirror and comb symbol. Where they do occur, multiple symbol pairs on Class I stones result from re-use of the stone. Old and new symbol pairs are sometimes carved on different sides of the stone. Sometimes the whole stone was turned upside-down before the new set of symbols was added. This re-use is done in such a way as not to obliterate the old message – the older symbols are still visible, as for example on Eastertown of Roseisle, Aberdeenshire [3.27, 3.28]. These are the multiple lives of Pictish stones.[70]

Class II cross-slabs break away from this Class I convention of the single pair of symbols and can feature

Figs 3.27–3.28: The Eastertown of Roseisle, Moray, symbol-stone whose 'multiple lives' included use as a slab for a burial cist and two sets of symbol messages carved on different sides and at different orientations.

EARLY MEDIEVAL SCOTLAND

166

multiple sets of symbols.[71] The Class II multiple pairs of symbols, referred to here as 'complex messages', seem to be mostly part of the original design, not re-use or additions. Dressed surfaces on Class II cross-slabs provided increased capacity for display and the figural art appears to have also provided more opportunities for the use of symbols. Symbol pairs appearing in close relation to depictions of people, such as the rider and seated figures on the Dunfallandy cross-slab, Perthshire, supports the theory that some symbol pairs are names or identifiers.

There are fewer Class II cross-slabs in northern Pictland than south of the Mounth, but amongst this northern group complex messages are widespread and proportionally more prominent than in southern Pictland.[72] This is not really surprising as Class I stones were also more popular in northern Pictland and various experts have hypothesised that symbols originated in either Aberdeenshire or the Golspie/Dornoch Firth area.[73] The cross-slab from Golspie [3.29] is similar to the hybrid Aberdeenshire cross-slabs in that the cross is carved in shallow relief, but the complex message of eight symbols on the dressed back are all incised. There is also an ogham inscription around the edge of the slab, but it is unclear whether this is part of the original design, a translation or a later addition.

Ogham was developed in a pre-Christian context, probably in the south of Ireland, furthest from the influence of the Roman Empire.[74] In geographical terms this seems a good analogy for the development of the Pictish symbol script in northern Pictland, far beyond the frontier, but probably developed with knowledge of Latin grammar and Roman script.[75]

Meigle 1 is perhaps the only southern cross-slab of comparable complexity with a main symbol message writ large and two smaller ancillary pairs of symbols arranged between the larger symbols. This includes an otherwise unique and innovative symbol of a triquetra knot. There are varying definitions of what constitutes the corpus of symbols, but they are normally defined as those that occur on Class I stones.[76] This limited definition has impeded the identification of innovative symbols on Class II and denies the capacity for change through time that we see in all other contemporary scripts (such as ogham and runes). A more open view would allow the introduction of new Class II symbols like the lion appearing with traditional, i.e. Class I, symbols on the cross-slabs from Golspie [3.29] and Ulbster.

The pairing of symbols seems so fundamental to the function of the script that it has been suggested this should determine whether or not a design should be regarded as part of the symbol set. Consequently the many single bulls from Burghead [3.30] and the single horse from Inverurie have been discounted.[77] Much of the distinctive Pictish animal art – such as boar, wolf and deer [3.31] – do not transfer to Class II stones as symbol script, although they do appear in the narrative scenes, especially the deer. Only snake, bird/eagle and fish continue in use as symbol script on Class II cross-slabs [3.29].[78]

Some popular Class I symbols, such as the arch, do not appear on Class II stones and have been suggested as the most archaic symbols.[79] The potentially archaic symbols are, however, found among symbols carved on cave walls in Fife and at Covesea, Moray. They are also found on portable artefacts such as the notched rectangle on the Whitecleugh silver chain [3.32], the rare s-shaped ogee on the terminal of the Parkhill silver chain, and the disc with an

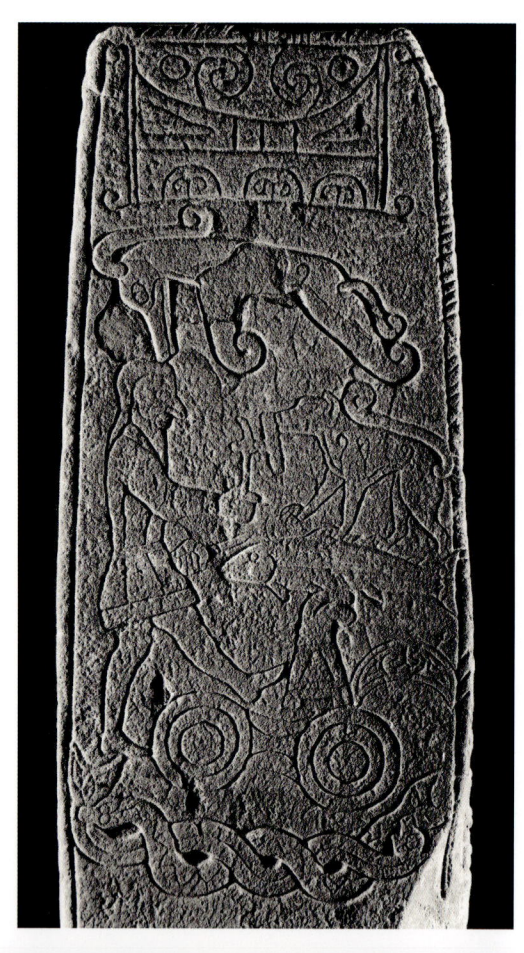

EARLY MEDIEVAL SCOTLAND

168

Fig. 3.29 (opposite, left, above): The back of the cross-slab from Golspie, with its complex messages in ogham and symbol script.

Fig. 3.30 (opposite, left, below): One of six slabs depicting bulls that survive from the fort at Burghead.

Fig. 3.31 (opposite, right): A relatively plain example of the rectangle symbol and the beautifully incised deer on the Grantown-on-Spey symbol-stone.

Fig. 3.32 (right): The symbols on the penannular clasp of the Whitecleugh silver chain.

indented rectangular projection on the Broch of Burrian bone.[80] Other Early Medieval scripts, such as runes, were used on portable objects for centuries before they were first carved on stone monuments.[81] The decorated rectangle has also been suggested as an archaic symbol, with the only Class II example being the complex inscription from Golspie [3.29]. Most of these archaic symbols are from north of the Mounth.

Many of the portable objects that carry symbols (for example, the Norries Law plaques [3.50] and Whitecleugh chain); and those incised on outcrops (such as at Dunadd, Argyll, and Trusty's Hill, Kirkcudbright, or in the Fife caves), are beyond the normal distribution of Class I, at the periphery of what we might consider to be Pictish political influence. How do we explain this largely peripheral distribution?

The two classes of symbols are usually conflated and used to define the extent of Pictish ethnicity, but there are numerous other curiosities beyond this simplistic use. For instance, Class I and II stones rarely appear at the same site. Is this a separation related to different time periods of use, different communities of use, or just plainly different use?

There are greater numbers of Class I symbol-stones north of the Mounth, particularly Strathdon and the Garioch, and yet comparatively few cross-slabs in northern Pictland. This can be contrasted with the popularity of Class II cross-slabs in southern Pictland, particularly Strathmore, but with far fewer symbol-stones. Some areas in northern Pictland, such as Inverness-shire, have no Class II cross-slabs at all, and the Mounth itself creates a gap in the distribution with little sculpture of any kind between the rivers North Esk and Aberdeenshire Dee. How are we to understand this different emphasis between north and south and the smaller regional variations?

There are always more questions than answers with the enigmatic Pictish symbols and they remain an area ripe for research.

IDEAS AND IDEOLOGIES

DIFFERENT CHRISTIANITIES: STONE CROSSES

Early Medieval Scotland is particularly rich in sculptural remains. The ideas and ideologies these embody have been well rehearsed. Stone crosses represent the most abundant form of evidence for the successful spread of Christianity. Referring to 'Christianity' often depersonalises what was people's lived faith – Christianity becomes an institutional phenomenon, almost thought of as an entity in itself. Rather than a product of a detached institutional force shaping people's lives, the creation of Christian sculptured monuments should be seen as representative of specific times and places: they reflected the needs of people living within those particular circumstances. These monuments remained part of people's lives and, as was suggested for Hilton of Cadboll, they could continue to be the focus for ceremony and action long after their creation.

As with literacy and manuscript arts, stone-carving represents new skills introduced through contact with the Roman world. Later, in the second half of the first millennium, established Christian communities enthusiastically engaged with these new technologies, often in the service of the new religion. From a European perspective, the styles of decorated crosses of the 'Celtic' north and west are seen as a distinctive product of the dynamic artistic context of the 7th to 10th centuries AD in Early Medieval Britain and Ireland. These stone monuments generally did not move far in comparison to the portable art of metalwork or manuscript, and because of this we can more easily see differences in style and form, and different regional expressions of Christianity.[82] Even a universal religion such as Christianity is subject to regional differences and localised variation. People still managed to portray something of their local or regional identity using a wide repertoire of art and symbolism.

The regional differences in cross types and monumental sculpture within Early Medieval Scotland are often portrayed in terms of the ethnic labels that have been transmitted through the historical record. For instance, cross-shafts from southern Scotland – such as those from Aberlady, East Lothian, or Ruthwell, Dumfriesshire – are perceived as northern examples of the styles of cross popular further south in the Anglo-Saxon kingdoms. The Scottish examples of this type are then related to the expansion of Northumbrian political control in southern Scotland. There are no monuments of this type north of the Firth of Forth, which would support the contemporary Anglo-Saxon chronicler Bede's notion of the Forth being the boundary of Pictland from the beginning of the 8th century.

Different types of cross were preferred in Anglo-Saxon kingdoms and Ireland.[83] Anglo-Saxon free-standing crosses consist of an equal-armed cross surmounting a pillar-shaft, whereas Irish crosses are tall Latin crosses where the long lower arm of the cross forms an elongated shaft. This is regardless of the addition of a ring linking the arms of the cross-head, which is often mistakenly seen as the defining characteristic of 'Celtic' crosses. The Gaelic-speaking west of Scotland appears to follow the Irish style.

The Picts embraced the format of the cross-slab and on these they carved a variety of crosses that presumably reflected choices of affiliation and their various relationships with neighbours to the west and south. Most cross-slabs have a cross on one side only, with the other broad, flat, dressed face used for the display of the symbol script and a wealth of other symbolism. The popularity of the cross-slab perhaps results from this need to display prominently both cross and symbol script.

Pictish symbols do not appear on any types of Christian monument other than cross-slabs. On cross-slabs the symbols are never depicted directly on the Christian cross. They can appear in the smaller framed spaces created by the intersecting cross; they can also appear in association with figures in the panelled scenes, and as large and bold messages on the back. But whatever the symbols meant in these positions, they were certainly inappropriate for display on the body of the cross itself. It is unclear why this might be, but there are other comparable conventions, such as animal interlace rarely decorating the cross itself.[84]

Because Pictish symbols never appear on the cross, they were therefore never likely to be used on free-standing crosses, whose entire form is the prime Christian symbol. The popularity of the free-standing cross at Iona and in Ireland has led to them being seen as a Gaelic-style monument of the Columban Church. There are, however, also many fragments of free-standing crosses in Pictland. Free-standing crosses need not be ethnically Gaelic, and contrasting them with Pictish cross-slabs creates a false ethnic division.[85]

It was only conventions about the display of Pictish symbols that did not allow them to be depicted on free-standing crosses. Certainly, the display of symbols suited the format of the cross-slabs, but ultimately ideas about what was appropriate for depiction on the cross meant that the form of the free-standing cross did not allow the inclusion of Pictish symbols. Rather than the ethnic labelling of different types of monuments, this general observation of form and function explains why symbols only occur on cross-slabs and the corresponding lack of symbols on free-standing crosses.

The famous intact free-standing cross from Dupplin [3.35] – Constantine's cross – also shows the difficulties of applying ethnic labels to monuments.[86] This monument provides a fixed and dated example for Scottish Early Christian sculpture through its dedication to Constantine, son of Fergus, a contemporary of the Carolingian Emperor Charlemagne.[87] Constantine held both the kingships of Dál Riata and Pictland when he died in AD 820. Constantine's cross therefore represents a cultural amalgam that was appropriate for the king who, for the first time, united the east and west of what was to become Scotland.

The variety of cultural influences on Constantine's cross include a majestic rider in a distinctive figural style with an over-sized head and a large moustache;[88] a dedication to Constantine, son of Fergus, in Roman letters;[89] an ogham-inscribed base; the uppermost capping feature reminiscent of some Irish High-crosses with a tiled roof; the Pictish preference for equestrian imagery, hunting dogs and the Old Testament hero David; and a Northumbrian-style equal-armed cross demarcated from its shaft and decorated with vine-scroll.[90]

Functional features of stone monuments have often been ignored in favour of their wealth of decoration and symbolism. Much more comment has been spent on the iconography of Meigle 2 [2.8] and Woodwray [3.33], for example, than on the tenons that project from the sides and top surfaces of the monuments.[91] Constantine's cross, Dupplin, is another case in point. Why is its socket stone

Fig. 3.33: The Woodwray cross-slab with its projecting tenon on the top edge.

Fig. 3.34: The bottom of the back of the Aberlemno 3 cross-slab is uneven in the layout of its panels.

asymmetrical, with a square surface projecting out at the front? Did this act as a focus for devotion or prostration? Could it also have acted as a platform for proclamation?

Likewise, there has been little comment on the oblique facet missing from the bottom corner of Constantine's cross-shaft. This 'flaw' [3.37] is an obvious feature projecting above the level of the socket stone. The carved decoration respects this feature, with the harrying hounds leaping towards it. The carving does not continue onto the facet, as the interlace does on the similar oblique facet of the back left corner of the Maiden stone, Aberdeenshire [3.38]. These may be quarrying flaws that were later integrated into the decorated monument, but they are not isolated examples. The cross-slab with complex symbol composition from Golspie also has its back left bottom corner worn away to an oblique surface, although in this case the decoration that had originally carried over the surface has been eroded to nothing. It is also the back left corner that retained the ancient cup-marked surface on Meigle 1, again at an oblique angle to the dressed surface of the rest of the cross-slab. Aberlemno 3 also has a worn oblique facet on the back left bottom corner. On the cross-slab, the David panel is bordered higher up than the larger centaur panel opposite, as if the facetted area below was an existing feature or it was deliberately set aside [3.34]. There are enough examples to suggest that these facets are a recurrent feature that requires more study. Did they have a purpose – were they meant to facilitate certain actions, or do they mark them?

On Constantine's cross from Dupplin, the oblique facet [3.37] creates an angular vacuum within the carefully cut rectangular socket stone. This space would be wide

EARLY MEDIEVAL SCOTLAND

172

Figs 3.35–37: Among the rich iconography of the Dupplin cross is an inscribed panel (3.36, right, above). This panel was thought to have been weathered blank until Katherine Forsyth deciphered the inscription in 1995, which dedicates the cross to Constantine son of Fergus, King of Pictland (died AD 820). The oblique facet at the bottom corner (3.37, right, below) is an unexplained, but apparently deliberate feature.

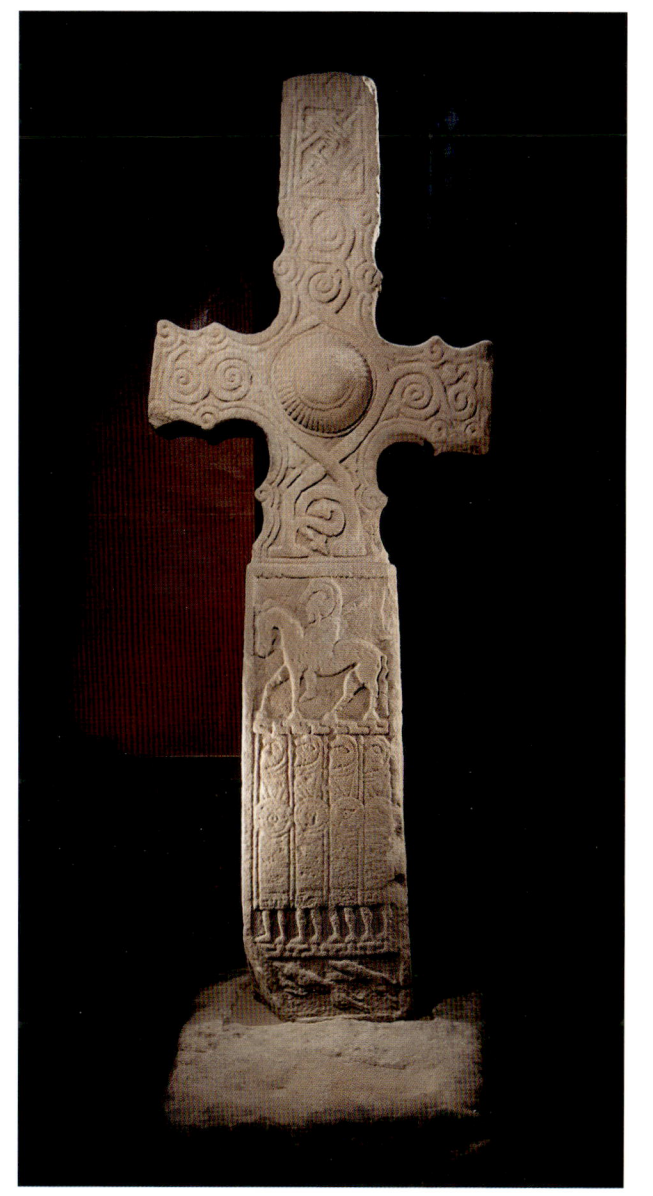

IDEAS AND IDEOLOGIES

Fig. 3.38: The Maiden stone, Aberdeenshire, also has a decorated oblique facet (if the cross is viewed from the front, this is the bottom left of the back of the slab).

enough to reach into. Water flowing off the cross would have collected in this space were it not for an oval hole cut in the base of the socket stone. This hole lines up with the oblique angle of the facet and appears to be related. Could something have been inserted or withdrawn? Many Irish stone monuments bear sword scars and similarly worn or polished areas. These have been interpreted recently as the result of rituals surrounding peace and warfare, involving swords being alternately blunted and sharpened on the stone.[92] However, the V-shaped sword marks are more clearly secondary on the Irish examples, whereas, decorated or otherwise, the oblique facets noted on Scottish sculpture seem either to be part of the original design or adapted features that were part of the function of the monuments.

DIFFERENT CHRISTIANITIES: DIFFERENT EVIDENCE

Christianity is undoubtedly one of the most important ideas and the big ideological change that occurs during the Early Medieval period. Scotland was witness to the same fundamental changes in belief and religious practice as elsewhere, and, like the rest of Europe, has been shaped by this ever since. Conversion to Christianity would have occurred as a decision during a person's lifetime, with the cumulative effect of every conversion leading to the eventual triumph of Christianity as it spread across Early Medieval Europe. In Early Medieval Scotland, the beliefs that Christianity was merging with, suffer from the pervasive problem of a lack of historical documentation. However, there is also a lack of archaeological evidence for Christianity in Scotland until the poorly-dated development of Christian sculpture in the second half of our period. Both of these factors have served to make the chronology of conversion unclear.

There are certain features of how Christianity adapted within northern Britain that may reflect the influence and interplay with existing traditions of practice and belief. The new faith came as a comprehensive philosophical package through its central texts, but it was one that was still open to debate and modification through the centuries. From the 1st to the 4th centuries AD, Roman imperial colonisation brought three main innovations in religious practice to southern Britain: specially dedicated sacred buildings, religious inscriptions for named deities, and statues of gods. In much of Scotland there was no Roman transition to introduce these Mediterranean models of practice and worship that Christianity later used and adapted across the rest of the Europe. Instead, we must expect a more direct interface between Christianity and existing belief systems of people beyond the frontier. Religion in later prehistoric Britain has proven difficult to characterise because it lacks these types of evidence – temples, statues and inscriptions – which are easily recognised as 'ritual' by archaeologists. These same absences of evidence that characterise later prehistoric religion in northern Britain also typify the earliest evidence for Christianity.

An assumption is often made that the earliest churches in Scotland must underlie modern churches. This might explain why there is so little archaeological evidence for early churches.[93] However, the lack of early churches is not so surprising when we realise that there was also no previous tradition of creating specially dedicated sacred space or temples in later prehistoric northern Britain. The early appearance of church architecture in southern Britain can be attributed to the existing inheritance of substantial sacred architecture from the Roman period and the adaptation of the Roman *basilica* to Christian worship.[94]

Similarly, the lack of human representations of Christ in Early Christian art in northern Britain does not seem so unusual, given that there was no pre-existing tradition of representing deities in human form. The *Book of Durrow* lacks any representation of Christ in human form, in comparison to later manuscripts such as the *Book of Kells*. The popularity of the formula '*in nomine*', 'in the name of', inscribed on a variety of objects, may be due to an aversion to saying or to inscribing the name of the deity. If this were the case, then the phrase would be compatible with both Christian and previous practices.

The suggestion that Pictish identity may have been formed in opposition to Rome and have glorified non-Roman practices, might reasonably lead us to expect other material points of contact between old and new ritual practices.[95] Despite being Christian monuments, some details of Pictish cross-slabs are suggestive of lingering differences from Mediterranean models of practice. There is little use of Roman script in Pictish sculpture. As well as lacking Latin inscriptions, cross-slabs also lack common Christian symbols such as the *Agnus dei*, *Chi-Rho* or *alpha* and *omega* that might have been easily co-opted into any existing symbol system. Many cross-slabs retain the traditional system of communication – the Pictish symbols.[96] These were obviously compatible with the Christian message and were presumably proclaiming complementary ideological messages using the regionally appropriate script.

Cross-slabs are manifestly not a church, though they often incorporate features associated with the house of God [1.40–1.41]. Some are church-shaped with sloped sides, an apex pediment [2.3–2.4], framing beasts or interlace with opposed zoomorphic terminals [3.25]. Pictish cross-slabs were obviously focal points for Christian worship. Did they serve as substitutes for stone churches, reflecting the earlier tradition that avoided sacred architecture?

The main feature of a cross-slab is always the figure-less cross, decorated with abstract designs, and never with representation of the crucified human body of Christ. There are also few clear examples of iconography depicting the events of the four Gospels, unlike the heavily scriptural Irish High crosses.[97] However, the reading of the hunt scenes proposed above shows that these monuments could be suffused with hidden Christian meaning. While the rider on some cross-slabs has a Christological aspect, it is often an opaque message within a more easily understood composition depicting everyday secular activity.[98] Pictish cross-slabs are unequivocal evidence for the success of Christianity, but they also suggest that traditional ideas about buildings, inscriptions and iconography may have continued to influence the representation of Christianity in Pictland.

Different social conditions beyond the imperial frontier created different Christianities.[99] Interpretation has often focused on the differences between 'Celtic' or Columban Christianity and 'Roman' Christianity, using the historically documented debates of the Synod of Whitby in AD 664 as a basis. This meeting of important Church figures was concerned with certain differences in Christian practice, but ultimately was about ecclesiastical authority. The debate was concerned with wider trends of reform and bringing the Churches of Britain and Ireland in line with Continental practice at the expense of the traditions of the revered saints who converted these communities. The Northumbrian king was to decide whether his kingdom would continue to follow the example of the British and Irish Churches whose missionaries first converted them, but who differed from the rest of European Christendom in their method of tonsure (the hairstyle given to monks as a sign of devotion) and in their reckoning of the date of the central Christian feast of Easter.[100]

In the 8th century, Bede records a letter from the Pictish King Nechtan seeking advice from Abbot Ceolfrith at Monkwearmouth concerning the same reform of the calculation of Easter that had been the focus at Whitby fifty years earlier. This incident is usually discussed in terms of another stage in the conflict between Columban and Roman authority. Nechtan also made a request for masons to build a church in the Roman tradition and this incidental detail is used by some art historians as a starting point for Pictish sculpture and the transfer of stone-carving skills.[101] Nechtan's request for masons certainly suggests that there were no stone churches in Pictland, but we might then wonder about what other 'Roman' traditions were still missing? Other than his currently unlocated stone church, does Nechtan's reign herald other changes in the evidence for Christianity in Pictland?

The tonsure was a visible and physical manifestation of difference between the Columban tradition and Roman orthodoxy, but it is largely incidental when compared to the question about the timing of the celebration of Easter, which united all of Christendom in common worship. The question of the Columban tonsure has been implicated with the transition from Druid to Christian cleric in Britain and Ireland. The tonsure favoured by the Columban party has been suggested as an inheritance from the Druidic past.[102] This unusual detail of physical appearance has received far too much focus and often provides the starting point for all sorts of wild theories about timeless Celtic continuity from pagan Celt to Celtic Christianity.

THE PAGAN-CHRISTIAN INTERFACE

Early Medieval people had to reconcile their pagan past with becoming Christian. Pre-Christian religion in northern Britain would normally fall under the well-rehearsed topic of Celtic religion.

There is much popular interest in this subject, with many fanciful and romantic conflations using a variety of evidence from widely different times and places, all distant from Early Medieval Scotland. The intermediary of Roman period hybrid cults were never introduced to Scotland and this goes some way to explaining why the evidence for the transition to the new Christian religion differs from that in southern Britain. A detailed treatment of the features of prehistoric religion in Scotland is not possible here, but people, places and practices would have provided certain points of contact with Christianity as it became established in Early Medieval Scotland.

Hagiography, the writing of saints' lives such as Adomnán's *Life of St Columba*, contains snippets of information about the last vestiges of pre-Christian beliefs as people of northern Britain were being converted to the new religion.

There are bound to be biases in these tales. Christianity was obviously the winner in this battle between old and new religions and many accounts were written generations after the conversion period they describe. However, there are also some surprising correspondences. Adomnán refers to Columba's adversaries as *magi*, and the Druids had also been equated with *magi* from the earliest Greek sources.[103] The position of the *magi* Broichan as foster father of the Pictish King Bridei, also strikes a chord with Julius Caesar's earlier account of the social position of Druids. Tirechan's account of St Patrick's mission tallies with other Irish traditions about the social prominence of the Druids. Early Christian missionaries could have exploited the respect and social standing that holy and learned men already had in these societies.[104]

There is evidence from later prehistoric Scotland for particular practices associated with curating and manipulating fragments of human remains. Previous interpretation of this evidence focused on skulls as evidence for 'The cult of the head', supposedly a key feature of prehistoric Celtic religion.[105] A recent study showed that much more than skulls were involved – many different parts of human bodies were incorporated into archaeological and structural features on Scottish later prehistoric sites.[106] The cult of Christian relics that developed into the Medieval period involved similar practices of curating and breaking up the bodily remains of saints.[107] Judging by the later prehistoric evidence, using human remains as tangible reminders of other important lives and ancestral figures would not have seemed alien to the converting communities of Early Medieval Scotland. As with the transition from Druid to Christian cleric, we are seeing an interface between old

Fig. 3.39: The only surviving piece from the bronze hoard discovered at Tarnavie, Perthshire, is an enamelled ring with an inset triskele decoration.

and new, albeit with different implications within the new framework of Christianity.

The place-name element *nemeton* is variously translated as 'sanctuary' or 'sacred place' and also features regularly in general accounts of Celtic religion.[108] The ancient place-name Drunemeton (oak sanctuary), recorded in ancient sources as the central sanctuary for the tribes of Celts who settled in Galatia (Asia Minor), is the classic example of religious site designated by this pan-Celtic place-name.[109] *Nemetons* are recorded in ancient sources broadly scattered throughout Europe and also survive in numerous modern place-names, including a host of *nemeton* place-names in Scotland.[110] This broad geographic distribution has been used to link the furthest extremes of the Celtic world into a common narrative of Celtic religion.

However, the Scottish evidence suggests that the place-name element *nemeton* requires more detailed study. Occasional finds of Roman Iron Age metalwork in association with *nemeton* sites provide hints at the archaeological potential of this place-name group. There is, for example, an antiquarian report about burials and bronze armour associated with Tarnavie,[111] an unusual, long, hump-backed mound of glacial till at the foot of Rossie Law, one of the high hillforts of the Ochil escarpment bordering the southern side of Strathearn. The discovery of 'bronze armour' is presumably a reference to some sort of sheet bronze artefacts.[112] The only surviving item from Tarnavie is an enamelled ring decorated with a tri-coloured triskele design [3.39] dating to the early centuries AD.[113] Of similar date are two massive bronze armlets recovered from the entrance fill of the Castle Newe souterrain, part of a cluster of *nemeton* place-names surrounding the mountain Ben Newe in western Aberdeenshire.[114]

Nemeton place-names are found both in northern and eastern Scotland, but not in the Gaelic-speaking west. It is also rare as a place-name element in Ireland and Wales. This suggests that the Pictish language maintained the term and renewed the use of these sites into the Early Medieval period.[115] There are hints of supporting archaeological evidence from a few associations between *nemeton* place-names and sculptured stones inscribed with Pictish symbols (Class I). The cluster of Nevay/Newtyle place-names on the lower slopes of Kinpurney hill in the Sidlaws, indicate a *nemeton* in the area, and the Keillor inscribed symbol-stone may mark the south-western boundary of this cluster.[116] The Ardross and Stittenham symbol-stone fragments are from farmland adjacent to another cluster of *nemeton* compound place-names surrounding the hill Cnoc Navie in Easter Ross, with another fragment of Class I sculpture coming from the south side of the hill at Nonakiln, 'the chapel of the *nemeton*'.[117] St Ninian's Chapel, Navidale, Sutherland, has also produced a Class I symbol-stone. An earlier study suggested that a large proportion of *nemeton* place-names had close associations with early church sites.[118]

A *nemeton* need not be a natural site, a Druid's secluded oak grove. Finavon hill in Angus (originally *fidnemed*, the 'wood sanctuary'[119]) represents extreme levels of alteration to a *nemeton* site. The hill has a complex sequence of enclosures including a massive oblong stone bank. These are the remains of timber-laced walls that had been heated to such intense temperatures that the stonework became

EARLY MEDIEVAL SCOTLAND

molten and fused into glassy masses – a process known as vitrification. Large rock-cut shafts interpreted as cisterns or wells are a common feature within later prehistoric forts of this type,[120] and the only one so far excavated, at Finavon, produced a fragment of human skull.[121] The fragment may have accidentally ended up in the shaft, but, as already noted, there is plenty of other evidence from later prehistoric Scotland of the selective manipulation of human remains. When combined with linguistic and landscape studies, the archaeological evidence hints at the benefits of further investigation of these *nemeton* sites as a group within Scotland.

Martin Carver, the excavator of the monastery at Portmahomack, has argued that Early Christian sites need to be understood in terms of the existing prehistoric landscape.[122] Early Medieval sculptured stones from Woodray and Aberlemno, in the landscape surrounding the hill of Finavon, indicate that the later Christian focus of activity had shifted away from the hilltop site and into the lower-lying surroundings. The place-name element 'Aber-' indicates a confluence where a smaller tributary meets a river, and this is a prominent element in early parish names. The place-name Aberlemno indicates the confluence where the River South Esk meets the Lemno Burn, the stream that wraps around three sides of Finavon. The confluence is the lowest point in the surrounding landscape – the polar opposite of Finavon in landscape terms.[123] Retaining both a general connection and, at the same time, a distance from the older site of Finavon, emphasises the complex relationship of Christianity with landscapes of existing significance and the preceding belief system.

Connections from pagan past to earliest Christianity would have been necessary for the new religion to adapt to existing social and cultural conditions in northern Britain. Therefore we should not be surprised that certain features of later prehistoric practice were renewed within the framework of Christianity. We should also not be surprised that the evidence for earliest Christianity is limited in terms of substantial architecture, inscriptions,[124] and representations of God in human form, when these types of evidence had never previously existed in northern Britain. Some of the characteristics interpreted from Pictish cross-slabs suggest lingering influences over religious expression and practice, long after the ideas of Christianity have been accepted. This does not mean that people in Early Medieval Scotland were not fervent and devout Christian believers. Rather, their Christianity was initially different and they were slower to take up the increasingly uniform Christian expressions of faith that had developed in Rome and on the Continent.[125] But the eventual triumph of Christianity shows that it was capable of adapting to the new circumstances at the edge of the known world, while still retaining its core structure. Roman cults and imperial forms of governance had never been established in Scotland and so there was no social, political and religious structure to inherit from the Roman world. Different Christianities were possible where there was no Roman heritage to adapt easily.

TAKING FROM ROME

So what role did Rome play? Rome is not just the 'end of' or 'fall of' at the beginning of any narrative about Early Medieval Scotland, but should instead be considered as a continual presence of varying influence. Through most of our period, Rome was not projecting a specific imperial ideology anymore, but the idea of Rome was being reinvented as the metropolitan heart of western Christendom (with varying degrees of success and in competition with the eastern imperial city of Constantinople/Byzantium). The legacy of Rome's imperial past was a particularly dominant expression of power, but this was never subsequently achieved on the same scale anywhere in Europe, although it was often aspired to and emulated. At the beginning of our period, as the range of Latin culture reached its height in the Roman province of Britain, the political influence of Rome was in decline. Yet the ultimate paradox is that in the following centuries, the idea of Rome, as the ideological heart of Christendom, would exert a greater influence over northern Britain and Ireland than the might of Rome's armies had ever managed.

Rather than the direct cultural inheritance of the imperial provinces, the areas that had been beyond the frontiers developed strategies of taking what was useful from Rome – an active choice, selectivity, rejection or even an invention of participation in a common Roman inheritance. Conversion and the creation of Christian identities were enmeshed in this attitude. The spread of Christianity must have depended on this adaptable way of thinking more than on distant memories of the realities of late Roman diplomacy and frontier politics. In general, Christianity provided the most stable ideological connection with a Roman past, even in northern Britain and despite its history of intermittent incorporation within the imperial boundaries. In the post-imperial period, Rome was a part of the common cultural legacy that most of Europe shared, but it was a past that could be invented, inverted, contested, rejected and reinvented anew. In societies where there was otherwise little Roman legacy, the enthusiastic appropriation of technologies originating within the Empire will be referred to as 'taking from Rome'.

Sculpture undoubtedly played an important role in the expression of new Christian identities in the societies that flourished beyond what had been the frontiers of imperial Rome. But it was an innovation, an affectation of *Romanitas* – an idea taken from Rome. Wherever the people of northern Britain travelled within the former imperial boundaries, they would have seen the visible monumental remains of the glory of the Roman Empire, especially on pilgrimage to metropolitan Rome and the near east. Roman Christianity had also appropriated many older forms of religious representations from the 4th century AD onwards. Pilgrims would have seen this as a visible continuity between imperial past and Christian present. As we saw with the use of *Adventus* imagery on Pictish cross-slabs, Early Medieval Christianity continued the tradition of associating a Christian identity and Christian representation with the Roman past.

In Scotland, where there were very little Roman remains (*spolia*) to appropriate, and certainly no Roman Christian art, 'taking from Rome' involved mimicry in its finest form, producing stunning new artistic creations that came to define Christian worship in northern and western Britain. To the classically trained eye, these Christian monuments might appear barbaric and foreign, but to the local populace they presented that perfect amalgam of their place in the world and their relationship to the faith that was uniting Europe. Their place in the world was rooted in their ancestry and position beyond the former imperial boundaries, represented through the visually distinctive Insular art. But this was not just the re-emergence of prehistoric Celtic art. Nearly four centuries of contact and occasional occupation meant that Insular art had a Romano-British legacy[126] combined with a host of influences and motifs that transferred from Continental and Mediterranean sources of inspiration – some via Anglo-Saxon and Irish contacts. These reference points also established their place in the world. To the people of Early Medieval Scotland, their monumental art was the perfect vision and realisation of *their* Christianity, with all its universal themes and local idiosyncrasies. The summary of the motifs used on the Hilton of Cadboll cross-slab captures those various scales of reference perfectly (see pp 151–54).

SILVER

Discussion so far has focused on stone sculpture and the wealth of symbolism, but we will see that 'taking from Rome' was equally important for another material innovation – silver as the symbol of wealth. While only ever sporadically occupied, northern Britain had lived hard by and dealt with imperial Rome for over three centuries. People's way of life in later prehistoric Scotland could apparently survive the massive influx of soldiers during the shortlived Roman military occupations of the first two centuries AD, but it could not resist the more insidious changes brought about by diplomatic relations, access to new forms of wealth, often in the form of silver, and the prestige accrued from raiding and negotiating with its imperial neighbour in the 3rd and 4th centuries AD.

Contemporary references to northern Britain in the later classical sources hint at new political arrangements, with fewer groups mentioned and new names suggesting the political coalescence of the kingdoms and peoples that became known as the Picts, the Scots and the Britons. The presence of Rome without actual occupation had a similar destabilising and consolidating effect on frontier societies throughout Europe.[127] The boundaries with *barbaricum* were permeable, and both *imperium* and beyond were fundamentally changed by their relationship with one another. The supply of silver into Early Medieval Scotland has its basis in these relations between *barbaricum* and *imperium*.

Silver was not yet mined in Scotland, but several centuries of contact with the Roman Empire led to the introduction of this new exotic material through coins, and more rarely hacksilver bullion. These would have been acquired during raids on the Empire, or used by imperial officials to buy peace beyond the northern frontier. The most recent analysis of moulds and crucibles suggests that silver was not being reworked by native craftsmen until the 4th or 5th centuries AD when the supply of silver was presumably dramatically reduced with the decline of the western Roman Empire.[128] The continuing circulation of silver led to the development of new forms of dress object, such as silver chains, pins and penannular brooches. There was no monetary currency produced in Scotland during this time and there would not be for several centuries after, so objects made from silver became an important means of creating portable wealth.

The use of silver is an important phenomenon for exploring ideologies in Early Medieval Scotland. Bronze and enamelling had been common during the Roman Iron Age [3.39], but silver rapidly replaced bronze as the metal of choice for expressing wealth, rank, prestige and social standing. While fluctuations in the availability and use of silver may well be concealed by our vague sense of chronology, it remained prominent in the making of prestigious dress objects across the entire period (and beyond into the Viking Age). It was made into the massive silver chains, into brooches, pins, finger-rings, armlets and bowls [3.40]. It was hoarded – as treasuries of whole (if damaged and worn) objects, as in the St Ninian's Isle hoard from Shetland [1.51] – or as collections of mostly broken fragments of silver, as in the Norrie's Law hoard from Fife [3.49].

We might crudely characterise the use of silver across the period in terms of quantity and quality. The early phase is typified by the conspicuous quantity of the silver chains, whereas in the later part of our period visual quality was enhanced through the development of a more polychrome repertoire using gold, glass and amber insets that adapted jewellery techniques and materials appropriated from the Anglo-Saxon world.

During the Early Medieval period there are obvious aesthetic differences between contemporary Anglo-Saxon and Insular art. Anglo-Saxon metalwork displays a strong preference for gold and red garnets, and styles of animal ornament that appear much less frequently in Ireland and Scotland. Unlike the Anglo-Saxon kingdoms, gold in Scotland played a supporting rather than a starring role.

Fig. 3.40 (belwo): The surviving remnants from the Gaulcross hoard, Banffshire.

Gold was applied thinly to gild copper-alloy and sometimes silver objects, and used to make very fine wire for the forming of intricate decoration called filigree [1.1]. Modern connotations about the relative value of gold and silver should be ignored – they may well each have had different symbolic values to people in the past. Silver, as a material, may have long retained an association, a memory of the Roman world. Silver certainly has a story to tell as part of the ideologies of Early Medieval Scotland.

EARLY MEDIEVAL SCOTLAND

Fig. 3.41 (right): A folded package of hacksilver from the Traprain Law hoard.

Fig. 3.42 (below): A dribble of melted silver from the Traprain Law hoard.

TRAPRAIN LAW

One of the most complex stories is that of the Traprain Law hacksilver hoard. Traprain Law is a hill in East Lothian with a range of archaeological material that sets it apart from other contemporary sites in Scotland. There are centuries of settlement evidence and fortification, but also large gaps in this evidence over several millennia. Much of the material is of an unusual character, including Neolithic rock art, hoards of Bronze Age metalwork and the large hoard of hacksilver for which the hill is perhaps best known. Hacksilver is the term used when silver objects have been chopped up for their bullion value, as a substitute for coinage.[129]

Much of the hoard assemblage [2.78, 3.43–45] started life as fine silverware suitable for lavish feasting; it was decorated with the mythological traditions of the Mediterranean world and more recent Christian ideology. There are also some elements of Late Roman belt equipment [3.44]. At some point in their travels towards Traprain Law, the ideologies associated with these objects lost their potency. Subsequent owners decided to treat the material as hacksilver, cutting it up and packaging it into parcels.

The silver objects in the hoard originated far away within the Late Roman Empire and their biographies must have been diverse and complex.[130] Some of the objects are notably older than others and had been in circulation for over a century before other items in the hoard had even been made. The processes of accumulation are obscure, but a number of trajectories must have brought the material in the hoard together before it was buried on Traprain Law sometime around or after the mid-5th century AD. At that time the western Roman Empire was in terminal decline. At least a generation had passed since the legions had left Britain, and it was possibly more than a century after they last set foot in Scotland.

The Traprain Law hoard is often discussed with reference to the hill's occupation during the Roman Iron Age. Traprain Law is differentiated from any other contemporary site by the amount and range of Roman material available to this community. The hoard is just one aspect of this favoured relationship with the Roman world. The hill sits in the middle of one of the richest agricultural regions in Scotland, favoured by good fertile soils and a relatively mild climate, undoubtedly a factor in the status of this hillfort throughout its history. The site assemblage includes the precocious appearance of many forms of metalwork that were to prove popular throughout Late Roman Britain and Ireland,[131] with clay moulds indicating that some of these were being produced on the hill.[132] Part of that metalworking and manufacturing also involved the re-use of Roman silver for new objects. A small dribble of silver found with the hoard tells us that immediately before burial some of it was being melted down. The silver was being transformed into new creations, new objects to act as vehicles for new ideologies [3.42].

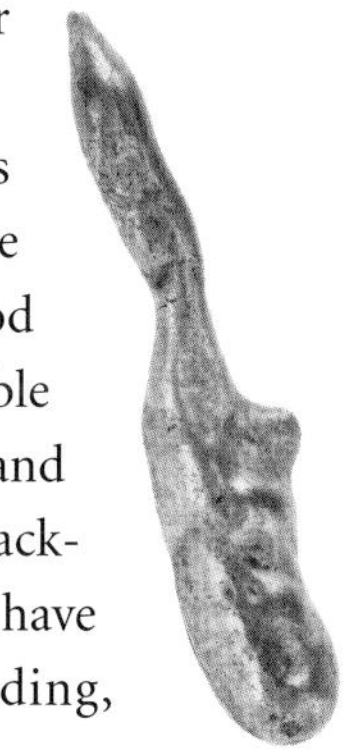

The social and political conditions that led to this wealth being buried on the hill and never recovered are difficult to reconstruct. The hoard is best understood as part of a European-wide phenomenon comparable with similar finds of hacksilver hoards from Ireland and beyond the Continental imperial frontiers. With hacksilver hoards it is difficult to distinguish what could have been pay-offs to avoid the military threat of raiding,

IDEAS AND IDEOLOGIES

Fig. 3.43–3.45: A selection of Late Roman silverware from the Traprain Law hoard, East Lothian.

3.46 (below): The silver chain discovered during quarrying on Traprain Law.

EARLY MEDIEVAL SCOTLAND

184

or rewards to barbarian warriors for service in imperial armies. The Traprain Law hoard could have resulted from either of these scenarios.[133]

What we can be more definite about from the modern survival of the hoard is that it lay unacknowledged and unclaimed for centuries. Why was it never recovered? What does such a loss of wealth suggest for the individual who buried it, and for the community who had occupied the site? Can the non-retrieval of the hoard be related to the site's subsequent history?

SILVER CHAINS

In the 1930s an Early Medieval massive silver chain was found during preparation for quarrying at the opposite corner of Traprain Law from the hoard [3.46]. Such massive silver chains are found only in Scotland, normally as single finds. Most have been found in south-east Scotland with over half of the total coming from south of the Forth.

Apart from Traprain Law, there is an old poorly-recorded find from somewhere near Haddington, three from the hills and valleys on the northern side of Tweedale[134] and two from south Lanarkshire, making seven out of the total of eleven. The other four are scattered north of the Mounth, with one from Aberdeenshire, one from Kincardineshire, one (now lost) from Banffshire, and one from Invernessshire. This leaves a significant gap in what traditionally would be considered as southern Pictland, between the Forth and the Mounth. Terminology and ethnic labelling again become important. They are often referred to as Pictish silver chains because two are incised with Pictish symbols [3.47]. The dispersed distribution argues against an ethnic label, however – it is not helpful to view them as either British or Pictish.[135]

Can these massive silver chains from Scotland be considered anything other than symbols of power? What other clues can they reveal? Why and how were they produced? How would they have been worn, by whom, and on what sort of occasions? These are the sorts of questions that this type of object is begging to be asked. In doing so, new stories about Early Medieval Scotland may emerge. Chain symbolism does not necessarily have positive connotations. Despite the valuable material, the form of the object suggests restraint coupled with weight: literary associations are with betrothal and bondage.[136] The narrow neck circumference of the chains (as far as they can be reconstructed from their fragmentary remains) suggests that they were not worn by big powerful men. The two most complete chains, Hoardwel and Torvean, have neck circumferences of approximately 32–34 centimetres (equivalent to a 13-inch shirt collar) [3.51]. These chains would have been a more suitable size for adolescents or women. Some of the massive silver chains may have been implicated as gifts, pledges or assurances in social processes that are otherwise archaeologically invisible, such as bridewealth, dowries, hostaging or fostering. This important class of objects that have rarely been considered beyond the museum case, or the disconnected view provided by a distribution map, are undoubtedly more complex than simple bold statements of wealth and power.[137]

Chains would have required the use of large amounts of raw material (over three kilograms for the Torvean, Inverness-shire, chain). This could only be supplied from

EARLY MEDIEVAL SCOTLAND

Fig. 3.47: Four massive silver chains from (left to right) Whitecleugh, South Lanarkshire; Hoardweel, Berwickshire; Parkhill, Aberdeenshire; and Borland, South Lanarkshire.

Fig. 3.48: Roman silver fragments from the Norrie's Law hoard, confirmed by recent analysis. The only previously recognised fragment of Roman spoon is top left. The new fragment discussed here is located centre below.

within the Roman world and it is commonly accepted that the chains are made from Late Roman silver.[138] But if so, what sort of silver?

The occurrence of both a massive silver chain and the Late Roman silver hoard at Traprain Law has led to the justifiable assumption that the hoard material was being melted down to make exactly this type of large silver object. Although comparable to the wider phenomenon of hacksilver hoards, the Traprain Law silver is almost unique in Scotland. There is another silver hoard – the Norrie's Law hoard – whose silver is of poorer quality and which was probably deposited slightly later than the Traprain Law hoard. The Norrie's Law hoard also contains a few fragments of Roman silver, which suggests this material may have continued to circulate in northern Britain for some time. Can the chains be considered as proxy evidence for the supply of Roman silver, and if so, which sort? Were they made from Late Roman hacksilver like that from Traprain Law, or more mixed and poorer quality silver like the Norrie's Law hoard?

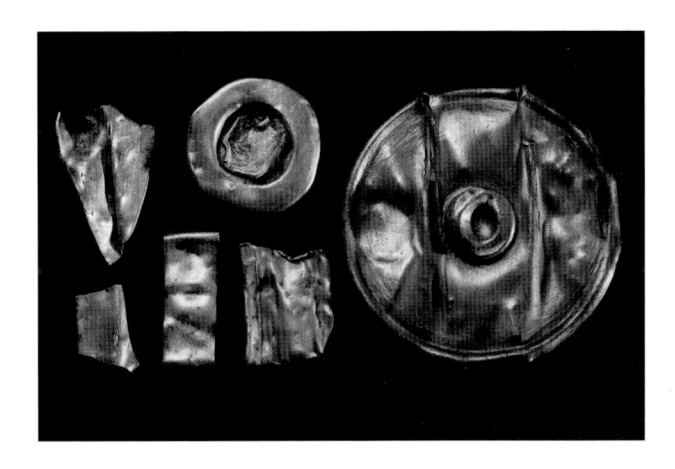

THE FRAGMENTARY BIOGRAPHY OF ONE PIECE OF SILVER

Some objects are remarkably well studied, while others have seen surprisingly little detailed work. Some sculpture, such as the Hilton of Cadboll cross-slab and the Traprain Law silver hoard, have been the subject of major studies.[139] In contrast, the Norrie's Law silver hoard has never been fully catalogued and knowledge of its context is severely lacking.

Norrie's Law is a large cairn (presumably of Bronze Age origin) at the end of a ridge near the boundary between Largo and Ceres parishes in Fife. The hoard was reported for the first time in 1839, twenty years after it was discovered, but the find details are sketchy and much of it had been stolen, sold and melted down by the time it came to the attention of scholars. Since then, for over 150 years, scholarly focus has been drawn to a few eye-catching items from the hoard – the embossed *repoussée* spirals, the handpins, and of course the unique plaques with their Pictish symbols decorated with interlocking triple spirals [3.50]. However, the bulk of the hoard as it survives consists of small fragments of thin silver sheet which have been largely ignored.

Having talked about the Roman past and the importance of the introduction, supply and re-use of silver, a new story can now be told by looking at a single uninspiring object, one small fragment of silver from the Norrie's Law hoard [3.48, centre below]. Taking a single fragment of scrap silver will provide a starting point, but as our perspective widens outwards, it will become obvious that even tiny broken objects reveal much about ideas and ideologies.

IDEAS AND IDEOLOGIES

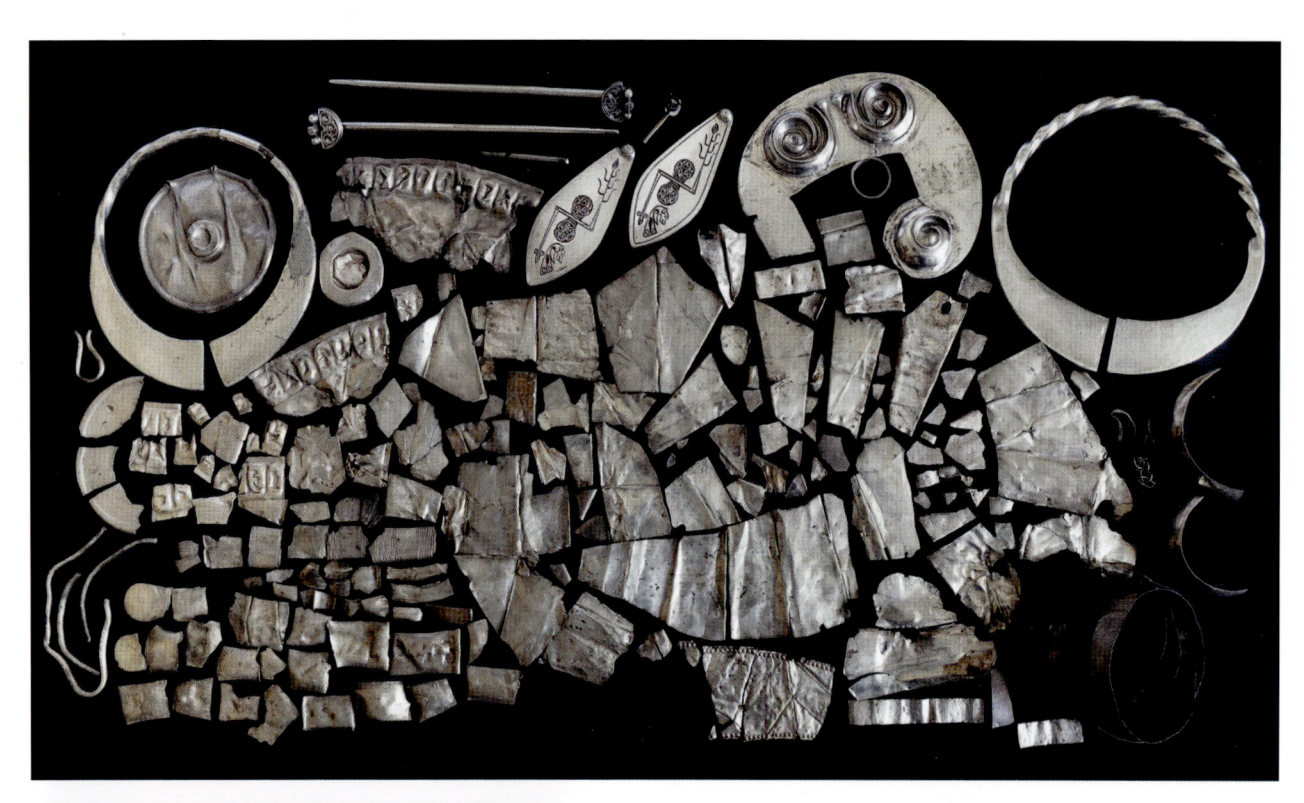

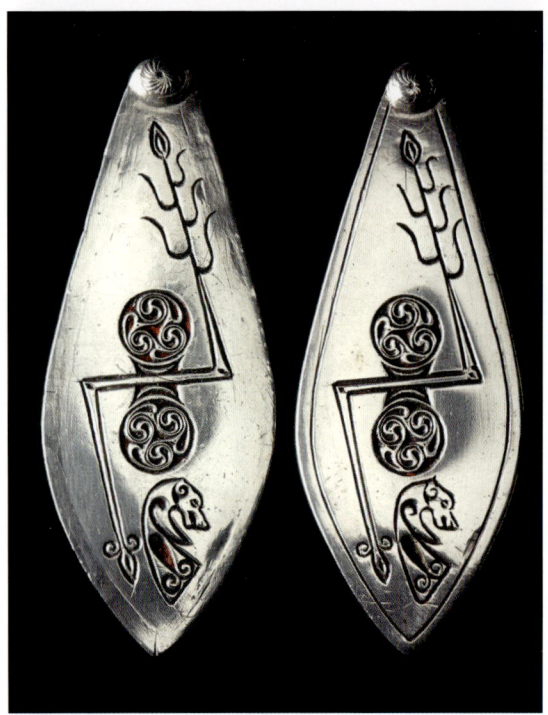

EARLY MEDIEVAL SCOTLAND

Fig. 3.49 and 3.50 (opposite): The surviving remnants of the Norrie's Law hoard (above) and the two enigmatic plaques from the Norrie's Law hoard (below, left).

Fig. 3.51: The Hoardweel silver chain is the only complete example of the type, although one of its end-rings was broken when it was discovered

Fortunately, modern scientific analysis provides new insights. As part of the Glenmorangie Research Project, National Museums Scotland is pursuing a programme of X-ray fluorescence analysis, designed to measure the chemical composition of this fragment, the quality of the silver, and the types of trace elements present. Preliminary results suggest that this scrap of silver is unlike most of the other pieces of sheet silver in the Norrie's Law hoard, in that it is purer, with a high percentage of silver (92–95%) which is comparable to the high-quality Roman silver of the Traprain Law hoard.[140]

Only one fragment of Roman silver had been previously recognised among the Norrie's Law hoard material – an inscribed spoon fragment [3.48, top left]. The newly analysed fragment has no inscribed letters, but when compared with the known piece of Roman spoon, the thickness and folding patterns suggests they are both from the same object. Although just two scraps of an original silver object, the Norrie's Law spoon was no everyday cutlery item. Roman silver spoons are rare in Scotland and only appear otherwise in the Traprain Law hoard. While this provides a point of comparison between the two hoards, there are also significant differences in the degree of fragmentation – the Traprain spoons are more intact.

Roman spoons occur in large numbers in hoards of silverware in southern Britain, often with other pieces of silver dinner service such as large dishes. These hoards are normally interpreted as wealth buried at times of stress, but never retrieved. In the declining monetary economy of the Late Roman province, the easily portable size of a spoon may have provided a convenient and measurable token of wealth of a fairly uniform size and weight.[141]

The world of the Norrie's Law spoon fragments had changed dramatically through many human lifetimes. The spoon was made several centuries earlier somewhere to the south, within the Roman Empire. It may have graced a table in a villa along with other fine silverware used for serving food in the elaborate dinner services and feasting rituals of the Roman world. But it was later taken out of its normal culture of use, and no longer valued for its original craft or function. At what point the spoon was first broken is unknown and it is impossible to say how many hands the Norrie's Law spoon fragments had passed through on their way to Fife. They may have been accompanied on stages of the journey by other elements of the table service that the spoon had been part of, in a collection of hacksilver like the Traprain Law hoard. However, in the Norrie's Law hoard the Roman silver is in fragments and only a minority component among the main body of the hoard which consists largely of thinner and lower quality sheet silver. The difference was only detected through the XRF analysis.

The Roman spoon fragments eventually joined a collection of silver objects gathered together in Fife from diverse sources. The Roman spoon was no longer intact but cut up, suitable for use as recycled raw material for the production of new silver objects from old. The spoon's original use, form and meaning had been rendered obsolete, but the raw material was still valued in its new context beyond the frontier. Some of the silver objects in the Norrie's Law hoard had already been made from recycled Roman silver. Indeed, X-ray and microscopic analysis of one of the plaques (FC34) suggests that it was hammered flat from a shallow, dished, tear-drop shaped object (a spoon perhaps?) before being decorated with the chased design of Pictish symbols. Hammering and polishing of the plaque failed to completely remove the residual presence of an incised border – again a common feature of Roman spoons.

Despite being just a single scrap of precious metal, the previously unrecognised fragment of Roman spoon in the Norrie's Law hoard acts as a metaphor for the Roman legacy within northern Britain. Rome provided influence, raw materials, styles and ideological models for Early Medieval Scotland, but these were actively transformed by the societies that lived beyond the imperial frontiers. The supply of Roman silver coming into Scotland would have declined after the province of Britannia was left to govern itself from around AD 410. As far as we know, native silver resources were not exploited until the Late Medieval period and new supplies of Continental silver were not readily available until after AD 800 when northern Britain and Ireland became part of Viking trade networks. From the 5th to the 9th centuries AD, silver became a finite resource. The Norrie's Law hoard is situated in this gap in the supply of silver, and the analysis and publication of the hoard will help to provide further detail to this sketch.[142]

Although the objects in the Norrie's Law hoard may have been treasured, worn or used by a previous generation, being gathered together in their worn and fragmentary state probably meant that they were destined for the crucible – material of various ages and from numerous places, intended to go through yet another transformation. The accumulation of the hoard, with well-worn items and scraps from a variety of sources (including highly fragmented Roman pieces still in circulation) was presumably intended as raw material for the manufacture of the very latest fashions, objects to be used for the display of new ideologies developing when the hoard was buried.

The Norrie's Law hoard may have been intended to be melted down and made into ingots like that recovered from the fort of Clatchard Craig in northern Fife. Analysis has shown that the quality of this ingot is lower than Roman silver, which suggests it was formed from silver of variable quality, much like the bulk of the Norrie's Law hoard. Silver ingots, like the one from Clatchard Craig, in turn may have provided the gradually debased raw material for the next generation of personal ornament, the penannular brooches with large panelled terminals [3.52]. The enlarged terminals of these new symbols of prestige became popular vehicles for Early Medieval art motifs. Clay moulds for making these penannular brooches were also found at Clatchard Craig.[143]

Later biography

The Norrie's Law hoard never made it to an Early Medieval crucible to be melted down. It lay for centuries in its place of burial at the prehistoric mound on the end of a ridge encircling Largo Bay. Over a millennium after its burial, around 1819, a labourer digging for sand discovered the silver. His fortune now made, he spirited most of the treasure away, and it passed through several hands on its way to jewellers who melted it down to make new objects to grace 19th-century Scottish tables and outfits. By luck, our spoon fragment again survived the crucible. It was left at Norrie's Law amongst the scattered remains collected later on behalf of the local landowner, General Durham.

Fig. 3.52: Penannular brooches from the Cluny hoard, Perthshire.

It is these fragments that survive today. Durham was a rich man and did not need to melt the silver down and sell it for its contemporary bullion worth. Thus he made a rare choice, but one that was becoming increasingly fashionable – to save such antiquities for posterity. Discoveries of treasure made before the 19th century were unlikely to be preserved – they were subject to the values of the time. Many treasures would have been melted down soon after their discovery because the precious materials were deemed more valuable to the finder than any historical or archaeological value.[144]

After Durham's death, his relatives allowed the hoard to be exhibited at the Great Industrial Exhibition in Dublin (1853) and one of the first major archaeological exhibitions in Edinburgh (1856).[145] The science of archaeology may have been in its infancy, but the early antiquarians were enthusiastic about the hoard and commented regularly on its link to the fascinating sculptured stones.[146] They tried to reconstruct the events of the hoard's discovery before the details were lost from living memory, and scholars today are solely reliant on (and grateful for) their belated efforts. Durham's niece, Mrs Dundas Durham, donated most of the hoard to the national collection in 1864. The aforementioned spoon fragment then went into a museum case, with most of the other fragments, where it was viewed by generations of visitors from Scotland and around the world.

This brief summary will have raised more questions than answers. Why were the objects buried at Norrie's Law, already a site of great antiquity in the Early Medieval period, and why were they never recovered? The hoard contains a mixture of unique objects and silver versions of rare and exotic objects more commonly made in copper

IDEAS AND IDEOLOGIES

191

alloy, very local symbols on the plaques, and old objects like the Roman silver fragments. There is not space here to cover all of these stories.

Even with its depleted survival, the combined effect of the Norrie's Law fragments embodies the range of connections, long histories, innovation and transformation that were part of the ongoing processes of cultural renewal in Early Medieval Scotland. In terms of general themes, the Norrie's Law fragments evoke a similar range of ideas as the Hilton of Cadboll cross-slab. Thinking about the ideas and ideologies surrounding silver allows us to interpret the meaning of the Norrie's Law hoard, both in the past and what it means to us now.

Future scientific developments may unlock more clues about the Norrie's Law hoard and new interpretations will be proposed.[147] The ability to measure non-destructively the relative purity of the fragments from the Norrie's Law hoard and compare them with other silver objects, has allowed scholars an insight into changing values and the use of silver. And new questions can be posed, such as when was native silver first exploited in Scotland? The publication of a complete catalogue with the comprehensive analysis of the Norrie's Law hoard will provide a solid foundation for future work.

The value of values

It often seems obvious that certain objects should be valued as expressions of wealth and power, normally because of the precious material they are made from. The Torvean, Inverness-shire, silver chain was made from over three kilograms of silver and now would be valued more highly than the Haddington chain, which is less than a quarter of that weight. The Hunterston brooch has a range of materials added to its silver body, including amber insets that must have been acquired from a great distance, and the technically difficult use of gold through gilding and minute filigree. With this type of brooch, the materials used emphasise value, but the technical ability poured into the creation of the object magnifies that value beyond material worth. However, wealth, material worth and technical skill represent particularly materialistic understandings of value; values also exist as thoughts, ideas and codes of behaviour: for example, Christian values. Other intangible elements of value relate to the history of an object – who owned it and what it has been used for. These affect how the object has been treasured and how it was valued, both in the past and more recently. The Early Christian handbells, for example, were not made of particularly valuable material, and although making them requires technically advanced blacksmithing and the ability to braze (apply a copper-alloy coating), it is the association with a particular person, a saint, that has made them valued objects to the point of their veneration as holy relics.

There are other objects, like the Monymusk reliquary, that have been constantly treasured because they were thought to be representative of the most powerful ideas – the ideologies whose shared values and beliefs shape the way people think, act and understand the world.

Christianity has provided a constant ideological link that people could still relate to from the Early Medieval period into the present.[148] The modern value we place on the Monymusk reliquary has more to do with its antiquity and the popular myths relating to St Columba and the Battle of Bannockburn (see page 36),[149] than the material worth of its precious metals and our judgements of the quality of its artistic embellishment. However, the value of the reliquary in the past would have stemmed from its uses and the relics it contained. Relics changed hands and travelled throughout the Medieval world. They were essential for the spread of saints' cults and the foundation of new churches, providing links to older churches that initially provided the relics. They provide a perfect example of how an ideological link can afford a much greater value to an object, whether it be the bones of the saint or objects associated with a holy person or place (see page 31).

With some objects, such as hand-bells, enshrinement changed their use, making them relics but unable to perform their original function. Perhaps the Monymusk reliquary served a different purpose before it became a reliquary (see page 38). Unlike many types of archaeological object, the Monymusk reliquary has been treated with great reverence. It survived the Reformation and has been constantly curated, creating the antiquity that we now value. However, motives and values shift through time. We can see wear patterns on the object from people touching it in reverence. This wear is a consequence of the beliefs about the holy properties of what was contained within the reliquary throughout much of its existence. Our modern sense of value and reverence treats the object completely differently; now we do not let anyone touch or use it for any of its previous functions.[150]

In the past some objects were accorded an importance far beyond what we might think of as their modern material value. Now, when we are deciding what we think are the most important objects to have survived from the past, we tend to impose our own values and beliefs onto the material; such subjectivity is a major limitation that scholars have to deal with. We must always be aware that potentially there were different systems of value at work in the past and that these might not appear rational to us or make modern economic sense, especially when they are based on different beliefs. The destruction of wealth represented by the prehistoric practice of votive deposition, where prestige metalwork was sacrificed to deities and often deposited in wet locations such as bogs and lakes, seems alien to modern economic sensibilities. The treatment of some objects only makes sense when we can get at the ideas and stories that people associated with them. This is difficult with prehistoric religions where we have no explanation of the beliefs that underlie the practices we can observe through archaeological evidence.

EVERYDAY LIVING AND DYING

Profound ideological shifts will be revealed not only through art, wealth and symbolism, but also everyday material and everyday practices.[151] Particularly where there has been sustained social, political or religious change, we might expect to see fundamental shifts in the basic ways that people conducted their lives. The demise of that most common artefact of Iron Age archaeology, the substantial roundhouse, represents one of the most important ideological shifts at the beginning of our period. Aerial photographs show us that the populated landscapes of later prehistoric northern Britain were peppered with agricultural communities who had invested substantial time and labour in their domestic buildings, souterrains (underground passages) and enclosures. Excavated examples show that by the 3rd century AD, the density of roundhouse communities was declining. They were replaced by more ephemeral structures that are harder to spot through archaeological survey. Early Medieval rural settlement is much less substantial and much more variable in comparison to the roundhouse settlements of later prehistory. For some reason, people no longer felt that they needed to put down substantial roots in the landscapes they lived in.

Roundhouses had been the focus for everyday activity throughout later prehistory with associated lifeways and world views that had been developing in northern Britain for over a millennium. Their eventual demise suggests not only that a traditional architecture had been abandoned during the move into the Early Medieval period, but along with it the entire theatre for everyday life had changed.

People had invested time and communal effort in the construction of their homes throughout later prehistory. A certain sense of security is implied in the expectation of being able to live in the same building for at least the course of a human lifespan or longer. Something caused these long-standing features of society and associated structural forms to change, and in many cases be abandoned, around the beginning of the Early Medieval period.

The demise of the prehistoric roundhouse is concrete material evidence of a severe destabilisation of the accompanying lifestyles, social structures and ideologies. The shift from round to rectangular architecture has affected the way people have lived in Scotland right up to the present day.[152]

Field cemeteries

Curiously, in tandem with the decline in evidence for living, there is an increase in the evidence for death and burial. The growth in evidence for field cemeteries – i.e., burial away from settlement – has usually been linked to the advent of Christianity.[153] In particular, the so-called long-cist cemeteries of the 5th to 7th centuries AD, where extended inhumation graves were lined with slabs, have been seen as evidence of Christian communities differentiating themselves through a new and distinctive form of communal burial practice.

However, there is a growing body of evidence for an earlier tradition of similar Iron Age burial that was more occasional, but widespread across Scotland, which used a variety of features including barrows, cairns and long-cists.[154] It is these burial forms that become more prevalent during the Early Medieval period. This has only really come to light in the last twenty years through developer-funded excavations and through the growing reliability and increased use of radiocarbon dating.[155]

The dead body could be laid out in stone-lined graves (cists with extended inhumations) or dug graves. These are not always accompanied by above-ground features, but either of these grave forms could be covered with a stone cairn (often kerbed, sometimes with corner-posts) or earthen barrow (often ditched, sometimes with interrupted or causewayed corners). The shape in plan can be round, oval, square or trapezoidal, and sometimes these cairns and barrows have no visible form of burial and may have received scattered cremations.[156] The components of the burial features are interchangeable, making them difficult to assign to clear groups and types,[157] and there is often a mixture of forms within the same cemetery.

Iron Age burials had tended to be isolated or clustered in very small groups. However, from the 5th century AD and lasting into the 7th century AD, we begin to see the growth of field cemeteries, away from settlement but without any formal boundary. They are often dominated by one type of monument such as barrows or long cists, but not exclusively.[158] What do these new communities of the dead tell us about changes in ideologies, especially when combined with the changes in settlement construction highlighted above? And what led to such a shift in emphasis, with decreasing investment of time and resources in places for the living, and the increasing appearance of communal places for the dead?

Despite the numbers of archaeologically visible burials, these by no means represent the whole of society. Were these rites reserved for a selected element within Early Medieval society?[159] The suggestion that long cist cemeteries represent early Christian communities differentiating themselves through a distinctive communal burial rite has increasingly been questioned.[160] Only the scale of the cemetery sites and numbers of burials are new – the burial form had pre-Christian origins. This is better understood in a much wider context, as part of an increase in inhumation burial sweeping across the Late Roman world and the North Sea littoral, pre-dating the official recognition of Christianity in the Roman Empire. Christians may have been buried in the field cemeteries with increasing frequency through time, as more people in northern Britain became Christian, but these burials were not primarily dependent on the adoption of Christianity.

Within many cemeteries one or two burials are often significantly older than the majority. These were more characteristic of the scattered Late Iron Age burial pattern. Published plans of excavated cemeteries often show the different periods of burial conflated together.[161] Some circumstance or characteristic of the people in these early inhumations led to their location later becoming the focus for many more burials.[162] Late Iron Age burial was highly selective, with very few people chosen for inhumation. These individuals remained important in the lives of those participating in funeral rites.

Not all Late Iron Age burials attracted later cemetery development, but those that did must have been remembered by the generations that followed in order for later people to be buried in association with them. Graves very rarely inter-cut one another, suggesting that the cemeteries grew from clusters around several well-tended plots. A sense of community and lineage stimulated the further development of the cemeteries, not Christian ideology.

The people buried later may well have been Christians, but the restricted number and selective placement of burials suggests the relationship with the oldest burial was of paramount concern. The growth of field cemeteries in the 6th century AD represents attempts by certain sections of communities to establish connections with older, more exclusive burial rites through proximity and repeating the form of the grave. The cemeteries might then be considered as sites of ancestral memory growing around foundation burials of perceived ancestors (see page 131). Christianity undoubtedly contributed to changing concepts of life, death, and time,[163] but existing social factors relating to changes in community expression and a growing sense of the importance of lineage would be equally important. Ancestry and a focus on lineage are features of the later vernacular literature, with documents like the Pictish king-lists attempting to stretch their genealogies back to these earlier times when field cemeteries began to grow.

Early Medieval graves were usually unfurnished and people were buried without any material signs of wealth. In contrast to the richly furnished burials from contemporary Anglo-Saxon England, the Scottish burial record demonstrates that powerful ideas are not always expressed in terms of wealth and expensive materials. Although this is difficult to recognise or quantify in material terms, the number of people who gather for a funeral is a testament to the importance of that deceased individual to their kin-group, within their extended network and associated communities.

MAKING CHOICES IN EARLY MEDIEVAL SCOTLAND

The two major factors that have been discussed within this chapter are the most common explanations for social and political changes at the beginning of the Early Medieval period: proximity to the Roman Empire from the 1st to the 4th centuries AD, and the slightly later advent of Christianity. Both have been used to explain diverse topics such as the demise of circular architecture and the growth of field cemeteries. Both are external influences, but a balance needs to be found with internal reception of these ideas and existing trajectories of change.

The diffusion of ideas and ideologies away from the civilised Mediterranean has too often been seen as the only way that change could have occurred in prehistoric and Early Medieval Scotland. This outdated methodology for explaining change is still frequently used in academic literature, even though it denies the past peoples of Scotland a will of their own, and makes them slaves to external forces. We should be cautious, however, about such blanket explanations as there are always a variety of factors at work in any given historical situation. In this case, two factors stand out: Scotland was only sporadically colonised by Rome, and the people of Early Medieval Scotland chose to become Christians.

Choice is key. There were Christian missionaries from elsewhere, such as St Columba, but no invasion and no external power forcing people to adopt new beliefs, in contrast to how the Carolingian emperors forced conversion on the Slavs and pagan Saxons through warfare. We can also see distinct choice in other matters. The people of Early Medieval Scotland chose not to adopt coinage, and a monetary economy only emerged in Scotland over a thousand years after their neighbours in southern Britain had started using coinage. This cannot be dismissed as primitivism – although incredibly rare, coins have been found in Scotland dating back to their earliest uses in southern Britain.[164] Coins were certainly available during the Roman period and have been found throughout Scotland, often as substantial hoards. But exposure to coins and the market economies of the imperial world did not substantially change the different economic conditions that prevailed beyond the frontier.[165]

Powerful people in Early Medieval Scotland would have been familiar with the idea of coinage, but they did

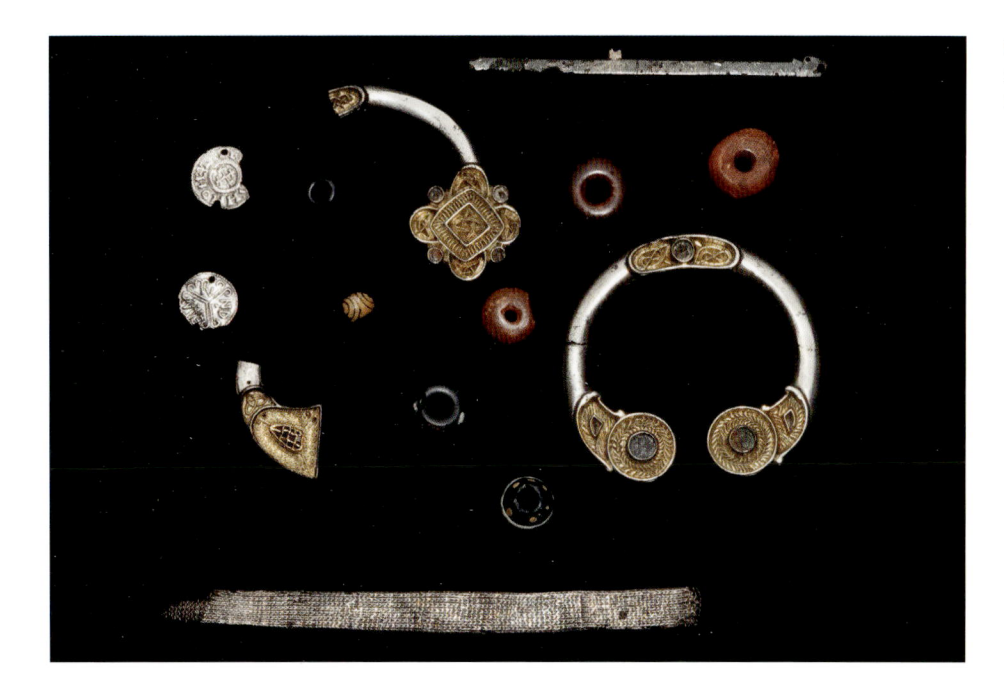

Fig. 3.53: The Croy hoard, Inverness-shire, contains coins that were minted in England.

not introduce the use of coins for everyday trade and exchange. It was not until several centuries later, in the High Medieval period, that Scottish kings began to mint their own coins. The people of northern Britain chose to convert to Christianity over half a millennia before they converted to a monetary economy because such choices suited the social, political, economic and cultural situation at those different times.

Proximity to imperial power was undoubtedly one of the factors that stimulated the emergence of new ideologies in northern Britain. Post-imperial Christianity opened up Early Medieval Scotland to a new, shared Christian identity and participation in wider networks of influence that had previously been restricted by the power politics of the imperial boundaries. However, the way that both the legacy of Rome and conversion to Christianity has often been understood is as the diffusion of a superior culture and passive acceptance by more primitive societies. In reality, external factors are always interacting with a host of internal factors and in the process become internalised; the people beyond the frontiers of the former empire were open to change on their own terms – earlier referred to here as 'taking from Rome' and 'different Christianities'. In order to understand ideological change better – and especially the advent of Christianity – these two factors have been emphasised during this discussion.

'Taking from Rome' is the active choice in transforming the legacy of the Roman Empire. Christianity is another idea taken from the late Empire, but it too had to engage with, adapt, subvert and renew the ideas, belief and value systems that already existed in northern Britain. Although the Roman Empire had provided the platform for Christianity's success and a long-lasting model of power for later ideologies, societies that existed beyond the former frontiers had a great deal of choice in how they became Christian and how they used both the legacy of Rome and their own past histories. Balancing inside with outside influence is also a gross simplification, but looking at objects through these large-scale lenses has shown the complexities of processes of change, the legacy of the past and the local manifestation of what had once been distant and foreign ideas of power and authority.

IDEAS AND IDEOLOGIES

NOTES

1. Thomas Edison, popularly thought to have been the inventor of the light-bulb, which has become the symbol for an idea.
2. Burke 2006, 130.
3. Related terms that might have been used would be 'culture' or 'society', but these belong more with a community perspective, and culture especially has a long and complicated usage in archaeological literature. 'World view' is a more understandable term, but this tends to be a very individual perspective and, if not, shared or collective world views are the scope of religion and belief, which is only a part, albeit an important part, of the topic I am trying to cover.
4. Bells have their origin as percussion instruments accompanying ceremonies throughout the ancient world and were introduced to Britain by the Romans.
5. Ivan Pavlov demonstrated in his experiments that the sound of a bell in association with a dog's meals would condition the dog to expect food being delivered, and consequently the sound of the chime alone could trigger the physical response of salivation.
6. Bourke 1983.
7. The historical trajectory for this probably ran in tandem with the development of Medieval thanages and parishes. The evidence for these is later than our period, but some have speculated that these institutions have an Early Medieval origin (see Driscoll 1992).
8. Imbolc on 1 February became St Bridget's day, although its practical relevance to the agricultural cycle remained unchanged in that it marked the beginning of the lactation period of ewes. Samhain became All Hallow's Eve, the day before All Saint's day, a festival that tenaciously continues to reinvent itself. Beltane/May day (1 May) is still a bank holiday, but it has its origins as a festival celebrating excess when pre-industrial dairy production was at its seasonal height (see Lysaght 1994).
9. Thacker 2002.
10. The focus of Marxist philosophy's use of ideology.
11. Burke 2006.
12. For example, Thomas 2000.
13. Carver and Spall 2004, 193–94.
14. Carver 2008, 134.
15. The tools themselves are the basics used for many types of fine leather-craft and minimalist interpretation would suggest no more than this. It is the wider context of a monastery that has allowed Professor Martin Carver to pursue the interpretation of parchment and manuscript production.
16. Higgit 1982, 310–15.
17. The *Book of Kells* was also once suggested as originating at Portmahomack (see Brown 1972). The evidence for vellum-working is not enough legitimately to raise Portmahomack's claim above any other candidate sites for its production.
18. Although the purpose of the carving is unknown, the decorated phalanges have been suggested as bone gaming-pieces (see David Clarke, pers. comm. in MacGregor 1974, 88). The form and the symbolism raises the humble phalanges into the category of elite leisure activities practised by those whose status and accumulated wealth (probably measured in numbers of cattle) gave them the lifestyle that could afford to indulge in more than just subsistence activities.
19. Radford 1962. (National Museums Scotland [NMS] accession no. X.GB 227)
20. Bone is best carved when fresh as it becomes more brittle with age and drying out (see Clarke and Heald 2008).
21. In the realities of life, ideologies have much to do with the exercise of power as one of the constant features of human behaviour. Marxist interpretations of ideologies have often focused on the uneven distribution of wealth as an expression of power and rank.
22. Burke 2006, 136.
23. *Ibid.*, 132.
24. Williams 2003; Hingley 1992.
25. Chapter one ('Individuals') of this book explains '*in nomine*' as an abbreviated but potent Christian phrase.

26 Campbell 1987.
27 Ó Carragáin 2005.
28 James et al. (eds) 2008, 208.
29 Ó Carragáin 2005, 259.
30 *Ibid.*
31 *Ibid.*, 282.
32 *Ibid.*, 120–26.
33 This is probably overly simplistic, given that a full 422-page monograph on the stone has been published recently (James et al. [eds] 2008).
34 *Ibid.*
35 On some cross-slabs an implicit connection is made between the motifs used to decorate the cross also being used to decorate the symbols: for example Aberlemno 2 where the notched rectangle above the 'battle scene' contains the same triple spirals as those which decorate the roundel on the front of the cross (Henderson and Henderson 2004, 179). This relationship might lead us to speculate about the decoration of the centre of the lost cross of Hilton of Cadboll.
36 Foster 1996, 93–95.
37 Henderson 2008b, 179 in James et al. (eds) 2008.
38 Kantorowicz 1944.
39 Henderson and Henderson 2004, 179.
40 Henderson 2008b, 184; see Alcock 1993 for terminology of 'athwart' versus 'side-saddle'.
41 Stevenson (1993), however, saw it as a Persian deity.
42 Kantorowicz 1944, 217; Henderson 2001.
43 *Hosanna filio David: Benedictus qui venit in nomine Domini* (Matthew 21: 9).
44 Kantorowicz 1944, 217.
45 The classic paper on the subject (Kantorowicz 1944) outlined two basic ways of representing an *Adventus*, termed 'historical' and 'eschatological' models.
46 *Ibid.*, 217–20.
47 Mathews 1999.
48 The 4th-century sarcophagus of Junius Bassus shows a classic example of the Entry into Jerusalem. This realistic depiction of one of the pivotal moments of the New Testament proved exceptionally popular and ensured the integration of Late Antique *Adventus* into early Christian art. See Mathews 1999 and MacCormack 1972.
49 Foster 1996, 74–75.
50 Mathews 1999, 115–41.
51 Henderson and Henderson 2004, 201–202.
52 Carrington 1996.
53 Roddy 2001.
54 *Ibid.*, 174.
55 Tamburr 2007.
56 O'Carragáin 2005.
57 See Allen and Anderson 1903, and Mack 2007. One major issue with Pictish symbols is that there is no agreement as to what the range of symbols are.
58 The double-disc and Z-rod has become common parlance for what might be better described as a double-disc and double-bent rod. The majority of double-bent rods would be more usefully described as S-rods or reverse Z-rods, as this would better describe the orientation of the rod. Almost all Class I uses of this symbol are S-rods and most of the Class II cross-slabs too. This might seem like a minor point, but conventions in symbol-carving and variations away from them may be one clue to a relative chronology or at least relative competence. One of the few examples that has a Z-rod is the Drosten stone from St Vigeans whose inscription Clancy (1993) tentatively dated to the mid-9th century AD. After such consistency for several centuries of use, the script, or at least one of its most common symbols, does not appear to be have been transmitted correctly by the mid-9th century AD at St Vigeans.
59 In the same way, the bottom half of the slab is tied together by the theme of Baptism through the harried deer, the four rivers of paradise springing out from the centre of the spiral panel and the sprouting vegetal motif of the lower border. All three motifs – deer, four rivers of paradise and vegetal/tree of life – can be seen together on contemporary apse mosaics in Rome, for example San Clemenza.

60 Allen and Anderson 1903; and many consider it obsolete. (See Henderson and Henderson 2004, 10–12.)
61 Noble and Gondek 2010.
62 St Vigeans 1 is not included because it is on a slightly smaller scale and broken, the symbols are similar (although the crescent has no v-rod), and there is a harried deer and rider. This has been dated to 837/42 by inscription. (See Clancy 1993.)
63 Henderson and Henderson 2004, 179.
64 Meyer 2010.
65 O'Riain 1972.
66 Clancy 2008.
67 Yet politically St Andrews and Iona would have frequently been under Pictish political authority. (See Clancy 2004.) The Class I and Class II differences in distribution in Fife may reflect the changes in 7th- to 8th-century political arrangements on the southern boundary of Pictland.
68 Fraser and Halliday 2010.
69 *Ibid.*, 307.
70 Clarke 2007.
71 In a pithy summary of the symbols, Allen and Anderson (1903, 109) observed that 'the groups of symbols on the upright cross-slabs are often numerically much larger'.
72 North of the Mounth – Golspie, Ulbster, Skinnet, Rosemarkie, Hilton (if the interlace roundels are an innovative Class II symbol), Tarbat in inscription position, Glenferness, Mortlach?, Dyce, Migvie. There is a small cluster in Strathmore – Glamis 1 and 2, Eassie?, St Vigeans 1 and Meigle 1; in Perth and Kinross, there are Fowlis Wester, Dunfallandy, St Madoes, Gask? (see Fraser 2008).
73 Allen and Anderson (1903) thought that the symbol system originated in Aberdeenshire, and Isobel Henderson (1958) the firthlands north of Inverness.
74 Charles-Edwards 2000.
75 *Ibid.*
76 Alice Blackwell, pers. comm. Allen and Anderson (1903) were much more inclusive than more recent commentators. The latest RCAHMS survey of Pictish symbols (Fraser 2008) seems to only use Class I symbols, although they never clearly state their rationale.
77 Forsyth 1997.
78 These were possibly of Christian significance, similar to the three orders of creation Stevenson (1974) observed in the filigree of the Hunterston brooch.
79 Allen and Anderson 1903, 109.
80 Allen and Anderson (*ibid.*) did not define what time-frame they considered archaic, but they may have thought it earlier than the Burrian phalange, which has been radiocarbon dated to AD 570–655.
81 Imer 2010.
82 Brown 2003.
83 Kelly 1993.
84 Henderson and Henderson 2004, 175.
85 Gondek 2006, 129–33. Do the many fragments of free-standing crosses in Pictland that match Kelly's form for Irish crosses factionally mark Christian communities who used or were influenced by sculptural schools with Columban connections?
86 Henderson and Henderson 2004, 190–91.
87 Forsyth 1995.
88 Dupplin-Benvie (Alcock 2003). This style of moustache had become popular among contemporary Carolingian nobility. The Germanic world was riddled with ideological associations and identities that surrounded certain hairstyles (see Dutton 2004).
89 Forsyth 1995.
90 Henderson and Henderson 2004, 190–91
91 *Ibid.*, 189.
92 Newman 2009.
93 Recently summarised by Foster (in press).
94 For example, the succession of structures at Uley, Gloucestershire (Woodward and Leach 1993), and in general the adoption of the *basilica*, the Roman meeting place, as the preferred building style for Christian worship.
95 Fraser 2009.
96 Forsyth 1998.

97 See Alcock 2003, 75–76. The Picts seem to have preferred Old Testament or Apocryphal tales.
98 Early Medieval controversies about the divine and human status of Christ, such as iconoclasm, may also have played some role in the issue of how to depict religious scenes.
99 This is what Peter Brown referred to as 'micro-Christianities' (Brown 2003).
100 *Ibid.*, 360–61.
101 Mac Lean 1993, 247.
102 Herren and Brown 2002.
103 Sharpe (trans.) 1995.
104 Charles-Edwards 2000, 195.
105 Armit 2005, 86–88. The stereotype of head-hunting warriors was used by classical writers in descriptions of many barbarian nations. There was a widespread belief in the ancient world about the head as the seat of the soul. The archaeological evidence stretches beyond the limits of 'Celtic Europe' and there is also a surprising amount of evidence for similar practices within the Roman Empire.
106 Armit and Ginn 2007; Shapland and Armit 2012.
107 These are different attitudes when compared to Wales and Brittany, where saints' bodies were not fragmented, and these suggest that the different heritages of the Celtic-speaking areas and different history of incorporation in the Roman Empire might have influenced these later practices (Edwards 2001).
108 Watson 1926; Taylor, pers. comm.
109 Drunemeton (Green 1992).
110 Barrow 1998a; Taylor, pers. comm.
111 Simpson 1970.
112 This is similar to the Norrie's Law hoard being described in initial antiquarian reports as silver armour.
113 NMS X.FA 109.
114 Castle Newe: British Museum accession no. 1946.4–2.2.
115 Taylor, pers. comm. The origin of the *nemeton* place-name element must pre-date Gaelic linguistic expansion that shaped later Medieval Scotland and saw the demise of Pictish language and culture.
116 What the original feature or site was that denoted the term *nemeton* is difficult to pinpoint, but the clusters of compound place-names indicate that whatever the focus was, the importance of the ideas associated with these places meant that they could come to define quite a wide surrounding region. This would consequently justify a wider archaeological survey of the surrounding landscapes.
117 The original has gone missing and the only record is preserved in a cast in the National Museums Scotland (X.IB 216).
118 Barrow 1998a, 27.
119 Watson 1926.
120 Feachem 1966.
121 Childe 1935.
122 Carver 2009.
123 Rivers are mentioned in Bede as sites of mass Baptism and the initial act of conversion in rivers and holy springs may have been a convenient point of contact between old and new through the continuing significance of water. The prehistoric reverence for springs is an area that still requires testing through excavation, as does the Christian veneration of holy wells. Of course, practices like Baptism or ritual cleansing might not leave any material evidence.
124 The exception is the Latin inscriptions of Southern Scotland (Forsyth 2005) and particularly famous examples such as the 5th-century Latinus stone from Whithorn – Scotland's first named Christian (*Ibid.*, 115). These are part of the earliest post-Roman phase of conversion of Brittonic-speaking people stretching from the Isle of Man to Wales, Somerset, Devon, Cornwall and Brittany.
125 Similar processes have been noted in Ireland (Carey 1999) and this may help to explain the early emphasis on the monastic model for Christian communities in Britain and Ireland (see Carver 2009).
126 Laing 2010.
127 Heather 1994; Fraser 2008.
128 Heald 2005 (PhD thesis).
129 Hunter and Painter (eds) 2013.

130 The forthcoming comprehensive publication of the hoard (*ibid*.) will explore these issues through more detailed analysis than we have space for here.
131 These include enamelled zoomorphic stick-pins, rosette-headed pins, proto-hand-pins, and zoomorphic penannular brooches.
132 Burley 1956.
133 It could be the pay-off from civilian southern Britain, to a potential military threat from the north, or it could be payment for military service given to a group of northern (Christian?) Britons based in the Lothians, who could act as a buffer against the raids of the Picts. The military equipment in the hoard might support the latter interpretation, but our lack of historical sources stops us from deciding with any certainty. The full publication of the hoard will undoubtedly draw more nuance from this rather bald historical sketch (that also lacks any real historical support).
134 One of these – Greenlaw, Berwickshire – is lost.
135 Thomas 1995, 5–6.
136 Ross 1959; Youngs 2013.
137 Even basic details, such as the number of chains, has been misreported. One of the more recent commentaries (Breeze 1998) got the accounts of discovery hopelessly confused and ended up with a total of thirteen instead of eleven. For an authoritative statement and accurate list, see Youngs 2013.
138 Stevenson 1956.
139 However, these solid foundations are by no means the final word. As has been shown here, even more can be said about how these sculptured stones functioned in practice.
140 Troelan and Tate 2009.
141 Hobbs 2005.
142 From the 5th to the 9th centuries AD, it has been assumed that the high-quality Roman silver originally available in Scotland was gradually debased. This assumption is based on only one previous compositional analysis of the brooches in the St Ninian's Isle hoard, where the silver was of remarkably low quality (in some cases less than 30%) and dated to the late 9th century AD (McKerrell, appendix B, in Small et al. 1973). The NMS Glenmorangie Research Project programme of analysis hopes to widen out and investigate these wider issues surrounding the long-term use and availability of silver from the 5th to 9th centuries AD.
143 Close-Brooks 1986.
144 See chapter 8 on 'Losses' in Henderson and Henderson 2004, especially pp. 221–25.
145 Sally Foster, pers. comm.
146 Buist 1839.
147 Blackwell and Goldberg 2013.
148 Many cross-slabs will have been damaged or destroyed during the Reformation as changes in material practice and veneration of objects swept through the later Medieval Christian world. Much of the wealth of the Church, including reliquaries and liturgical objects, will also have been seized and melted down. Catholic countries have tended to preserve more ecclesiastical treasures.
149 Caldwell 2001.
150 One of the Continental house-shaped shrines remains part of an abbey treasury in Italy, appearing still to contain various relics.
151 Burke 2006, 129–34.
152 Although substantial rectangular buildings were built in Britain during the Neolithic period, roundhouses had been the dominant architectural form since the Middle Bronze Age.
153 Henshall 1956; Thomas 1971, 48–51.
154 *Ibid*.
155 Maldonado 2011 has gathered together the radiocarbon dates and information about these late prehistoric burials.
156 Ashmore 1980.
157 *Ibid*., table 1.
158 Maldonado 2011.
159 *Ibid*., 261: Maldonado has suggested that, in the early phases, the age profile is young adults and only becomes more representative of wider society in the later phases.
160 Henshall 1956; Thomas 1971, 48–51.
161 Maldonado 2011 shows colour-coded plans that demonstrate development of cemeteries over the centuries of interment.

Below: The rotary quern from Dunadd, Argyll, taken from a different angle (see Fig. 3.8).

162 Thomas (1971) saw this as a founder saint, or the missionary responsible for the conversion of the community, but the concept of a founder is plausible without this figure having to be a Christian, especially in the context of emerging lineages and increasingly hierarchical social structures.

163 Driscoll 1998.

164 For example, the gold bullet coins from Gaul that were part of the Netherurd hoard dating to the 1st century BC (see Feachem 1966).

165 Coins were used in existing practices of hoarding and votive deposition (see Hunter 2001).

EARLY MEDIEVAL SCOTLAND

CONCLUSION
Early Medieval Scotland

Objects were fundamental parts of people's lives in Early Medieval Scotland. How objects were used, how they were – and are – interpreted and how they were disposed of can reveal much about individuals, communities and ideas in the past. A myriad of stories about the people of Early Medieval Scotland emerge from the objects that have survived. Artefacts should never be regarded as just providing pretty pictures in history books. Instead they should be allowed to reveal some of their own stories about people who lived in the past, the people the objects belonged to, the communities that created, inherited and discarded them, and the ideas that objects can embody. The primary aim of this book has been to show the wide range of topics and questions that we can ask of the material traces of this important period of Scotland's past.

As the detritus of past lives, the mass of archaeological evidence can be used to construct fragmentary jigsaws of everyday activities. But much of the evidence is missing, especially from everyday organic artefacts such as textiles, clothing, bone, leather and wooden objects that would have made up the bulk of people's possessions. What often survives in archaeological deposits is the result of specific moments, perhaps sometimes life-defining events – at least for the lives of the objects if not their owners.

This evidence can provide a bridge from the present to the memories, thoughts, knowledge, values, beliefs and ideas of people in the past. Some objects might be created for a particular purpose, with a specific idea in mind, by a particular craftsman, and supported by a network of supply and assistance. However, it is largely through ownership, associations with people, places and communities, and how they were put to use by them, that the objects can communicate ideas. Objects themselves do not contain universal meaning; meaning is generated through the use of the object. Whether in the present or the past, people will use the same object differently and attach a variety of subjective meanings to it because of each person's unique background, circumstances, experiences and perception of the material world.

Opposite: A symbol-stone on Peterhead Farm, Gleneagles, Perthshire.

Objects could have long lives during the Early Medieval period. Many will have lasted for more than one lifetime and been owned by more than one person, as we can see with the Hunterston brooch and its runic inscription added more than two centuries after its creation. Objects could carry the ideas and the ideologies they embody into succeeding generations through curation by individuals and their inheritance by new communities. But like historical documents, objects are also open to rejection, reinterpretation, misunderstanding and misappropriation by succeeding generations, in the past and in the present. We see this in Late Roman silver being melted down for the production of new Early Medieval objects or the adoption of Pictish symbols onto Christian monuments, and the diverse interpretations of this transformation.

Many of the objects featured in this book could be used to illustrate any one of the three interwoven themes of individuals, communities and ideas. For instance, the Hilton of Cadboll cross-slab is a monument that has literally set Early Medieval ideas and ideologies in stone. It features extensive and complex Christian imagery, realising the doctrine of the religion that had spread across Scotland in the preceding centuries. It combines motifs and ideas that are international and local, old and new. It was made for and by groups of people, a church and its followers. It features the newly adopted art of depicting people, albeit for very particular means. Certainly this one object is capable of drawing together our three perspectives.

We are not suggesting that the framework of this book – individuals, communities, and ideas and ideologies – is the only way to study the period. While it provided a framework which suited our material evidence, others might supplement the topics, or provide a different framework altogether. But we believe that one viewpoint will only ever provide a fragmentary picture – the past is better understood through a kaleidoscope of perspectives.

Bibliography

Abdy, R and Williams, G 2006. 'A catalogue of hoards and single finds from the British Isles, c. AD 410–675', in Cook and Williams (eds) 2006, 11–73.

Abernethy, D 2009. 'Bruach an Druimein, Poltalloch, Argyll: excavations directed by the late Eric Cregeen, 1960–2'. Scottish Archaeological Internet Report 27.

Aitchison, N 2003. *The Picts and Scots at war*. Sutton Publishing.

Aitken, W G 1955. 'Excavations of a chapel at St Ninian's Point, Isle of Bute', *Transactions of the Buteshire Natural History Society* 14, 62–76.

Alcock, L 1988. 'The activities of potentates in Celtic Britain, AD 500–800: a positivist approach', in Driscoll and Nieke (eds) 1988, 22–46.

Alcock, L 1993a. *The neighbours of the Picts: Angles, Britons and Scots at war and at home.* Rosemarkie: Groam House Museum.

Alcock, L 1993b. 'Image and icon in Pictish sculpture', in Spearman and Higgitt (eds) 1993, 16–26.

Alcock, L 1995. *Cadbury Castle, Somerset: the early medieval archaeology.* Cardiff: University of Wales Press.

Alcock, L 1996. 'Ur-symbols in the pictographic-system of the Picts', *Pictish Arts Society Journal* 9, 2–5.

Alcock, L 1998. 'From realism to caricature: reflections on Insular depictions of animals and people', *Proceedings of the Society of Antiquaries of Scotland* 128, 513–36.

Alcock, L 2003. *Kings and Warriors, Craftsmen and Priests in Northern Britain AD 550–850*. Edinburgh: Society of Antiquaries of Scotland.

Alcock, L and Alcock, E A 1992. 'Reconnaissance excavations on early historic fortifications and other royal sites in Scotland', 1974–84, 5: 'A, Excavations and other fieldwork at Forteviot, Perthshire, 1981'; 'B, Excavations at Urquhart Castle, Inverness-shire, 1983'; 'C, Excavations at Dunottar, Kincardineshire, 1984', *Proceedings of the Society of Antiquaries of Scotland* 122, 215–87.

Alcock, L, Alcock, E A and Foster, S M 1986. 'Reconnaissance excavations on early historic fortifications and other royal sites in Scotland, 1974–84: 1: 'Excavations near St Abb's Head, Berwickshire, 1980', *Proceedings of the Society of Antiquaries of Scotland* 116, 255–79, fiche 1, D1–G9.

Alexander, D 2005. 'Redcastle, Lunan Bay, Angus: the excavation of an Iron Age timber-lined souterrain and a Pictish barrow cemetery', *Proceedings of the Society of Antiquaries of Scotland* 135, 41–118.

Armit, I 2005. *Celtic Scotland: Iron Age Scotland in its European Context*. London: Batsford.

Allen, J R and Anderson, J 1903. *The Early Christian Monuments of Scotland.* Edinburgh: Society of Antiquaries of Scotland, reprinted 1993. Balgavies: Pinkfoot Press.

Allen, J R and Anderson, J 1903a. 'Part II: general results arrived at from the archaeological survey of the early Christian monuments of Scotland', in *The Early Christian Monuments of Scotland*. Edinburgh: Society of Antiquaries of Scotland, 1–414.

Allen, J R and Anderson, J 1903b, 'Part III: classified, illustrated, descriptive list of the monuments, arranged by counties', in *The Early Christian Monuments of Scotland*. Edinburgh: Society of Antiquaries of Scotland, 1–518.

Armit, I 2012. 'Headhunting and social power in Iron Age Europe', in Moore and Armada (eds) 2012, 590–607.

Armit, I, Campbell, E and Dunwell, A 2008. 'Excavation of an Iron Age, early historic and medieval settlement and metalworking site at Eilean Olabhat, North Uist', *Proceedings of the Society of Antiquaries of Scotland* 138, 27–104.

Armit, I and Ginn, V 2007. 'Beyond the grave: human remains from domestic contexts in Atlantic Scotland', *Proceedings of the Society of Antiquaries of Scotland* 73, 115–36.

Ashbee, J and Luxford, J M (eds) 2013. *Newcastle and Northumberland*, BAA Conference Transactions XXXVI.

Ashmore, P 1980. 'Low cairns, long cists and symbol stones',

Proceedings of the Society of Antiquaries of Scotland 110, 346–55.

Bagnoli, M 2011, 'The stuff of heaven: materials and craftsmanship in Medieval reliquaries', in Bagnoli et al. 2010, 137–47.

Bagnoli, M, Klein, H, Mann, G and Robinson, J (eds) 2011. *Treasures of Heaven: Saints, Relics, and Devotion in Medieval Europe*. The Cleveland Museum of Art, The Walters Art Museum and The British Museum. New Haven: Yale University Press.

Ballin Smith, B (ed.) 1994. *Howe, four millennia of Orkney prehistory: excavations 1978–1982*. Edinburgh: Society of Antiquaries of Scotland, monograph 9.

Barber, J 1981. 'Some observations on early Christian footwear', *Journal of the Cork Historical and Archaeological Society* 86, 103–106.

Barnes, M P and Page, R I 2006. *The Scandinavian Runic Inscriptions of Britain*. Runrön 19 (Uppsala: Institutionen for nordiska språk, Uppsala Universitet).

Barnwell, P (ed.) (in press). *Buildings for Worship in Britain: Celtic and Anglo-Saxon*.

Barrow, G W S 1998a. 'Religion in Scotland on the Eve of Christianity', in Borchardt and Bunz (eds) 1998, 25–32.

Barrow, G W S 1998b. 'The uses of place-names and Scottish history – pointers and pitfalls', in Taylor (ed.) 1998, 54–73.

Benton, S 1931. 'The excavation of the Sculptor's Cave, Covesea, Morayshire', *Proceedings of the Society of Antiquaries of Scotland* 65 (1930–31), 177–216.

Berg, G 1951. 'Wooden traps', *Folk-Liv* 14–15 (1950–51), 31–59.

Binski, P and Noel, W (eds) 2001. *New offerings, ancient treasures: studies in medieval art for George Henderson*. Stroud: Sutton Publishing.

Bitel, L M 2004. 'Ekphrasis at Kildare: the imaginative architecture of a seventh-century hagiographer', *Speculum* 79/3, 605–27.

Black, G F and Thomas, N W 1903. *Examples of printed folk-lore concerning the Orkney & Shetland Islands*. London: Folk-Lore Society and David Nutt.

Blackwell, A 2010. 'Anglo-Saxon Dunbar, East Lothian: a brief reassessment of the archaeological evidence and some chronological implications', *Medieval Archaeology* 54, 361–71.

Blackwell, A 2011. 'The iconography of the Hunterston brooch and related early medieval material', *Proceedings of the Society of Antiquaries of Scotland* 141.

Blackwell, A and Goldberg, M 2013. 'The different histories of the Norrie's Law Hoard', Proceedings of the 2011 Insular Art Conference, University of York.

Blindheim, M 1984. 'A house-shaped Irish-Scots reliquary in Bologna, and its place among the other reliquaries', *Acta Archaeologica* 55, 1–53.

Bone, P 1989. 'The development of Anglo-Saxon swords from the fifth to the eleventh centuries', in Hawkes (ed.) 1989, 63–70.

Borchardt, K and Bunz, E (eds) 1998. *Forschungen zur Reichs-, Papst- und Landesgeschichte*, part 1. Stuttgart: Hiersemann.

Bourke, C 1983. 'The hand-bells of the early Scottish church', *Proceedings of the Society of Antiquaries of Scotland* 113, 464–68.

Bourke, C (ed.) 1995. *From the Isles of the North: Medieval Art in Ireland and Britain*. Belfast: HMSO.

Bowes, K 2008. *Private worship, public values, and religious change in Late Antiquity*. Cambridge: Cambridge University Press.

Boyle, J W 2004. 'Lest the lowliest be forgotten: locating the impoverished in early medieval Ireland', *International Journal of Historical Archaeology* 8: 2, 85–99.

Bramwell, D 1994. 'The bird remains', in Ballin Smith (ed.) 1994, 153–57.

Breeze, A 1998. 'Pictish chains and Welsh forgeries', *Proceedings of the Society of Antiquaries of Scotland* 128, 481–84.

Brown, P 2003. *The Rise of Western Christendom*. Oxford: Blackwell.

Brown, T J 1972. 'Northumbria and The Book of Kells', *Anglo-Saxon England* 1, 219–46.

Bruce-Mitford, R 2005. *The Corpus of Late Celtic Hanging Bowls*. Oxford: Oxford University Press.

Buckley, A (ed.) 2015. *Hibernia Cantans: Music, Liturgy, and the Veneration of Irish Saints in Medieval Europe*. Turnhout: Brepols.

Buist, G 1839. *The Silver Armour of Norrie's Law*. Cupar: Fifeshire Journal Office.

Burke, H 2006. 'Ideology and the material culture of life and death', in Hall and Silliman (eds) 2006, 128–46.

Burley, E 1956. 'A catalogue and survey of the metal-work from Traprain Law', *Proceedings of the Society of Antiquaries of Scotland* 89, 118–226.

Caldwell, D 2001. 'The Monymusk reliquary: the Breccbennach of St Columba?', *Proceedings of the Society of Antiquaries of Scotland* 131, 267–82.

Campbell, E 1987. 'A cross-marked quern from Dunadd and other evidence for relations between Dunadd and Iona', *Proceedings of the Society of Antiquaries of Scotland* 117, 105–17.

Campbell, E 1996. 'Trade in the Dark Age West. A peripheral activity?', in Crawford (ed.) 1996, paper 6, 79–91.

Campbell, E 2001. 'Were the Scots Irish?', *Antiquity* 75, 285–92.

Campbell, E 2007. *Continental and Mediterranean imports to Atlantic Britain and Ireland, AD 400–800*. York: Council of British Archaeological Research Report 157.

Campbell, E and Heald, A 2007. 'A "Pictish" brooch mould from North Uist: implications for the organisation of non-ferrous metalworking in the later 1st millennium AD', *Medieval Archaeology* 51, 172–78.

Campbell, E and Lane, A 2000. *Dunadd: An Early Dalriadic Capital*. Oxford: Oxbow Books.

Carey, J 1998. *King of Mysteries: Early Irish Religious Writings*. Dublin: Four Courts Press.

Carey, J 1999. *A single ray of the sun: religious speculation in early Ireland*. Andover and Aberystwyth: Celtic Studies Publications.

Carr, R D, Tester, A and Murphy, P 1988. 'The Middle-Saxon settlement at Staunch Meadow, Brandon', *Antiquity* 62, 371–77.

Carrington, A 1996. 'The horseman and the falcon: mounted falconers in Pictish sculpture', *Proceedings of the Society of Antiquaries of Scotland* 126, 456–68.

Carver, M 2004. 'An Iona of the east: the early medieval monastery at Portmahomack, Tarbat Ness', *Medieval Archaeology* 48, 1–30.

Carver, M 2008. *Portmahomack: Monastery of the Picts*. Edinburgh: Edinburgh University Press.

Carver, M 2009. 'Early Scottish monasteries and Prehistory: a preliminary dialogue', *Scottish Historical Review* 88, 332–51.

Carver, M and Spall, C 2004. 'Excavating a parchmenerie: archaelogical correlates of making parchment at the Pictish monastery at Portmahomack, Easter Ross', *Proceedings of the Society of Antiquaries of Scotland* 134, 183–200.

Case, H 2003. 'Beaker presence at Wilsford 7', *Wiltshire Archaeological & Natural History Magazine* 96, 161–94.

Casey, J 1984. 'Roman coinage of the fourth century in Scotland', in Miket and Burgess (eds) 1984, 295–304.

Cavers, G 2010. *Crannogs and later prehistoric settlement in western Scotland*. Oxford: British Archaeological Reports, British Series 510.

Charles-Edwards, T 2000. *Early Christian Ireland*. Cambridge: Cambridge University Press.

Charles-Gaffiot, J 2011. *Trônes en majesté: l'autorité et son symbole*. Paris: Cerf.

Childe, G V 1935. 'Excavation of the vitrified fort of Finavon, Angus', *Proceedings of the Society of Antiquaries of Scotland* 69, 49–80.

Christison, D and Anderson, J 1899. 'On the recently excavated fort on Castle Law, Abernethy, Perthshire', *Proceedings of the Society of Antiquaries of Scotland* 33 (1898–99), 13–33.

Christison, D, Anderson, J and Ross, T 1905. 'Report on the Society's excavations of forts on the Poltalloch Estate, Argyll, in 1904–05', *Proceedings of the Society of Antiquaries of Scotland* 39 (1904–05), 259–322.

Clancy, T O 1993. 'The Drosten Stone: a new reading', *Proceedings of the Society of Antiquaries of Scotland* 123, 345–53.

Clancy, T O (ed.) 1998. *The Triumph Tree: Scotland's Earliest Poetry AD 550–1350*. Edinburgh: Canongate Press.

Clancy, T O 2001. 'The real St Ninian', *Innes Review* 52, 1–28.

Clancy, T O 2004. 'Iona in the kingdom of the Picts: a note', *Innes Review* 55, 73–76.

Clancy, T O 2008. 'Deer and the early church in north-eastern Scotland', in Forsyth (ed.) 2008, 363–97.

Clancy, T O and Márkus, G 1995. *Iona: The Earliest Poetry of a Celtic Monastery*. Edinburgh: Edinburgh University Press.

Clarke, D 2001. 'Defining and integrating sequences in site analysis: the evidence from hillforts and other sites', *Oxford Journal of Archaeology* 20 (3), 293–306.

Clarke, D 2007. 'Reading the multiple lives of Pictish Symbol Stones', *Medieval Archaeology* 51, 19–39.

Clarke, D 2008. *St Ninian's Isle Treasure*. Edinburgh: National Museums Scotland. With photography by Neil McLean.

Clarke, D and Heald, A 2008. 'A new date for Pictish Symbols', in *Medieval Archaeology* 52, 291–95.

Close-Brooks, J 1986. 'Excavations at Clatchard Craig, Fife', *Proceedings of the Society of Antiquaries of Scotland* 116, 117–84, fiche 1: B1–C14.

Coles, F R 1901. 'Report on the stone circles of the northeast of Scotland, Inverurie District, obtained under the Gunning Fellowship with measured plans and drawings', *Proceedings of the Society of Antiquaries of Scotland* 35 (1900–01), 187–248.

Colgrave, B (trans.) 1999. *Bede's The Ecclesiastical History of the English People*. Oxford: Oxford University Press.

Colgrave, B and Mynors, R A B (eds) 1969. *Bede's Ecclesiastical History of the English People* (revised edition 1992). Oxford: Oxford University Press.

Cook, B and Williams, G (eds) 2006. *Coinage and history in the North Sea world, c.AD 500–1250: essays in honour of Marion Archibald*. Leiden and Boston: Brill.

Coon, L 2008. 'Gender and the body', in Nobel and Smith (eds) 2008, 433–52.

Cooney, G, Becker, K, Coles, J, Ryan, M and Sievers, S (eds) 2009. *Relics of old decency: archaeological studies in later prehistory. Festschrift for Barry Raftery*. Dublin: Wordwell.

Cormack, W F 1989. 'Two recent finds of exotic porphyry in Galloway', *Transactions of the Dumfries & Galloway Natural History & Antiquarian Society*, 3rd series, 64: 43.

Cowley, D C 1996. 'Square barrows in Dumfries and Galloway', *Transactions of the Dumfries & Galloway Natural History & Antiquarian Society*, 3rd series, 71, 107–13.

Cramp, R 2006. *Wearmouth and Jarrow monastic sites*, vol. 2. London: English Heritage.

Craw, J H 1930. 'Excavations at Dunadd and other sites on the Poltalloch Estate', *Proceedings of the Society of Antiquaries of Scotland* 64 (1929–30), 111–46.

Crawford, B (ed.) 1994. *Scotland in Dark Ages Europe*. University of St Andrews: The Committee for Dark Age Studies.

Crawford, B (ed.) 1996. *Scotland in Dark Age Britain*. St Andrews: St John's House, paper 6.

Crawford, S 1999. *Childhood in Anglo-Saxon England*. Stroud: Sutton Publishing.

Crone, A 1993. 'Crannogs and chronologies', *Proceedings of the Society of Antiquaries of Scotland* 123, 245–54.

Crone, A 2000. *The History of a Scottish Lowland Crannog: Excavations at Buiston, Ayrshire 1989–90*. Edinburgh: Scottish Trust for Archaeological Research (STAR), monograph 4.

Crone, A and Campbell, E 2005. *A crannog of the 1st millennium AD: excavations by Jack Scott at Loch Glashan, Argyll, 1960*. Edinburgh: Society of Antiquaries of Scotland.

Crowfoot, G M and Harden, D B 1931. 'Early Byzantine and later glass lamps', *The Journal of Egyptian Archaeology* 17, 196–208, pls 28–30.

Cruickshank, G D R 1985. *Nechtansmere 1300: a commemoration: an essay on the Pictish victory at the battle of Nechtansmere or Linn Garan, fought at Dunnichen in Angus on 20 May 685*. Forfar: Fofar & District History Society.

Cruickshank, G D R 1999. *The Battle of Dunnichen: an account of the Pictish victory at the Battle of Dunnichen, also known as Nechtansmere, fought on the 20th of May 685, with an appendix on the Dunnichen stone*, second edition. Balgavies: Pinkfoot Press.

Crummy, N (ed.) 2005. *Image, Craft and the Classical World*. Montagnac: Monograph Instrumentum 29.

Cummins, J 2001. *The hound and the hawk: the art of medieval hunting*, paperback edition. London: Phoenix Press.

Curle, A O 1905. 'Description of the fortifications on Ruberslaw, Roxburghshire, and notices of Roman remains found there', *Proceedings of the Society of Antiquaries of Scotland* 39 (1904–05), 219–32.

Curle, A O 1920, 'Report of the excavation on Traprain Law in the summer of 1919', *Proceedings of the Society of Antiquaries of Scotland* 54, 102–24.

Curle, A O 1923. *The Treasure of Traprain: a Scottish hoard of Roman silver plate.* Glasgow: MacLehose, Jackson & Co.

Curle, C L 1982. *Pictish and Norse finds from the Brough of Birsay 1934–74.* Edinburgh: Society of Antiquaries of Scotland, monograph 1.

De Waal, E 2010. *The Hare with the Amber Eyes: A Hidden Inheritance.* London: Chatto and Windus.

Dockrill, S J, Bond, J M, Turner, V E, Brown, L D, Bashford, D J, Cussans, J E and Nicholson, R A. 2010. *Excavations at Old Scatness, Shetland, volume 1: the Pictish village and Viking settlement.* Lerwick: Shetland Heritage Publications.

Dodwell, C 1982. *Anglo-Saxon Art: a New Perspective.* Manchester: Manchester University Press.

Downes, J and Ritchie, A (eds) 2003. *Sea Change. Orkney and Northern Europe in the later Iron Age AD 300–800.* Balgavies: Pinkfoot Press.

Driscoll, S T 1992. 'Discourse on the frontiers of history: material culture and social reproduction in early Scotland', *Historical Archaeology* 26, 12–25.

Driscoll, S T 1998. 'Picts and prehistory: cultural resource management in Early Medieval Scotland', *World Archaeology* 30(1), 142–58.

Driscoll, S T 2010. 'Pictish archaeology: persistent problems and structural solutions', in Driscoll et al. (eds) 2010, 245–79.

Driscoll, S T and Nieke, M (eds) 1988. *Power and politics in Early Medieval Britain and Ireland.* Edinburgh: Edinburgh University Press.

Driscoll, S T, Geddes, J and Hall, M (eds) 2010. *Pictish Progress.* Leiden: Brill.

Dutton, P E 2004. *Charlemagne's Mustache and other Cultural Clusters of a Dark Age.* Basingstoke/New York: Palgrave Macmillan.

Eckhardt, H 2002. *Illuminating Roman Britain.* Montagnac: Editions Monique Mergoil.

Edwards, A J H 1925. 'Excavation of a chambered cairn at Ham, Caithness, and of a hut-circle and two earth-houses at Freswick Links, Caithness, obtained under the Gunning Fellowship, with a note on a winged horse carved on one of the lintels in the earth-house at Crichton Mains, Midlothian', *Proceedings of the Society of Antiquaries of Scotland* 59 (1924–25), 85–95.

Edwards, N 2001. 'Early medieval inscribed stones and stone sculpture in Wales: context and function', *Medieval Archaeology* 45, 15–39.

Edwards, N 2002. 'Celtic saints and Early Medieval archaeology', in Thacker and Sharpe (eds) 2002, 225–65.

Edwards, N 2007. *A corpus of early medieval inscribed stones and stone sculpture in Wales: volume II, south-west Wales.* Cardiff: University of Wales Press.

Edwards, N (ed.) 2009. *The archaeology of the early medieval Celtic churches.* Leeds: Maney Publishing and the Society for Medieval Archaeology.

Ellis-Fermor, U (trans.) 1958. *Henrik Ibsen, The Master Builder and other plays.* London: Penguin.

Etchingham, C and Swift C 2004. 'English and Pictish terms for brooch in an 8th-century Irish law-text', *Medieval Archaeology* 2004, 31–49.

Farmer, D (ed.) 1988. *The age of Bede*, 2nd revised edition. London: Penguin.

Farmer, D 2004. *The Oxford Dictionary of Saints.* Oxford: Oxford University Press.

Feachem, R W 1966. 'The hillforts of northern Britain', in Rivet (ed.) 1966, 59–87.

Fisher, I 2001. *Early Medieval Sculpture in the West Highlands and Islands.* Edinburgh: Royal Commission on the Ancient and Historical Monuments of Scotland and the Society of Antiquaries of Scotland.

Fitzgerald, M 1997. 'Insular dress in early medieval Ireland', *Bulletin of the John Rylands University Library* 79(3), 251, note 6.

Forsyth, K 1995. 'The inscriptions of the Dupplin Cross', in Bourke (ed.) 1995, 237–44.

Forsyth, K 1997. 'Some thoughts on Pictish symbols as a formal writing system', in Henry (ed.) 1997, 85–98.

Forsyth, K 1998. 'Literacy in Pictland', in Pryce (ed.) 1998, 39–61.

Forsyth, K 2005. '*HIC MEMORIA PERPETUA*: the inscribed stones of sub-Roman southern Scotland', in Foster and Cross (eds) 2005, 113–34.

Forsyth, K (ed.) 2008. *Studies in the Book of Deer.* Dublin: Four Courts Press.

Forsyth, K 2009. 'The Latinus stone: Whithorn's earliest Christian monument', in Murray (ed.) 2009, 483: 19–41.

Forsyth, K and Tedeschi, C 2008. 'Text-inscribed slates' in Lowe 2008, 128–51.

Foster, S M 1996. *Picts, Gaels and Scots*. London: Batsford.

Foster, S M 1998a. 'Before Alba: Pictish and Dál Riata power centres from the fith to late ninth centuries AD', in S M Foster et al. (eds) 1998, 1–31.

Foster, S M (ed.) 1998b. *The St Andrews sarcophagus: a Pictish masterpiece and its international connections*. Dublin: Four Courts Press.

Foster, S 2004. *Picts, Gaels and Scots*, 2nd edition. London: Batsford.

Foster, S 2015. Physical evidence for the early church in Scotland (in press), Barnwell P (ed.) *Places of Worship in Britain and Ireland, 300–950,* Buildings for Worship in Britain: Celtic and Anglo-Saxon, Oxford, 8.1.2010–10.1.2010, Donington: Shaun Tyas, 68–91.

Foster, S and Cross, M (eds) 2005. *'Able minds and practised hands': Scotland's Early Medieval Sculpture in the 21st century*. Society for Medieval Archaeology monograph series. Leeds: Maney Publishing and the Society of Medieval Archaeology.

Foster, S M, Macinnes, A and MacInnes, R (eds) 1998. *Scottish power centres from the early middle ages to the twentieth century*. Glasgow: Cruithne Press.

Fraser, I 2008. *The Pictish Symbol Stones of Scotland*. Edinburgh: Royal Commission on the Ancient and Historical Monuments of Scotland.

Fraser, I and Halliday, S 2010. 'The Early Medieval landscape of Donside, Aberdeenshire', in Driscoll et al (eds) 2010, 307–34.

Fraser, J E 2002a. *The battle of Dunnichen 685*. Stroud: Tempus Publishing.

Fraser, J E 2002b. 'Northumbrian Whithorn and the making of St Ninian', *Innes Review* 53, 40–59.

Fraser, J E 2009. 'From Caledonia to Pictland: Scotland to 795', *The New Edinburgh History of Scotland*, vol. 1. Edinburgh: EUP.

Freeman, M 1945. 'Lighting the Easter candle', *The Metropolitan Museum of Art Bulletin* 3, 194–200.

Friell, J G P and Watson, W G (eds) 1984. *Pictish studies: settlement, burial and art in Dark Age northern Britain*, Oxford: British Archaeological Report, British Series 125, 169–87.

Gabra-Sanders, T 2001. 'The Orkney hood, re-dated and re-considered', in Rogers et al. (eds) 2001, 98–104.

Gage, J 1999. *Color and Culture: Practice and Meaning from Antiquity to Abstraction*. Berkley: University of California Press.

Geary, P J 2009. 'What happened to Latin?', *Speculum*, 84, 859–73.

Gilchrist, R 2008. 'Magic for the dead? The archaeology of magic in Later Medieval burials', *Medieval Archaeology* 52, 119–59.

Glenn, V 2003. *Romanesque and Gothic decorative metalwork and ivory carvings in the Museum of Scotland*. Edinburgh: National Museums of Scotland.

Gondek, M 2006. 'Investing in sculpture: power in Early Historic Scotland', *Medieval Archaeology* 50, 105–42.

Gondek, M and Noble, G 2011. 'Together as one: the landscape of the symbol stones at Rhynie, Aberdeenshire', in Driscoll et al. (eds) 2010, 281–305.

Godman P (ed.) 1982. *Alcuin: the Bishops, Kings, and Saints of York*. Oxford: Oxford University Press.

Goubitz, O, van Driel-Murray, C and Groenman-van Waateringe, W 2001. *Stepping Through Time: Archaeological Footwear from Prehistoric Times Until 1800*. Zwolle: Stichting Promotie Archaeologie.

Graham-Campbell, J A 1973. 'The 9th century Anglo-Saxon horn mount from Burghead, Morayshire, Scotland', *Medieval Archaeology* 17, 43–51.

Graham-Campbell, J 1995. *The Viking-Age Gold and Silver of Scotland*. Edinburgh: National Museums Scotland.

Graham-Campbell, J 2001. 'Whithorn and the Viking World', The Eighth Whithorn Lecture. Whithorn: Friends of the Whithorn Trust.

Green, M 1992. *Symbol and Image in Celtic Religious Art.* London: Routledge.

Greig, C, Greig, M and Ashmore, P 2000. 'Excavation of a cairn cemetery at Lundin Links, Fife, in 1965–6', *Proceedings of the Society of Antiquaries of Scotland* 130, 585–636.

Grieg, S 1940. *Viking antiquities in Scotland.* Oslo: H Aschehoug.

Gwilt, A and Haselgrove, C (eds) 1997. *Reconstructing Iron Age societies: new approaches to the British Iron Age.* Oxford: Oxbow Books.

Hahn, C 1997. 'Seeing and believing: the construction of sanctity in early-medieval saints' shrines', *Speculum* 72, 1079–106.

Hall, D W 1995. 'Pre-burghal St Andrews. Towards an archaeological research design', *Tayside & Fife Archaeological Journal*, 1, 23–27.

Hall and Silliman (eds) 2006. *Historical Archaeology.* Oxford: Blackwell.

Hamerow, H and MacGregor, A (eds) 2001. *Image and power in the archaeology of early medieval Britain.* Oxford: Oxbow Books.

Hamling, T and Richardson, C (eds) 2010. *Everyday Objects: Medieval and Early Modern Material Culture and its Meanings.* Farnham: Ashgate.

Härke, H 1989. 'Early Saxon weapon burials: frequencies, distributions and weapon combinations' in Hawkes (ed.) 1989, monograph 21, 49–61.

Haselgrove, C C and Wigg-Wolf, D (eds) 2005. *Iron Age coinage and ritual practices.* Mainz: Studien zu Fundmünzen der Antike 20.

Hatherley, C 2009. 'Into the west: excavation of an early Christian cemetery at Montfode, Ardossan, North Ayrshire', *Proceedings of the Society of Antiquaries of Scotland* 139, 195–211.

Hawkes, J and Mills, S (eds) 1999. *Northumbria's Golden Age.* Stroud: Sutton Publishing.

Hawkes, S C (ed.) 1989. *Anglo-Saxon weapons and warfare.* Oxford: Oxford University Committee for Archaeology, monograph 21.

Heald, A 2005. 'Non-ferrous metal-working in Iron Age Scotland (*c.* 700 BC to AD 800)' (PhD thesis, University of Edinburgh).

Heald, A 2010. 'The interpretation of non-ferrous metalworking in Early Historic Scotland', in Driscoll et al. (eds) 2010, 221–44.

Heaney, S (trans.) 2002. *Beowulf: A new translation.* New York: Norton.

Heather, P 1994. 'State Formation in Europe in the First Millennium AD', in Crawford (ed) 1994, 47–63.

Hencken, H 1942. 'Ballinderry Crannog no 2', *Proceedings of the Royal Irish Academy* 47C: 1, 1–76.

Hencken, H 1950. 'Lagore Crannog: an Irish royal residence of the 7th to 10th centuries AD', *Proceedings of the Royal Irish Academy* 53C: 1, 1–247.

Henderson, G 1999. *Vision and Image in Early Christian England.* Cambridge: Cambridge University Press.

Henderson, G 2001. 'The Barberini Gospels (Rome, Vatican, *Biblioteca Apostolica Barberini Lat.* 570) as a paradigm of Insular art', in Redknap et al (eds) 2001, 157–68.

Henderson, G and Henderson, I 2004. *The Art of The Picts: Sculpture and Metalwork in Early Medieval Scotland.* London: Thames & Hudson.

Henderson, I 1958. 'The origin centre of the Pictish symbol stones', *Proceedings of the Society of Antiquaries of Scotland* 91, 44–60.

Henderson, I 1987. 'Early Christian monuments of Scotland displaying crosses but no other ornament', in Small (ed) 1987, 45–58.

Henderson, I 1998. '*Primus inter pares:* the St Andrews sarcophagus and Pictish sculpture', in Foster (ed) 1998b, 97–167.

Henderson, I 1999. 'The Dupplin Cross: a preliminary consideration of its art-historical context', in Hawkes and Mills (eds) 1999, 161–77.

Henderson, I 2001. '"This wonderful monument": the cross slab at Nigg, Easter Ross, Scotland', in Binski and Noel (eds) 2001, 114–47.

Henderson, I 2005. 'Fragments of significance: the whole picture', in Foster and Cross (eds) 2005, 69–84.

Henderson, I 2008a. 'The cataloguing of the Hilton of Cadboll cross-slab', in James et al. (eds) 2008, 75–126.

Henderson, I 2008b. 'The art-historical context of the Hilton of Cadboll cross-slab', in James et al. (eds), 127–204.

Henderson, I 2008c. 'Understanding the figurative style and decorative programme of the Book of Deer', in Forsyth (ed.) 2008, 32–66.

Henry, D (ed) 1997. *The worm, the germ and the thorn: Pictish and* related studies presented to Isabel Henderson. Balgavies: Pinkfoot Press.

Henshall, A S 1956. 'A long cist cemetery at Parkburn Sand Pit, Lasswade, Midlothian', *Proceedings of the Society of Antiquaries of Scotland* 89 (1955–56), 252–83.

Henshall, A S 1966. 'Second report on cist burials at Parkburn Sand Pit, Lasswade, Midlothian', *Proceedings of the Society of Antiquaries of Scotland* 98 (1964–66), 204–12.

Herren, M W (ed. and trans.) 1974. *The Hisperica Famina: I The A-Text, a New Critical Edition.* Toronto: Pontifical Institute of Mediaeval Studies.

Herren, M and Brown, S 2002. *Christ in Celtic Christianity, Britain and Ireland from the fifth to the tenth century.* Woodbridge: Boydell.

Higgitt, J 1982. 'The Pictish Latin inscription at Tarbat in Ross-shire', *Proceedings of the Society of Antiquaries of Scotland* 112 (1982), 300–21.

Hill, P 1997. *Whithorn and St Ninian: Excavations of a Monastic Town 1984–91.* Stroud: Sutton Publishing.

Hobbs 2005. 'Why are there always so many spoons? Hoards of precious metals in late Roman Britain', in Crummy (ed) 2005, 197–208.

Hingley, R 1992. 'Society in Scotland from 700 BC to AD 200', *Proceedings of the Society of Antiquaries of Scotland* 122, 7–53.

Holmes, N M McQ 2006. 'Two denarius hoards from Birnie, Moray', *British Numismatic Journal*, 76, 1–44.

Hourihane, C (ed.) 2001. *From Ireland Coming: Irish Art from the Early Christian to the Late Gothic Period and its European Context.* New Jersey: Princeton University Press.

Hourihane, C (ed.) 2004. *Irish Art Historical Studies in Honour of Peter Harbison.* Dublin: Four Courts Press.

Hourihane, C (ed.) 2011. *Insular and Anglo-Saxon Art and Thought in the Early Medieval Period.* New Jersey: Princeton University Press.

Huff, C 1998. 'The introduction of falconry to the Anglo-Saxon kingdoms: a consideration of the evidence from Anglo-Saxon and Continental sources', *Medieval Life* 10, 7–12.

Hunter, F 1997. 'Iron Age hoarding in Scotland and northern England', in Gwilt and Haselgrove (eds) 1997, 108–33.

Hunter, F 2001. 'Roman and Native in Scotland: New Approaches', *Journal of Roman Archaeology* 14, 289–309.

Hunter, F 2005. 'The image of the warrior in the British Iron Age – coin iconography', in Haselgrove and Wigg-Wolf (eds) 2005, 20, 43–68.

Hunter, F 2008. 'The Roman tile fragment', in James and Yeoman 2008, monograph 6, 122–23.

Hunter, F and Painter, K (eds) 2013. *Late Roman Silver Within and Beyond the Frontier: The Traprain Treasure in Con-text.* Edinburgh: Society of Antiquaries of Scotland.

Hunter, J 2007. 'Investigations in Sanday, Orkney, vol. 1: excavations at Pool, Sanday. A multi-period settlement from Neolithic to late Norse times'. Kirkwall: *The Orcadian*.

Ibsen, Henrik [see Ellis-Fermor (trans.) 1958].

Imer, L M 2010. 'Runes and Romans in the north', *Futhark: International Journal of Runic Studies* 1, 41–64.

James, H 1999. 'Excavations of a medieval cemetery at Skaill House, and a cist in the Bay of Skaill, Sandwick, Orkney', *Proceedings of the Society of Antiquaries of Scotland* 129, 753–77.

James, H, Henderson, I, Foster, S and Jones, S (eds) 2008. *A Fragmented Masterpiece: Recovering the Biography of the Hilton of Cadboll Pictish Cross-slab.* Edinburgh: Society of Antiquaries of Scotland.

James, H F and Yeoman, P 2008. *Excavations at St Ethernan's monastery, Isle of May, Fife, 1992–7.* Perth: Tayside & Fife Archaeological Committee, monograph 6.

Kantorowicz, E 1944, 'The "King's Advent" and the enigmatic panels in the doors of Santa Sabina', *The Art Bulletin* 26 (4), 207–31.

Kelly, D 1993. 'The relationships of the crosses of Argyll: the evidence of form', in Spearman and Higgitt (eds) 1993, 219–29.

Kelly, E and Sikora, M 2011. *Reading the Faddan More Psalter: An Introduction.* Dublin: National Museums of Ireland.

Kelly, S 2010. 'In the sight of an old pair of shoes', in Hamling and Richardson (eds) 2010, 57–70.

Keppie, L 1979. *Roman distance slabs from the Antonine Wall: a brief guide.* Glasgow: Hunterian Museum.

Kessler, H L 2004. *Seeing Medieval Art.* Broadview: Ontario.

Kitson, P 1978. 'Lapidary traditions in Anglo-Saxon England: part I, the background; the Old English lapidary', *Anglo-Saxon England* 7, 6–90.

Kitson, P 1983. 'Lapidary traditions in Anglo-Saxon England: part II, Bede's *Expanatio Apocalypsis* and related works', *Anglo-Saxon England* 12, 73–123.

Kitzinger, E 1993. 'Interlace and icons: form and function in early Insular art', in Spearman and Higgitt (eds) 1993, 3–15.

Koch, J T 1997. *The Gododdin of Aneirin: Text and Context from Dark-Age North Britain.* Cardiff: University of Wales Press.

Koslin, D G and Snyder, J E (eds) 2002. *Encountering Medieval Textiles and Dress: Objects, Texts, Images.* New York: Palgrave Macmillan.

Krueger, D 2010. 'The religion of relics in Late Antiquity and Byzantium', in Bagnoli et al. (eds) 2011, 5–17.

Laing, L 1994. 'The hoard of Pictish silver from Norrie's Law, Fife', *Studia Celtica* 28, 11–38.

Laing, L 2000. 'The chronology and context of Pictish relief sculpture', *Medieval Archaeology* 44, 81–114.

Laing, L 2001. 'The date of the Aberlemno churchyard stone', in Redknap et al (eds) 2001, 241–51.

Laing L, 2010. *European Influence on Celtic Art: Patrons and Artists.* Dublin: Four Courts Press

Laing, L and Longley, D 2006. *The Mote of Mark: a Dark Age hillfort in south-west Scotland.* Oxford: Oxbow Books.

Lane, A and Campbell, E 2000. *Dunadd: An Early Dalriadic Capital.* Oxford: Oxbow Books.

Lang, J T 1988. *Viking-Age decorated wood: a study of its ornament and style.* Dublin: Royal Irish Academy.

Lang, J 1991. *Corpus of Anglo-Saxon sculpture, volume 3: York and eastern Yorkshire.* Oxford: Oxford University Press.

Lapidge, M, Blair, J, Keynes, S and Scragg, D (eds) 2001. *The Blackwell Encyclopaedia of Anglo-Saxon England.* Oxford: Blackwell.

Leyerle, B 2008. 'Pilgrim eulogiae and domestic rituals', *Archiv für Religionsgeschichte* 10, 223–37.

Loveluck, C 2001. 'Wealth, waste and conspicuous consumption. Flixborough and its importance for Middle and Late Saxon rural settlement studies', in Hamerow and MacGregor (eds) 2001, 78–130.

Loveluck, C 2007. *Excavations at Flixborough, volume 4: Rural settlement, lifestyles and social change in the later first millennium AD: Anglo-Saxon Flixborough in its wider context.* Oxford: Oxbow Books.

Lowe, C 1999. *Angels, Fools and Tyrants: Britons and the Anglo-Saxons.* The Making of Scotland series. Edinburgh: Canongate Press with Historic Scotland.

Lowe, C 2006. *Excavations at Hoddom, Dumfriesshire: an ecclesiastical site in south-west Scotland.* Edinburgh: Society of Antiquaries of Scotland.

Lowe, C 2008. *Inchmarnock: An Early Historic Island Monastery and its Archaeological Landscape.* Edinburgh: Society of Antiquaries of Scotland.

Lucas, A T 1986. 'The social role of relics and reliquaries in ancient Ireland', *Journal of the Royal Society of Antiquaries of Ireland* 116, 5–37.

Lucy, S and Reynolds, A (eds) 2002. *Burials in early medieval England and Wales.* London: Society of Medieval Archaeology, monograph series 17.

Lynn, C J 1984. 'Some fragments of exotic porphyry found in Ireland', *Journal of Irish Archaeology* 2, 19–32.

Lysaght, P (ed.) 1994, *Milk and Milk Products from Medieval to Modern Times.* Edinburgh: Canongate Press.

Macaulay, J S 1996. 'A review of the Pictish crossbow', *Pictish Arts Society Journal* 10, 2–6.

MacCormack, S 1972. 'Change and Continuity in Late Antiquity: The Ceremony of Adventus', *Historia: Zeitschrift für Alte Geschichte* 21. 4: 721–52.

McEnchroe Williams, M 2002. 'Dressing the part: depictions of noble costume in Irish high crosses', in Koslin and Snyder (eds) 2002, 45–63.

MacGregor, A 1974. 'The Broch of Burrian, North Ronaldsay, Orkney', *Proceedings of the Society of Antiquaries of Scotland* 105, 63–118.

MacGregor, A 1976. 'Two antler crossbow nuts and some notes on the early development of the crossbow', *Proceedings of the Society of Antiquaries of Scotland* 107 (1975–76), 317–21.

McLaren, D 2012. 'Funerary rites afforded to children in Earlier Bronze Age Britain: case studies from Scotland, Yorkshire and Wessex', PhD Thesis, University of Edinburgh.

Mac Lean, D 1993. 'Snake-bosses and redemption at Iona and in Pictland', in Spearman and Higgitt (eds) 1993, 245–60.

McKitterick, R 2004. *History and memory in the Carolingian world.* Cambridge: Cambridge University Press.

McRoberts, D 1961. 'The ecclesiastical significance of the St Ninian's Isle treasure', *Proceedings of the Society of Antiquaries of Scotland* 94, 301–14.

Mack, A 2007. *Symbols and Pictures: The Pictish Legacy in Stone.* Brechin: Pinkfoot Press.

Maldonado, A 2011. 'Christianity and burial in Late Iron Age Scotland, AD 400–650', PhD thesis, University of Glasgow.

Márkus, G 2008. 'The sick and the dying in the Book of Deer', in Forsyth (ed.) 2008, 67–97.

Mathews, T 1999. *The Clash of Gods: A Reinterpretation of Early Christian Art.* Princeton: Princeton University Press.

Meaney, A 1981. *Anglo-Saxon Amulets or Curing Stones.* Oxford: British Archaeological Report, British Series 96.

Meehan, B 1994. *The Book of Kells: an Illustrated Introduction to the Manuscript in Trinity College Dublin.* London: Thames and Hudson.

Meyer, K 2010. 'Saints, scrolls and serpents: theorising a Pictish liturgy on the Tarbat peninsula', in Driscoll et al. (eds) 2010, 169–200.

Miket, R and Burgess, C (eds) 1984. *Between and beyond the Walls: essays on the prehistory and history of north Britain in honour of George Jobey.* Edinburgh: John Donald.

Moar, P and Stewart, J 1944. 'Newly discovered sculptured stones from Papil, Shetland', *Proceedings of the Society of Antiquaries of Scotland* 78 (1943–44), 91–99.

Moore, T and Armada, X L (eds) 2012. *Atlantic Europe in the First Millennium BC: Crossing the Divide.* Oxford: Oxford University Press.

Moorhead, S 2009. 'Early Byzantine copper coins found in Britain: a review in light of new finds recorded with the Portable Antiquities Scheme', in Tekin (ed) 2009, 263–74.

Munro, R 1882, *Ancient Scottish lake-dwellings or crannogs.* Edinburgh: David Douglas.

Murray, J (ed.) 2009. *St Ninian and the earliest Christianity in Scotland.* Oxford: British Archaeological Reports, British Series 483.

Murray, P and Murray, L 1998. *The Oxford Companion to Christian Art and Architecture.* Oxford: Oxford University Press.

Nash-Williams, V E 1950. *The early Christian monuments of Wales.* Cardiff: University of Wales Press.

Newman, C 2009. 'The Sword in the Stone: previously unrecognised archaeological evidence of ceremonies of the later Iron Age and early medieval period', in Cooney et al. (eds) 2009, 425–36.

Nieke, M 1993. 'Penannular and related brooches: secular ornament or symbol in action?', in Spearman and Higgitt (eds) 1993, 128–34.

Noble, G and Gondek, M 2010. 'Together as one: the landscape of the symbol stones at Rhynie, Aberdeenshire', in Driscoll et al (eds) 2010, 95–110.

Nobel, T and Smith, J (eds) 2008. *The Cambridge History of Christianity*, vol. 3. Cambridge: Cambridge University Press.

Ó Carragáin, É 2005. *Ritual and the Rood: liturgical images and the Old English poems of the dream of the Rood tradition.* London: British Library.

Ó Carragáin, T 2009. 'The architectural setting of the mass in Early-medieval Ireland', *Medieval Archaeology* 53, 119–54.

Ó Carragáin, T 2010. *Churches in early medieval Ireland: architecture, ritual and memory.* New Haven and London: Yale University Press.

O'Dell, A C, Stevenson, R B K, Brown, T J, Plenderleith, H J and Bruce-Mitford, R L S 1959. 'The St Ninian's Isle silver hoard', *Antiquity* 33, 241–68.

O'Donoghue, N X 2011a. *The Eucharistic in Pre-Norman Ireland.* Indiana: University of Notre Dame Press.

O'Donoghue, N X 2011b. 'Insular chrismals and house-shaped shrines in the early middle ages', in Hourihane (ed) 2011.

O'Reilly, J 1993. 'The Book of Kells, Folio 114r: a mystery revealed yet concealed', in Spearman and Higgitt (eds) 1993.

Organ R M 1973. 'Examination of the Ardagh Chalice – a case history', in Young (ed.) 1973, 238–71.

Ó'Riain, P 1972. 'Boundary association in Early Irish society', *Studia Celtica* 7, 12–29.

Owen, S and Welander, R 1995. 'A traveller's end? – an assorted group of early historic artefacts from Carronbridge, Dumfries & Galloway', *Proceedings of the Society of Antiquaries of Scotland* 125, 753–70.

Peers, C and Radford, C A 1943. 'The Saxon monastery of Whitby', *Archaeologia* 89, 27–88.

Perry, D R 2000. *Castle Park, Dunbar: two thousand years on a fortified headland*. Edinburgh: Society of Antiquaries of Scotland.

Petts, D 2002. 'Cemeteries and boundaries in western Britain', in Lucy and Reynolds (eds) 2002, 24–46.

Petts, D 2009. *The Early Medieval Church in Wales*. Stroud: The History Press.

Pine-Coffin, R S (trans.) 1961. *St Augustine Confessions*. Harmondsworth: Penguin.

Proudfoot, E 1996. 'Excavations at the long cist cemetery on the Hallow Hill, St Andrews, Fife, 1975–7', *Proceedings of the Society of Antiquaries of Scotland* 126, 387–454.

Pryce, H (ed.) 1998. *Literacy in Medieval Celtic Societies*. Cambridge: Cambridge University Press.

Pulliam, H 2011. 'Looking to Byzantium: light, color and cloth in Insular Art', in Hourihane 2011.

Pulliam, H 2012. 'Color' in *Medieval Art History Today – Critical Terms, A Special Issue of Studies in Iconography* 33, 3–14.

Pulliam, H 2013. Eyes of Light: Colour in the Lindisfarne Gospels' in Ashbee and Luxford (eds), 2013, 54–72.

Radford, C A R 1955. 'Two Scottish Shrines: Jedburgh and St Andrews', *Archaeological Journal* 112, 43–60.

Radford, C A R, 1962. 'Art and Architecture: Celtic and Norse', in Wainwright (ed.) 1962, 163–87.

Ralston, I 1986. 'The Yorkshire Television vitrified wall experiment at East Tullos, City of Aberdeen District', *Proceedings of the Society of Antiquaries of Scotland* 116, 17–40.

Ralston, I 2004. *The hill-forts of Pictland since 'The problem of the Picts'*. Rosemarkie: Groam House Museum.

RCAHMS 1994. *South-east Perth: an archaeological landscape.* Edinburgh: Royal Commission on the Ancient and Historical Monuments of Scotland.

Redknap, M, Edwards, N, Youngs, S, Lanes, A and Knight, J (eds) 2001. *Pattern and Purpose in Insular Art*. Oxford: Oxbow Books.

Redknap, M and Lewis, J M 2007. *A corpus of early medieval inscribed stones and stone sculpture in Wales: volume I, south-east Wales and the English border*. Cardiff: University of Wales Press.

Rees, A R 2002. 'A first millennium AD cemetery, rectangular Bronze Age structure and late prehistoric settlement at Thornybank, Midlothian', *Proceedings of the Society of Antiquaries of Scotland* 132, 313–55.

Reid, R W 1922. 'Ancient wooden traps from the Moss of Auquharney, Aberdeenshire', *Proceedings of the Society of Antiquaries of Scotland* 56 (1921–22), 282–87.

Rhynne, E 1962. 'National Museum of Ireland archaeological acquisitions in the year 1960', *Journal of the Royal Society of Antiquaries of Ireland* 92, 139–73.

Ritchie, A 1989. *Picts: an introduction to the life of the Picts and the carved stones in the care of the Secretary of State for Scotland*. Edinburgh: Her Majesty's Stationery Office.

Ritchie, A 1995. 'Meigle and lay patronage in Tayside in the 9th and 10th centuries AD', *Tayside & Fife Archaeological Journal* 1, 1–10.

Ritchie, A 2005. 'Clothing among the Picts', *Costume* 39, 28–42.

Ritchie, J N G 1969. 'Shields in north Britain in the Iron Age', *Scottish Archaeological Forum* 1, 31–40.

Rivet, A (ed.) 1966. *The Iron Age in Northern Britain*. Edinburgh: Edinburgh University Press.

Robertson, A S 1971. 'Roman coins found in Scotland, 1961–70', *Proceedings of the Society of Antiquaries of Scotland* 103 (1970–71), 113–68.

Robertson, A S 1983. 'Roman coins found in Scotland, 1971–82', *Proceedings of the Society of Antiquaries of Scotland* 113, 405–48.

Roddy, K 2001. 'Politics and religion in late Antiquity: The Roman

Imperial Adventus ceremony and the Christian myth of the Harrowing of Hell', *Apocrypha* 11, 147–80.

Rogers, P W, Jorgensen, L B and Rast-Eicher, A (eds) 2001. *The Roman Textile Industry and its Influence*. Oxford: Oxbow Books.

Rosehill, Lord 1870. 'Notice of an underground chamber recently discovered at Crichton Mains', *Proceedings of the Society of Antiquaries of Scotland* 8 (1868–70), 105–109.

Ross, A 1959. 'Chain symbolism in Pagan Celtic religion', *Speculum* 34.1, 39–59.

Ryan, M 1997. 'The Derrynaflan hoard and early Irish art', *Speculum* 72, 995–1017.

Samson, R 1992. The reinterpretation of the Pictish symbols, *Journal of British Archaeological Association* 145, 29–65.

Sayers, W 1991. 'Early Irish attitudes towards hair and beards, baldness and tonsure', *Zeitschrift Fur Celtische Philologie* 44, 154–89.

Sealey, Paul R 2007. *A late Iron Age warrior burial from Kelvedon, Essex*. Colchester: East Anglian Archaeology Report 118.

Shahar, S 1990. *Childhood in the Middle Ages*. London: Routledge.

Shapland F and Armit I 2012. 'The Useful Dead: Bodies as Objects in Iron Age and Norse Atlantic Scotland', *European Journal of Archaeology* 15 (1), 98–116.

Sharpe, R (trans.) 1995. *Adomnán of Iona: Life of St Columba*. London: Penguin Classics.

Sharples, N 1998. *Scalloway: A Broch, Late Iron Age Settlement and Medieval Cemetery in Shetland*. Oxford: Oxbow Books.

Sharples, N 2003. 'From monuments to artefacts: changing social relationships in the later Iron Age', in Downes and Ritchie (eds) 2003, 151–65.

Sheridan, J A 2005. 'Pitfalls and other traps … Why it's worth looking at museum artefacts again', *The Archaeologist* 58, 20–21.

Simpson, D D A and Scott-Elliot, J 1963. 'Excavations at Camp Hill, Trohoughton, Dumfries', *Transactions of the Dumfries & Galloway Natural History & Antiquarian Society*, 3rd series, 41 (1962–63), 125–34.

Simpson, M 1970. 'Some Roman-Iron Age finger rings', *Proceedings of the Society of Antiquaries of Scotland* 102, 105–108.

Small, A (ed.) 1987. *The Picts: a new look at old problems*. Dundee.

Small, A, Thomas, C and Wilson, D M 1973. *St Ninian's Isle and its treasure*, 2 vols. London: Oxford University Press.

Smith, J 1990. 'Oral and Written: saints, miracles and relics in Brittany, c.850–1250', *Speculum* 65, 309–43.

Smith, J 2005. *Europe after Rome: a new cultural history 500–1000*. Oxford: Oxford University Press.

Speake, G 1981. *Anglo-Saxon Animal Art and its Germanic Background*. Oxford: Oxford University Press.

Spearman, R M 1988. 'Early Scottish towns: their origins and economy', in Driscoll and Nieke (eds) 1988, 96–110.

Spearman, M and Higgitt, J (eds) 1993. *The Age of Migrating Ideas: Early Medieval Art in Northern Britain and Ireland*. Edinburgh: National Museums of Scotland.

Stevenson, R B K 1949. 'The nuclear fort of Dalmahoy, Midlothian and other Dark Age capitals', *Proceedings of the Society of Antiquaries of Scotland* 83 (1948–49), 186–98.

Stevenson, R B K 1955. 'Pictish art' in Wainwright (ed) 1955, 97–128.

Stevenson, R B K 1956. 'Pictish chains, Roman silver and bauxite beads', PSAS 88 (1954–56), 228–29.

Stevenson, R B K 1974. 'The Hunterston Brooch and its significance', *Medieval Archaeology* 18, 16–42.

Stevenson, R B K 1983. 'Further notes on the Hunterston and "Tara" brooches, Monymusk reliquary and Blackness bracelet', *Proceedings of the Society of Antiquaries of Scotland* 113, 469–77.

Stevenson, R B K 1993. 'Further thoughts on some well known problems', in Spearman and Higgitt (eds) 1993, 16–26.

Stevenson, R B K 1995. 'Pictish chain, Roman silver and bauxite beads', *Proceedings of the Society of Antiquaries of Scotland* 88, 228–30.

Stout, M 2000. *The Irish ringfort*, new edition. Dublin: Four Courts Press.

Stuart, J 1856–67. *The Sculptured Stones of Scotland*. Aberdeen: The Spalding Club.

Tamburr, K 2007. *The Harrowing of Hell in Medieval England*. Cambridge: Brewer.

Tate, J and Troalen, L 2009. *Investigating the Traprain Law Roman Treasure*. Eu-Artech: Technical Report.

Taylor, S (ed.) 1998. *The Uses of Place-Names*. Edinburgh: Scottish Cultural Press.

Tekin, O (ed.) 2009. *Ancient history, numismatics and epigraphy in the Mediterranean world: Studies in memory of Clemens E Bosch and Sabahat Atlan and in honour of Nezahat Baydur*. Istanbul: EGE Publications.

Thacker, A T 2002. 'The Making of a Local Saint', in Thacker and Sharpe (eds) 2002, 45–72.

Thacker, A T and Sharpe, R (eds) 2002. *Local Saints and Local Churches in the Early Medieval West*. Oxford: Oxford University Press.

Thomas, C 1963. 'The interpretation of the Pictish symbols', *Archaeological Journal* 120, 31–97.

Thomas, C 1967. 'An early Christian cemetery and chapel on Ardwall Islet, Kirkcudbright', *Medieval Archaeology* 11, 127–88.

Thomas, C 1971. *The Early Christian Archaeology of North Britain*. Oxford: Oxford University Press.

Thomas, C 1984. 'The Pictish Class I symbol stones', in Friell and Watson (eds) 1984, 169–87.

Thomas, C 1995. 'The artist and the people, a foray into uncertain semiotics', in Bourke (ed.) 1995.

Thomas, J 2000. *Interpretive archaeology: a reader*. London: Leicester University Press.

Tilley, C, Keane, W, Küchler, S, Rowlands, M and Spyer, P (eds) 2006. *Handbook of Material Culture*. London: Sage.

Trench Jellicoe, R 1999. 'A missing figure on slab fragment no. 2 from Monifieth, Angus, the A' Chill Cross, Canna, and some implications of the development of a variant form of the Virgin's hairstyle and dress in Early Medieval Scotland', *Proceedings of the Society of Antiquaries of Scotland* 129, 597–647.

Tucker, F and Armit, I 2010. 'Living with death in the Iron Age', *British Archaeology* 113, 42–47.

Tweddle, D 1992. *The Anglian helmet from 16–22 Coppergate*. London: Council of British Archaeology.

van Houtts, E 1999. *Memory and Gender in Medieval Europe 900–1200*. Toronto: University of Toronto Press.

Waddell, J J 1932. 'Cross-slabs recently discovered at Millport and Fowlis Wester', *Proceedings of the Society of Antiquaries of Scotland* 66 (1931–32), 409–12.

Wainwright, F T (ed.) 1955. *The Problem of the Picts*. Edinburgh: Nelson.

Wainwright, F T (ed.) 1962. *The Northern Isles*. Edinburgh: Nelson.

Walker Bynum, C and Gerson, P 1997. 'Body-part reliquaries and body parts in the Middle Ages', *Gesta* 36, 3–7.

Warren, F E 1987. *The liturgy and ritual of the Celtic church*, second edition, originally published in 1881. Woodbridge: Boydell.

Watson, W 1926. *The Celtic Place-names of Scotland*. Originally published by William Blackwood & Sons (reprinted 2005, Edinburgh: Birlinn Books).

Webster, L 1999. 'The iconographic programme of the Franks Casket', in Hawkes and Mills (eds) 1999, 227–46.

Webster, L 2001. 'The Anglo-Saxon hinterland: animal style in Southumbrian eighth-century England, with particular reference to metalwork', *Veröff Joachim Jungius-Ges Wiss Hamburg*, 90, 39–62.

Webster, L and Backhouse, L (eds) 1991. *The making of England, Anglo-Saxon art and culture AD 600–900*. London: British Museum Press.

Whitfield, N 1996. 'Brooch or cross? The lozenge on the shoulder of the Virgin in the Book of Kells', *Archaeology Ireland* 10 (10), 20–23.

Whitfield, N 2001. 'The "Tara" Brooch: an emblem of status in its European context', in Hourihane (ed.) 2001.

Whitfield, N 2004. 'More thoughts on the wearing of brooches in Early Medieval Ireland', in Hourihane (ed.) 2004.

Whitfield, N 2006. 'Dress and accessories in the Early Irish Tale "The Wooing of Becfhola"', *Medieval Clothing and Textiles* 2, 1–4.

Whitley, D 1998. *Reader in Archaeological Theory: Post-Processual and Cognitive Approaches*. London: Routledge.

Wiedermann, T 1988. *Adults and Children in the Roman Empire*. London: Routledge.

Wilkinson, J 2002. *Jerusalem pilgrims before the Crusades*. Warminster: Aris & Phillips.

Williams, M 2003. 'Growing metaphors: the agricultural cycle as metaphor in the Later Prehistoric period of Britain and north-western Europe', *Journal of Social Archaeology* 3, 223–55.

Wood, J 2003. 'The Orkney hood: an ancient re-cycled textile', in Downes and Ritchie (eds) 2003, 171–75.

Wooding, J 1996. *Communication and commerce along the western sea-lanes AD 400–800*. Oxford: British Archaeological Report, International Series S654.

Woodward, A and Leach, P 1993. *Uley Shrines Excavation of a Ritual Complex on West Hill, Uley, Gloucestershire, 1977–79*. London: English Heritage.

Woolf, A 2006. 'Dún Nechtain, Fortriu and the geography of the Picts', *Scottish Historical Review* 85, 182–201.

Woolf, A 2007. 'From Pictland to Alba 789–1070', *New Edinburgh History of Scotland*, vol. 2. Edinburgh University Press.

Yeoman, P 2009. 'Investigations on the May Island, and other early medieval churches and monasteries in Scotland', in Edwards (ed.) 2009, 227–44.

Young, D 2006. 'The colours of things', in Tilley et al. (eds) 2006, 173–85.

Young, W J (ed) 1973. *The Application of Science in Examination of Works of Art*. Boston: Boston Museum of Fine Art.

Youngs, S 1989. *The Work of Angels: Masterpieces of Celtic Metalwork, 6th–9th Centuries AD*. London: British Museum.

Youngs, S 2013. 'From chains to brooches: the uses and hoarding of silver in north Britain in the Early Historic period', in Hunter and Painter (eds) 2013.

Index

Aberdour, Fife 114
Aberlady, East Lothian 170
– cross-shaft 170
– crosier mount *32*
Aberlemno, Angus, sculpture 71
– churchyard stone (Aberlemno 2) 71, 79; *72*
– roadside stone (Aberlemno 3) 162, 172; *163, 172*
Ackergill, Caithness, sculpture 151; *151*
Adomnán
– description of the Holy Land 113
– *Life of St Columba* 33, 47, 51, 54–55, 70, 116, 118
Advent 157
Adventus 155–60
African Red Slipware (*see* pottery)
agriculture 89
– cycles 144, 148
– production 148
Aidan, St 51
Alcock, Leslie 81, 83–85, 87–88
Alexandrinus, Eusabius 159
Allen, J Romilly 121, 161
al-Muallaqa church, Cairo 158; *158*
altars 34, 45, 57–58
amber, beads 14; insets 26–27, 182
amulets 14, 29, 47, 52, 59
Anderson, Joseph 105, 161
angels 156–57
Anglo-Saxon England 71, 83, 95, 98, 112, 119, 182
– burial 12, 14, 52, 71, 76
– historical sources 13, 21–22, 43, 45, 47, 57, 153
– monasteries 55–57, 133
– objects 10, 14, 18, 22, 25, 58, 98, 119

– poetry xv, 150
– sculpture 38, 57–58, 119–20
animal art 13, 22, 25–29, 38, 40, 42, 58, 80–81, 83, 151, 154–55, 167
animal bones 83, 146–48, 169; *146*
antler 83
Ardagh hoard, Co. Limerick, Ireland
– chalice 52–53, 145
Ardifuar, Argyll, mould 100, 105; *105*
Ardross, Ross and Cromarty, sculpture 178
Ardwall, Dumfries and Galloway, church 95
Armoy, Co. Antrim, Northern Ireland, ring-headed brooch 27
Augustine, St 121, 154

Ballinderry, Co. Offaly, Ireland 89
Baptism 48, 52, 154
battles
– depictions of 71, 73, 79; *72*
– Bannockburn 36
– Dún Nechtain 71
beads
– amber 14
– glass 14
Bede 35, 47, 113, 116, 133, 170, 176
bells
– Early Christian 32, 35, 54, 142–44, 146, 192–93; *143*
– in modern times 142–43
Ben Newe, Aberdeenshire 178
Benvie, Angus, sculpture 74, 81; *74*
Beowulf xv
Bewcastle, Cumberland, sculpture 83
Bible, The
– New Testament 157
– Old Testament 51, 113, 157–59
Big Ben 142–43

birds (*see* animal art)
Birnie, Moray, ring-headed brooch 27
Birsay (*see* Brough of Birsay)
body/bodies 5, 7, 31–32, 36, 42–43, 49, 51, 53–54, 59
bogs, finds from 3, 7–8
bones (*see* animal bones) 145–148
Book of Deer, The 30, 48–49
Book of Durrow, The 175
Book of Kells, The 18, 35, 110, 175; *19, 35*
book satchels
– description in *Hisperica famina* 110–12
– fragments from Loch Glashan 110, 12
– modern re-creation 106, 110–12; *111*
– images on sculpture 70, 110; *31, 110*
Borland, Lanarkshire, silver chain *186*
bowls 47, 55, 59, 114
box shrines (*see* shrines)
Brandon, Suffolk 92
Brandsbutt, Aberdeenshire, sculpture 121
brazing 142, 192
bread (*see also* Eucharist) 51, 149
Breck of Hillwell, Shetland, sculpture 123
Bressay, Shetland, sculpture 110
Bridei, King 70, 118, 177
bride-price/-wealth (*see* marriage)
Bridgeness, West Lothian, Roman sculpture 79; *80*
Brigit, St 53
Britons 112
Brittany 32, 43, 54
Broch of Burrian, Orkney 146
– cattle bones/phalanges 146–48, 169; *146*
Broichan (wizard) 70, 118, 177
Bronze Age, cup-marks 156

brooches
- manufacture of 22, 99, 101–102, 112
- meanings of 19–29, 49, 101, 129
- uses 15–22, 129

brooches 3, 6, 10, 12, 18, 19, 21, 71, 101, 190
- Armoy, Ireland 27
- Birnie, Moray 27
- Carn Liath, Sutherland 133; *133*
- Carronbridge, Dumfries and Galloway 77
- Castlehill, Ayrshire 16
- Cluny, Perthshire *191*
- Croy, Inverness-shire, hoard 29; *x, 29*
- Dunbeath fragment, Caithness 26
- Hunterston, Ayrshire 15, 19, 24, 26–27, 29, 99, 100, 112, 119, 124; *vi, xiv, 2, 12, 16, 17, 23, 27*
- Isle of Mull, Argyll 29
- Rogart, Sutherland 29; *20, 28, 90*
- St Ninian's Isle hoard, Shetland 22, 24–25, 29, 47, 101, 119, 125–129; *25, 28, 101, 102, 103, 126, 127, 128*
- Tara, Ireland 15, 24

Brough of Birsay, Orkney XVII
- glass *tessera* 115
- metalworking workshop 89, 101–102
- porphyry fragment 115; *116*
- sculpture 9, 73–74; *73*

Bruach an Drumein, Argyll 100, 103
buckles 99
Buiston, Ayrshire, crannog 88–89, 106, 112
- cross-bow nut and bolt 83; *83*
- imported pottery 118
- shoes 8
- spearhead 79; *78*

bulls (*see also* animal art) 167
Burghead, Moray 167
- fort 85, 87
- horn mount 120; *120*
- sculpture 92; *93, 168*

burial 6, 12, 14, 48, 71, 124, 129–32, 161, 194–96; *131*

- grave goods 12, 14, 52
- long-cist 129–130, 134; *130*
- Anglo-Saxon 12, 14, 52, 71, 76
- Viking 71

Byzantine
- coins 114–115
- glass lamp 55
- motifs 151–53, 158
- relics 49, 53
- votive gifts 45; *45*

Campbell, Ewan 117, 118, 135
candles (*see* lighting)
Carn Liath, Sutherland, brooch 133; *133*
Carronbridge, Dumfries and Galloway
- brooch 77
- sword blade fragment 77

Carthage 114
Castlehill, Ayrshire, brooch 16
Castle Newe, Aberdeenshire, bronze armlets 178
Castle Rock, Dumbarton, fort 85, 116
Castle Law, Abernethy, Perthshire 134; *135*
cemeteries (*see also* burial) 6, 129–31
Ceolfrith, Abbot of Northumbria 95, 133, 176
chains (*see* silver chains)
chalice 58–59
- Ardagh, Ireland 52–53
- Derrynaflan, Ireland 27; *146*

chancel screen 45, 57, 95, 97, 158
chapes (see sword chapes)
Charlemagne, Emperor 171
children/adolescents 4, 6, 8–9, 13, 42–43, 49
chrismal 38, 40, 90
Christianity 3, 4, 6, 18, 25, 30–59, 70, 90–97, 113, 124, 129–30, 143–44, 146, 149–60, 174–81, 192–97
- calendar 144, 154, 160
- Columban 143–44, 164–65
- communities 143–46, 154, 170, 164–65, 194–5

- conversion to 95, 123, 174–75, 180, 177, 196–97
- Eucharist 30, 38, 49, 52, 58, 149, 151-53
- healing 3–4, 6, 30, 35, 38, 42–43, 45, 47–49, 51–54
- in the home 30, 48
- iconography 27–29, 154–60, 175
- inscriptions 25–26, 52, 123–24, 126, 133
- liturgy 144, 150, 157
- monasteries 30, 145–46
- in Pictland 174–76, 178–79
- pilgrimage 30, 144
- regional expressions of 170
- rituals/practices 30–33, 38, 48–49, 55, 58
- 'Roman' 144

churches 30, 45, 92, 125, 175–76, 193
- construction 95, 133–34
- interior decoration 57, 97

cists/long-cists (*see* burial)
Clatchard Craig, Fife, fort 85, 190
- silver ingot 190

Clonmacnoise, Co. Offaly, Ireland, sculpture 83
Clonoura townland, Co. Tipperary, Ireland, shield 79
clothing 3, 6–8, 12, 29, 49
- colour 10
- depictions on sculpture 9, 18, 73, 154
- Orkney hood 3, 7–8
- shoes 3, 8; *9*

Cluny, Perthshire, brooches *191*
Clyde, River 85
Clynekirkton, Sutherland, sculpture 123
Cnoc a' Comhdhalach, North Uist 101
Cnoc Navie, Ross and Cromarty 178
coins/coinage 49, 155, 196–97
- Byzantine 114–115
- pierced 14
- Roman 115, 132

- votive gifts 47
colour 10, 36, 40, 56, 58, 59
Columba, St 33, 47, 51, 53–55, 70, 90, 116, 118, 119, 177
Constantine, son of Fergus 171
Constantine's cross, Dupplin, Perthshire 74, 79, 81, 171–74; *79, 173*
copper-alloy 38, 99–100
Coppergate, York, helmet 71
coriander 48, 118
Cossans, Angus, St Orland's cross 33, 162; *164*
Covesea, Moray 167
crafts/craft-working
- bone 100
- jet 100
- leather-working 100, 112, 145
- metalworking 10, 12, 22, 87, 98–106, 112, 145
- sculpting 98, 100, 153
- wood 100, 109
- workshops 89, 100, 102, 112, 145
Craig Phadrig, Inverness, fort
- imported pottery 117
crannogs 88–90
- Ballinderry, Co. Offaly, Ireland 89
- Buiston, Ayrshire 8, 79, 83, 88, 89, 106, 112, 118; *78, 83*
- Dowalton Loch, Dumfries and Galloway 8
- Lagore, Co. Meath, Ireland 89
- Loch Glashan, Argyll 89, 100, 112
- Loch Leathen, Argyll *89*
- Lochspouts, Ayrshire 53; *52*
Craw Stane, Rhynie, Aberdeenshire 121, 161
Crichton Mains, Midlothian 134
crosier/crooks 32, 35, 125
- Kells Crosier *32*
- St Fillan 125; *125*
cross, as symbol 148–50
cross-marked pebble 51, 146; *52*
cross-slab (*see* sculpture)

cross-bow 81–83
- remains of 83; *83*
Croy, Inverness-shire, hoard 14, 29; *x, 14, 29, 197*
crucible (*see* metalworking)
Culbin Sands, Moray, sword pommel 77
cults (*see* saints)
curing (*see* healing)
Curle, Mrs C 115
currency (*see* coins)
Cuthbert, St 47–48

Dalmahoy, Midlothian, fort 85, 119
Dalmeny, City of Edinburgh
- Anglo-Saxon burial 14; *14*
- sword-fitting/sword ornament 77; *77*
Dál Riata 119
David 158–59, 171–2
- and the Harrowing of Hell 158–59
death/dying 5, 6, 141, 143, 154–5
- Christian preparation for 48–49
deer (*see* animal art *and* hunting)
Derrynaflan hoard, Co. Tipperary, Ireland 145
- chalice 27; *146*
- paten *146*
- strainer 52
doctors (*see* healing)
dogs/hounds (*see* animal art *and* hunting)
Dornoch Firth 167
Dowalton Loch crannog, Dumfries and Galloway, shoes 8
dowries (*see* marriage)
Drainie/Kineddar, Moray, sculpture 165
dress objects (*see also* individual object types) 10, 12, 49
drinking vessels 55, 58–59, 99
Drosten stone (*see* St Vigeans) 162
Druids 177–78
Drumlanrig, Dumfries and Galloway 105
Drunemeton, place-name 178
Dull, Perthshire, sculpture 79

Dumbarton Rock (*see* Castle Rock, Dumbarton)
Dumyat, Stirlingshire, fort 87
Dunadd, Argyll, fort 85, 87, 98, 119
- boar 169
- cross bow nut 83
- dyer's madder 118
- glass *tessera* 53, 115; *53*
- gold and garnet stud 120
- hand-quern 148–49; *149, 203*
- imported pottery 117–18, 135; *117*
- imported glass 117, 118
- incised stones 52; *12, 52*
- metalworking 98–100, 102, 103, 112; *99*
- orpiment 118
- sword blade fragment 77
Dun Ardtreck, Skye, imported pottery 117
Dunbar, East Lothian 98, 120
Dunbeath brooch fragment, Caithness 26; *XIII*
Dundurn, Perthshire, fort 85, 119; *86*
- shoes 8
Dunfallandy, Perthshire, sculpture 167
Dunkeld, Perthshire 165
Dunlop, Ian 110
Dún Nechtain (*see* battles)
Dunnichen (*see* battles, Dún Nechtain)
Dupplin, Perthshire, sculpture 74, 79, 81, 171–74; *79, 173*
Durham, General 190–91
Durham, Mrs Dundas 191
Durisdeer, Dumfries and Galloway 105; *104*
Dyce, Aberdeenshire, sculpture 165
dyes 118

Early People gallery (*see* National Museums Scotland) 151
Eassie, Angus, sculpture 80
Easter 54–55, 144, 150, 154, 159–60
- candle 54, 160
- Good Friday 159

- Sunday 154, 159
- vigil 154, 159–60

Eastertown of Roseisle, Moray, sculpture 165–66; *166*
Edderton, Ross and Cromarty, sculpture 121; *122*
Eilean Olabhat, North Uist 102
Elgin, Moray, sculpture 83; *163*
enamel/enamelling 40
eschatology 155, 157
Eucharist 30, 38, 49, 52, 58, 149, 151–53
eulogiae (*see* relics)
Europe 14, 24, 30, 32, 35, 43, 45, 49, 53–54, 57–58, 106, 113, 116–18, 120
E ware (*see* pottery)

Faddan More Psalter, Co. Tipperary, Ireland 3; *4*
falconry (*see* hunting)
families 4, 43
farming (*see* agriculture)
fashion (*see* clothing)
Fearn peninsula 151, 158, 162–64
feasting 59
filigree 22–24, 182
Fillan, St, crosier 125; *125*
Finavon hill, Angus 178–79
Firth, Orkney, sculpture 123; *123*
Fiskavaig, Skye, sculpture 161; *162*
Flixborough, Lincolnshire 92
Forteviot, Perthshire
 - arch 95; *94*
 - 'Pictish' palace 165
Forth, Firth of 170
forts
 - Burghead, Moray 85, 87, 92, 120, 167; *93, 120*
 - Castle Rock, Dumbarton 85, 116
 - Clatchard Craig, Fife 85, 190
 - Craig Phadrig, Inverness 117
 - Dalmahoy, Midlothian 85, 119
 - Dumyat, Stirlingshire 87

- Dunadd 52–53, 77, 83, 85, 87, 98–100, 102–103, 112, 115, 117, 118, 119, 120, 135, 148–49, 169; *12, 52, 53, 99, 117, 149*
- Dundurn, Perthshire 8, 85, 119; *86*
- Mither Tap o' Bennachie, Aberdeenshire 87; *87*
- Mote of Mark, Dumfries and Galloway 87, 115, 116, 117, 135
- Trusty's Hill, Dumfries and Galloway 169

Foster, Sally 98
Fowlis Wester, Perthshire 80, 83, 109; *108*
Franks casket 25
Fraoch Eilean, Loch Awe, Argyll, glass armlet fragment 119; *120*

gaming pieces
- Mail, Shetland 9; *8*
- Scalloway, Shetland 9

Garioch, Aberdeenshire, sculpture 169
garnet 77, 99, 120, 182
Gaulcross, Moray, hoard *182*
gender 5–6, 18–19, 43, 131, 157–58
Germanus, St 35
gesso 58
gift-giving 10, 19, 21–22, 99, 100–101, 103, 118
glass
- armlet fragment 119; *120*
- beads 14; *14*
- insets 29, 58, 129, 182
- lamps, 55
- *tesserae* 53, 115; *53*
- vessels 55, 58–59, 116–18, 135
- windows 56–57
- -working 145

Glenmorangie Research Project 106
Gododdin, The 14
gold 77, 99–100, 115, 120, 182
Golspie, Sutherland
- pin 9

- sculpture 167–69, 172; *168*

Good Friday (see Easter)
Gorton, Moray, sword 77; *78*
Govan, Glasgow, sarcophagus 45; *44*
graffiti/doodles (*see* slates, incised)
Granton-on-Spey, Moray, sculpture *168*
grave marker *131* (*and see* burial)

hacksilver bullion (*see* silver)
Haddington, East Lothian, silver chain 185
hagiography 4, 6, 30, 32–33, 42–43, 45, 47, 53–55
Hahn, Cynthia 134
hair/hairstyles 3
 - depictions of 9, 18, 73–74, 154, 158
Hallow Hill, St Andrews, Fife, cemetery 130–131
hand-bells (*see* bells)
hand-querns 148–49; *149, 203*
hanging bowls 55–56, 126; *56*
Harrowing of Hell 158–60
Harvieston, Clackmannan, sword 77
head, cult of 177
healing
 - Divine 3–4, 6, 30, 35, 38, 42–43, 45, 47–49, 51–54
 - medical 4, 48
heirlooms 12–13, 15, 18, 21, 77, 124, 126
Hell, Harrowing of 158–60
Henderson, George 97
Henderson, Isabel 84, 97
Hexham, Bishop of 48
Hiberno-Saxon art (*see* Insular art)
Hilton of Cadboll, Ross and Cromarty, sculpture 9, 18, 69, 97, 151–54, 157–58, 160–162, 181; *VIII, 18, 68, 152, 153, 161*
Hisperica famina 110
hoards
 - Ardagh, Ireland 52–53, 145
 - Croy, Inverness-shire 14, 29; *X, 14, 29, 197*
 - Derrynaflan, Ireland 27, 52, 145; *146*

- Gaulcross, Moray *182*
- Norrie's Law, Fife 133, 182, 187–92; *187, 188*
- St Ninian's Isle, Shetland 22, 24–26, 29, 47, 59, 77, 101, 119, 120, 125–29, 182; *25, 26, 46, 56, 57, 59, 60, 67, 77, 78, 101, 102, 103, 126, 127, 128*
- Talnotrie, Dumfries and Galloway 49; *50*
- Traprain Law, East Lothian 130, 132, 183–89; *132, 183, 184*

Hoardweel, Scottish Borders, silver chain 185; *186, 188*
Hoddom, Dumfries and Galloway, church 90, 92,
- cross-marked pebble 51

Holy Land
- Adomnán's description of 113
- reliquary from 113; *114*

horn mount, Burghead, Moray 120; *120*
home 30–31, 42, 49, 53–55
horses (*see also* riding/riders *and* hunting) 76, 80–81
housing (*see* home)
Howe, Orkney 83
Hunterston, Ayrshire, brooch 15, 19, 24, 26–27, 29, 99–100, 112, 119, 124; *VI, XIV, 2, 12, 16, 17, 23, 27*
hunting 160, 151, 154
- depictions of 18, 70, 74, 79–81, 151, 154–160, 171; *69, 81, 82, 155*
- objects for 79, 83; *83*
- symbolism of 80, 154–55, 160, 162

identity 5–7, 19, 30, 59
ideologies 141–44, 148, 190, 192, 196, 182–84
- nationalist 142
- and political control 144
- religious authority and economic exploitation 144
- as 'science of ideas' 141

illness (*see also* healing) 4–5, 30, 35, 42–43, 47–49, 51, 53–54
illuminated manuscripts 24, 30, 40, 42, 48, 146, 149, 153
- *Book of Deer, The* 30, 48–49
- *Book of Durrow, The* 175
- *Book of Kells, The* 18, 35, 110, 175; *19, 35*
- *Lindisfarne Gospels* 146; *147*

imports
- food stuffs 48, 118
- glass vessels 55, 58–59, 116–18, 135
- glass beads 14
- pottery 55, 58, 114–18, 135; *117*

incense 45, 54
Inchaffray, Perthshire, bell-shrine *143*
Inchcolm, Fife 114
Inchmarnock, Isle of Bute, monastery 6, 90, 92
- inscribed slates 5, 90, 92; *7*

Inchtuthil, Perthshire 134
inscriptions 5, 25, 52, 123–24
Insular art 153–54, 181–82
interlace 13, 22, 24, 27, 29, 38, 40
interpretation 141, 144–45, 150
Invereen, Inverness-shire, sculpture 149
Inverurie, Aberdeenshire, sculpture 81, 167
Iona, Argyll, monastery 18, 33, 55, 59, 113–14, 119, 124, 149; *91*
- imported pottery 59
- sculpture 33; *34*
- shoes 8

Ireland 32, 35, 38, 40, 53, 71, 89, 112, 119, 167
- churches, 56, 95
- historical sources 14, 18–19, 21, 33, 53, 58, 153
- objects 10, 15, 18–19, 24, 52–53, 58, 106, 109

iron/iron-working 100
Isle of May, Fife 92, 134
Isle of Mull, Argyll, brooch 29

Jarlshof, Shetland 90
- inscribed slate 9; *5, 9*

javelin (*see* spear)
Jedburgh, Scottish Borders, sculpture 57–58; *58*
Jesus 153, 158, 175–76
- depictions of 179
- Entry into Jerusalem 157–58

John the Baptist, St 157

Keillor, Perthshire sculpture 178
key-pattern 40, 154
Kingoldrum, Angus, bell *143*
kings/kingship 4, 21, 43, 51, 54–55, 70, 74, 76, 87, 95, 98, 100–101, 109, 118, 133, 148–49, 157, 159
Kinpurney Hill, Angus 178
kinship 84
Kirkmadrine, Dumfries and Galloway, sculpture *123*
Kirriemuir, Angus, sculpture 80; *80*
knotwork (*see* interlace)
Knowe of Burrian, Orkney
- bell *143*
- Pictish symbol-inscribed bone 146; *146*

lachet fastener 10; *10*
Lagore crannog, Co. Meath, Ireland 89
lake dwellings (*see* crannogs)
lamps (*see* lighting)
lance (*see* spear)
Lasswade, Midlothian 134
Lastingham, Yorkshire 109
Latin 25–26, 52, 59, 123–24, 126, 133, 150, 161
leather-working (*see* crafts)
lighting 45, 49, 54–57
Lindisfarne Gospels 146; *147*
literacy 3, 6, 92, 133, 145–46, 150, 153, 165, 170
liturgical vessel 52–53, 58–59, 145, 153; *146*

INDEX

225

Loch Glashan, Argyll, crannog 89, 100
- leather satchel fragments 110, 112
Lochhead Quarry, Auchterforfar, Angus *130*
Loch Leather, Argyll, crannog *89*
Lochspouts, Ayrshire, crannog
- rock crystal 53; *52*
long cist 129–30, 134;
Lundin Links, Fife 6

Maiden stone, Aberdeenshire, sculpture 172; *174*
Mail, Shetland, gaming piece 9; *8*
'majestic rider' 154–60, 171
manuscripts (*see also* illuminated manuscripts) 76, 92, 145–46, 149, 153, 170
marble 43, 57
Markle, East Lothian, sword mount 77
marriage
- gifts 19, 21–22, 185
McCurdy, Adrian 106
medicine (*see* healing)
Meigle, Perthshire, sculpture 70, 156–58
- Meigle 1 156–58, 167, 172; *156*
- Meigle 2 74, 97, 156–58, 171; *75, 97*
- Meigle 22 95; *94*
- lost panel *81*
Melrose, Scottish Borders 47
memory/memories 7
- role of burial 129–32, 195
- role of objects 12, 124–29, 182
- role of places
- role of sculpture 121–24
men 4, 6, 9, 18, 42–43
Menas, St, flasks 51
Meols, Cheshire, St Menas flask, 51
metalworking 87, 98–106, 145, 183, 190
- control/organisation of 12, 98, 100–103
- moulds and crucibles 10, 22, 99–103, 105–106, 112, 181, 183, 190; *99, 105*
- tools 106
mica, 52

Mither Tap o' Bennachie, Aberdeenshire, fort 87; *87*
miracles (*see* saints *and* healing)
monasteries 6, 59, 90, 92, 124, 143–44
- Hoddom, Dumfries and Galloway 51, 90, 92
- Inchmarnock, Isle of Bute 5–6, 90, 92
- Iona, Argyll 8, 18, 33, 55, 59, 113–14, 119, 124, 149; *91*
- Monkwearmouth and Jarrow, Tyne & Wear 55, 109, 113, 133
- Portmahomack, Ross and Cromarty 80, 90, 92, 95, 106, 145–46, 158, 162–64; *81, 147, 165*
- Whithorn, Dumfries and Galloway 43, 45, 47–49, 52–53, 55, 57, 59, 92, 98, 114, 130–31, 133, 135; *134*
Monkwearmouth and Jarrow, Tyne & Wear, monastery 55, 109, 113, 133
Montfode, Ardrossan, Ayrshire 131–32
Monymusk reliquary 25, 27, 29, 26–42, 90, 125, 192–93; *37, 39, 41*
mosaics 53
Moss of Auquharney, Aberdeenshire, wooden hunting trap 83
Mote of Mark, Dumfries and Galloway, fort 87
- glass tessera 115
- imported pottery 116–17, 135
moulds (see metalworking)
moustaches (see hair)
Mugdrum, Fife, sculpture 81

National Museums Scotland
- Early People gallery 151
Nechtan, King of the Picts 95, 133–35, 176
Nechtansmere (see battles, Dún Nechtain)
nemeton place-names 178–79
Ness, River 51
Nevay/Newtyle, Angus 178
Nicodemus, Gospel of 159

Nigg, Ross and Cromarty, sculpture 97, 162–64
Ninian, St 42–45, 48–49, 52, 53
Nonakiln, Highland, sculpture 178
Norrie's Law, Fife, hoard 133, 182, 187–92; *188*
- plaques 169, 187, 189–190; *188*
- Roman silver 187–90; *187*
- spoon fragment 187–90
Northumbria (see Anglo-Saxon England)

ogham 6, 123, 146, 151, 161, 165–67
Old Deer, Aberdeenshire, sculpture 123
Old Rosyth, Fife *105*
Old Scatness, Shetland 90
Orkney hood 3, 7–8; *8*
orpiment 118, 149
Oswald, St 51, 54–55

paganism 25, 47, 54, 154, 174–79
Papil, Shetland, sculpture 70, 110; *31, 70, 110*
parchment-making 92, 106
Parkhill, Aberdeenshire, silver chain 167; *186*
paten 58
Pavlov, Ivan 142
peat bogs (*see* bogs)
pebbles
- cross-inscribed 51, 146
- in healing 51–52
Petts, David 132
Pictish 151–54
- *Adventus* 154–60
- cross-slabs 151–54, 160–76
- free-standing crosses 74, 79, 81, 171–74
Pictish symbols 73, 121–24, 146–48, 151, 154, 160–69, 185, 190
- as script 123, 151, 162–69
- crescent and V-rod 123, 161–62
- double-disc and Z-rod 161
- mirror and comb 158, 161

- ogee 167
- on portable objects 146, 167–169; *146*
- rectangle 123, 169

Pictish symbol-stones (Class I) 121–24, 161, 165, 167–69

Pictland
- northern 164, 167–69
- southern 161, 167–69, 185

Picts 71, 83, 112, 120, 151
- matrilineal inheritance 5

pilgrimage 4, 42–43, 47, 49, 51–53, 113–16, 134

pins 9–10, 49, 98, 101–102, 187

Pool, Sanday, Orkney 90

porphyry 115; *116*

Portknockie, Aberdeenshire 85

Portmahomack, Ross and Cromarty, monastery 90, 158
- parchment manufacture 92, 106, 145–6
- sculpture 80, 95, 145–146, 162–64; *81, 147, 165*

pottery 55, 58
- African Red Slipware 59, 114, 116
- DSPA 117, 135; *117*
- E ware 117–18; *117*
- Late Roman Amphora 116

Pre-Christian (*see* paganism)

protective
- inscriptions 25–26, 52, 59
- motifs 22, 24–25, 59
- objects 14, 22–29, 38, 53, 59; *14*

Psalms 150, 154, 159–60

ramparts 85

Ravenna, Italy 53

Redcastle, Lunan Bay, Angus, cemetery 131; *131*

relics 3, 29, 30–33, 35–36, 43, 45, 47–49, 51–54, 125–26, 143, 192–93; *114*

reliquaries 3, 25, 32–33, 35–36, 51, 54, 59, 90, 113, 125, 192–93; *26, 114*

- Monymusk (*see* Monymusk reliquary)

replication 106–12; *107, 108, 109*

Resurrection 154

re-use
- objects 8, 12–15, 36, 49, 77, 99, 129
- Roman masonry 134
- Roman objects 131

Rhynie, Aberdeenshire
- imported pottery 116
- sculpture 121, 161

riding/riders (*see also* hunting) 70, 74–75, 81, 156–58

rock crystal 14, 51–53

Rogart, Sutherland, brooches 29; *20, 28, 90*

Roman 131
- brooch 133; *133*
- coins 115, 132
- cults 179
- Empire 180
- frontier 180–83, 190
- glass 14; *14*
- imperial adventus 155, 159
- imperial iconography 155, 157
- legacy 132–35
- military occupation 180–81
- remains (spolia) 134, 180
- sculpture 79, 155–57; *155*
- silver 130, 132–33, 181–83, 187–90; *132, 183, 184, 187*

Romanitas 180

Rome, Early Medieval 30, 113, 180

rood (*see* chancel screen)

Rosemarkie, Ross and Cromarty, sculpture 162, 164

roundhouses 88, 193–94

royal households/sites 87, 89, 98–100, 103

runes 151

runic inscription 15, 18, 124, 150, 160

Ruthwell, Dumfries and Galloway, sculpture 150–51, 160, 170; *150*

saints (*see under individual names*)

saints (*see also* relics) 31–33, 35–36, 38, 42–43, 45, 47, 53–55, 113, 143–44, 148
- days 36, 144
- saints' lives/hagiography 4, 6, 30, 32–33, 42–43, 45, 47, 53–55

salt 51, 53

Salvation 154–55

sarcophagi 35, 45, 83, 95, 155–57; *44, 82, 96, 155, 159*

Scalloway, Shetland, broch
- gaming piece 9
- spearhead 79

Scone, Perthshire 165

Scoonie, Fife, sculpture *81*

Sculptor's Cave, Covesea, Moray
- orpiment 118

sculpture 24, 30, 32–33, 38, 42, 57, 92, 95, 145–48, 150–76
- architectural 45, 57–58, 92, 95, 97
- Anglo-Saxon 38, 57–58, 119–20
- burial marker
- cross-bases 33, 171
- cross-slabs (Class II) 69, 71, 73, 76, 81, 83, 95, 97, 110, 134, 151–76
- elaboration of 33, 40, 58
- free-standing crosses 170–71
- inscribed 123–24, 133
- Irish High-crosses 38
- Roman 79, 155; *155*
- symbol stones (Class I) 121–24, 161–65

sculpted stones
- Aberlady, East Lothian 170
- Aberlemno, Angus 71, 79, 162, 172; *72, 163, 172*
- Ackergill, Caithness 151; *151*
- Ardross, Ross and Cromarty 178
- Benvie, Angus 74, 81; *74*
- Bewcastle, Cumberland 83
- Brandsbutt, Aberdeenshire 121; *122*
- Breck of Hillwell, Shetland 123

- Bressay, Shetland 110
- Bridgeness, West Lothian 79; *80*
- Brough of Birsay, Orkney 9, 73–74; *73*
- Burghead, Moray 92; *93, 168*
- Clonmacnoise, Co Offaly, Ireland 83
- Clynekirkton, Sutherland 123
- Craw Stane, Rhynie, Aberdeenshire 121, 161
- Drainie/Kineddar, Moray 165
- Dull, Perthshire 79
- Dunadd, Argyll 169
- Dunfallandy, Perthshire 167
- Dupplin, Perthshire 74, 79, 81, 171–74; *79, 173*
- Dyce, Aberdeenshire 165
- Eassie, Angus 80
- Eastertown of Roseisle, Moray 165–66; *166*
- Edderton, Ross and Cromarty 121; *122*
- Elgin, Moray 83; *163*
- Firth, Orkney 123; *123*
- Fiskavaig, Isle of Skye 161; *162*
- Forteviot, Perthshire 95; *94*
- Fowlis Wester, Perthshire 80, 83, 109; *108*
- Garioch, Aberdeenshire 169
- Golspie, Sutherland 167–69, 172; *168*
- Govan, Glasgow 45; *44*
- Grantown-on-Spey, Moray *168*
- Hilton of Cadboll, Ross and Cromarty 9, 18, 69, 97, 151–54, 157–58, 160–62, 181; *18, 68, 152, 153, 161*
- Invereen, Inverness-shire *149*
- Inverurie, Aberdeenshire 81, 167
- Iona, Argyll 33; *34*
- Jedburgh, Scottish Borders 57–58; *58*
- Keillor, Perthshire, 178
- Kirkmadrine, Dumfries and Galloway 123
- Kirriemuir, Angus 80; *80*
- Maiden Stone, Aberdeenshire 172; *174*
- Meigle, Perthshire 70, 74, 81 95, 97, 156–58, 167, 171–72; *75, 94, 97, 156*
- Mugdrum, Fife 81
- Nigg, Ross and Cromarty 97, 162–64
- Nonakiln, Highland 178
- Old Deer, Aberdeenshire 123
- Papil, Shetland 70, 110; *31, 70, 110*
- Portmahomack, Ross and Cromarty 80, 95, 145–46, 162–64; *81, 147, 165*
- Rosemarkie, Ross and Cromarty 162, 164
- Ruthwell, Dumfries and Galloway 150–51, 160, 170; *150*
- Scoonie, Fife *81*
- Shandwick, Ross and Cromarty 83, 95, 162–64
- St Andrews, Fife 45, 83, 95; *44, 82, 96, 159*
- St Peter's Church, South Ronaldsay, Orkney 121, 123; *122*
- St Orland's Cross, Cossans, Angus 33, 162; *164*
- St Vigeans, Angus 81, 162; *82*
- Stittenham, Ross and Cromarty 178
- Sueno's Stone, Forres, Moray 73
- Tillytarmont, Aberdeenshire 161
- Tore, Isle of Skye 161
- Wester Denoon, Angus 9
- Whithorn, Dumfries and Galloway 133; *134*
- Woodrae, Angus 97, 171; *172*

senses 3, 30–31, 54–55, 58
Shandwick, Ross and Cromarty, sculpture 83, 95, 162–64
shields 70–71, 73, 76, 79–80
shoes (*see* clothing)
shrine fragments 45, 57, 45, 83, 95
shrines 31–33, 35–36, 42–43, 45, 49, 51, 53–54, 57
sickness (*see* illness)
silver (*see also* silver chains) 13, 38, 40, 45, 47, 99, 100, 130, 181–192
- analysis of 100, 187–10
- armlets 182
- bowls 22, 24–26, 29, 182
- finger-rings 182
- hacksilver 181, 183, 189
- hoards 22, 24–26, 29, 47, 59, 77, 101, 119, 120, 125–30, 132–33, 182–92
- Roman 130, 132, 181–83, 187–89; *187*
- votive gifts 45, 47, 59

silver chains 10, 13, 167, 181–82, 185–87, 192; *11, 140*
- Borland, Lanarkshire *186*
- Haddington, East Lothian 185
- Hoardweel, Scottish Borders, 185; *186, 188*
- Parkhill, Aberdeenshire 167; *186*
- Torvean, Inverness-shire 185, 192
- Traprain Law, East Lothian 185–87; *184*
- Whitecleugh, Lanarkshire 167–69; *13, 169, 186*

Skaill burial, Orkney 48
skeletal remains 48
Skye, Isle of, 161
slates, incised 3, 6, 9, 92; *5, 7, 9*
slaves 117
spear 71, 76, 79
- depictions of 70, 73, 79
spiral (*see* triskele spiral)
spoons 59
Springmount Bog, Co. Antrim, Northern Ireland, writing tablets 3; *4*
springs (*see also* wells) 47, 51, 54
St Andrews, Fife 98, 165
- sculpture, 'sarcophagus' 45, 83, 95; *44, 82, 96, 159*
St Fillan's Church, Kilmacolm, Renfrewshire 114
St John's Cross, Iona, Argyll 33; replica *34*
St Martin's Cross, Iona, Argyll 33
St Ninian's Cave, Whithorn, Dumfries and Galloway, cross-marked pebble 51; *52*

St Ninian's Chapel sculpture, Navidale, Sutherland 178
St Ninian's Isle, Shetland, hoard 101, 125–26, 182; *46*
- bowls 47, 59, 126; *56, 57, 59, 60, 67*
- brooches 22, 24–26, 29, 47, 101, 119, 125–29; *25, 28, 101, 102, 103, 126, 127, 128*
- cone-shaped mounts 77; *77*
- porpoise bone 47
- spoon 59
- sword pommel 77, 120; *78*
- sword chapes 25–26, 47, 77, 120, 126; *26, 78*

St Ninian's Point, Isle of Bute 45
St Oran's Cross, Iona, Argyll 33
St Orland's Cross, Cossans, Angus 33, 162; *164*
St Peter's Church, South Ronaldsay, Orkney, sculpture 121, 123; *122*
St Vigeans, Angus, sculpture 81, 162; *82*
Stittenham, Ross and Cromarty, sculpture 178
stone sculpture (*see* sculpture)
Strathdon 169
Sueno's Stone, Forres, Moray, sculpture 73
sword 71, 76
- depictions of 70, 73
- surviving examples 77

sword fittings 71, 77, 126
- chapes 25–26, 47, 77, 120, 126
- pommel 77, 120
- scabbard 25, 71, 77, 126

symbols (*see* Pictish symbols)
symbol-stones (*see* Pictish symbol-stones)
Synod of Whitby (AD 664) 144

Talnotrie, Dumfries and Galloway, hoard 49; *50*
Tara brooch, Ireland 15, 24

Tarnavia, Perthshire, finger-ring 178; *178*
tenons, on sculpture 97, 171
textiles (*see* clothing)
Thornybank, Midlothian, cemetery 129, 131–34
thrones
- depictions on sculpted stones 109; *108*
- modern reconstruction 106–110; *107, 108*

Tillytarmont, Aberdeenshire, sculpture 161
Tirechan 177
tombs (*see* shrines)
Torbeck Hill, Ecclefechan, Dumfries and Galloway, sword 77
Tore, Skye, sculpture 161
Torvean, Inverness-shire, silver chain 185, 192
trade (*see also* imports) 117–18, 120
Traprain Law, East Lothian
- Late Roman hacksilver hoard 130, 132, 183–89; *132, 183, 184*
- silver chain 185–87; *184*

triskele spiral 13, 24, 40, 151–54, 178
Trusty's Hill, Dumfries and Galloway, fort 169

vellum production 92, 106, 145–46
verde antico (*see* porphyry)
Vikings/Viking Age
- burial 71
- swords 77

vine-scroll 151–54, 161, 171
Virgin Mary 18, 19
votive gifts 45, 47, 59, 129

Wales 32, 43, 54
warfare 71, 79
warriors 4, 14, 76, 79–80
water
- and Baptism 52
- healing power of 47, 53–54
- malign influence of 47

wax writing tablets 3
weapons 25, 47, 70–73, 76–77, 79–83, 126
wear 26, 29, 42, 126, 129
weights 49
wells 47, 51, 54
Wester Denoon, Angus, sculpture 9
Whitecleugh, Lanarkshire, silver chain 167–69; *13, 169, 186*
Whithorn, Dumfries and Galloway, monastery 57, 92, 98
- burial 130–31
- coins 47
- glass tessera 115
- imported foods 48, 118
- imported glass 55, 59, 116, 135
- imported pottery 55, 59, 114, 116–17
- *Latinus* stone 133; *134*
- mica fragments 52
- St Ninian's healing shrine 43, 45, 48–49, 52–53, 116
- window glass 56–57

Wilson, David 119
Wilton, Norfolk 115
window glass 56–57
wine (*see also* Eucharist) 59, 153, 160
women 4–6, 12–13, 18–19, 42–43, 185
wood-working (*see* craft-working)
wooden crosses 95, 98
Woodrae, Angus, sculpture, 97, 171; *172*
written sources
- Anglo-Saxon 13, 21–22, 43, 45, 47, 57
- Classical 52
- Irish 14, 18–19, 21, 33, 53, 58
- Italian 54
- saints' lives 4, 6, 30, 23–33, 42–43, 45, 47, 53–55

Acknowledgements

✶

The publisher is grateful to the following sources for permission to use their images or text within this publication. No reproduction of material in copyright is permitted without prior contact with the publisher or with the original sources.

IMAGE CREDITS

© NATIONAL MUSEUMS SCOTLAND

for all images used within this publication, except for the following:

© AOC ARCHAEOLOGY

for Figure 2.75

THE BRITISH LIBRARY

© The British Library Board

for Figure 3.7

THE BRITISH MUSEUM

© The Trustees of the British Museum

for Figures 1.11, 1.36, 1.37

© B J STEWART

for Figures 1.8, 1.9

© THE COPTIC MUSEUM, CAIRO, EGYPT

for Figure 3.18

© DOUG SIMPSON/STILL PRINT
www.stillprint.co.uk

for Figures 2.6, 2.7, 2.8, 2.16, 2.18, 2.21, 2.22, 2.31, 2.32, 2.33, 2.36, 2.37, 2.39–2.40, 2.46–2.49, 3.10, 3.37

HISTORIC ENVIRONMENT SCOTLAND

© Crown Copyright HES

for Figures 1.39, 1.47, 1.48, 1.49, 1.59, 2.3, 2.4, 2.24, 2.25, 2.29, 2.59, 2.61, 2.76, 2.77, 2.80, 3.17, 3.19, 3.20, 3.23, 3.24, 3.25, 3.29, 3.34, 3.35, 3.36, 3.38 and page 204

© KILMARTIN MUSEUM COMPANY LTD

for Figure 2.26

© MARION O'NEIL

for Figures 1.31, 1.46

MUSÉE DÉPARTEMENTAL ARLES ANTIQUE

© M. Lacanaud

for Figure 3.16

NATIONAL MUSEUM OF IRELAND

© Reproduced with the kind permission of the National Museum of Ireland

for Figures 1.2, 1.3, 3.4

NATIONAL TRUST FOR SCOTLAND

© National Trust for Scotland, Iona

for Figure 2.28

© SHETLAND MUSEUM & ARCHIVES LICENSOR www.scran.ac.uk

for Figure 2.2

© SOCIETY OF ANTIQUARIES OF SCOTLAND

for Figure 2.81

We are grateful to the Society of Antiquaries of Scotland for permission to reproduce this image.

TRINITY COLLEGE DUBLIN

© The Board of Trinity College Dublin

for Figures 1.22, 1.40

THE VATICAN MUSEUMS

© Courtesy of the Vatican Museums

for Figures 2.50, 2.51

© THE WALTERS ART MUSEUM

for Figure 1.50

© WILSON McSHEFFREY

for Figures 1.15, 1.55, 3.48, 3.49, 3.53 and page 203

TEXT CREDITS

ANOVA BOOKS
for permission to reproduce extracts from S M Foster 2004. *Picts, Gaels and Scots.* Batsford.

ASHGATE PUBLISHING
for permission to reproduce an extract from Riello and McNeil, quoted in S Kelly 2010: 'In the sight of an old pair of shoes', in T Hamling and C Richardson (eds) 2010. *Everyday Objects: Medieval and Early Modern Material Culture and its Meanings.*

EWAN CAMPBELL
for permission to reproduce extracts from A Lane and E Campbell 2000. *Dunadd: an Early Dalriadic Capital.* Oxbow Books.

CANONGATE BOOKS
for permission to reproduce extracts from T O Clancy 1998. *The Triumph Tree: Scotland's Earliest Poetry* AD 550–1350.

EDINBURGH UNIVERSITY PRESS
for permission to reproduce extracts from L Alcock 1988. 'The activities of Potentates in Celtic Britain, AD 500–800: A Positivist Approach', in S T Driscoll and M Nieke (eds). *Power and Politics in Early Medieval Britain and Ireland.*

FOUR COURTS PRESS
for permission to reproduce an extract from J Carey 1998. *King of Mysteries: Early Irish Religious Writings.*

GROAM HOUSE MUSEUM
for permission to reproduce an extract from L Alcock 1993. *The Neighbours of the Picts: Angles, Britons and Scots at War and at Home.*

ALAN LANE
for permission to reproduce extracts from A Lane and E Campbell 2000. *Dunadd: an Early Dalriadic Capital.* Oxbow Books.

MANEY PUBLISHING
for permission to reproduce an extract from I Henderson 2005. 'Fragments of significance: the whole picture', in S M Foster and M Cross (eds). *Able Minds and Practised Hands: Scotland's Early Medieval Sculpture in the 21st Century,* monographs series, volume 23 (Society of Medieval Archaeology). By permission of Maney Publishing (www.maney.co.uk).

THE METROPOLITAN MUSEUM OF ART
for permission to reproduce an extract from M. Freeman 1945. 'Lighting the Easter Candle'. *The Metropolitan Museum of Art Bulletin* 3.

W W NORTON & COMPANY, INC
for permission to reproduce an extract from S. Heaney (trans) 2002. *Beowulf. A Verse Translation.*

OXBOW BOOKS
for permission to reproduce extracts from J Wilkinson 2002. *Jerusalem Pilgrims before the Crusades.* Aris & Phillips.

OXFORD UNIVERSITY PRESS
for permission to reproduce extracts from B Colgrave (trans) 1999. *Bede's The Ecclesiastical History of the English People*; B Colgrave and R A B Mynors (eds) 1969. *Bede's Ecclesiastical History of the English People*; and P Godman, (ed) 1982. *Alcuin: the Bishops, Kings, and Saints of York.* By permission of Oxford University Press.

PALGRAVE MACMILLAN
for permission to reproduce extracts from P E Dutton 2004: *Charlemagne's Mustache and Other Cultural Clusters of a Dark Age.* Reproduced with permission of Palgrave Macmillan.

PENGUIN BOOKS
for permission to reproduce an extracts from R S Pine-Coffin (trans) 1961. *St Augustine Confessions*; and R Sharpe (trans) 1995: *Adomnán's Life of St Columba.* Reproduced by permission of Penguin Books Ltd.

THE RANDOM HOUSE GROUP
for permission to reproduce an extract from E De Waal 2010. *The Hare with the Amber Eyes: A Hidden Inheritance* (Chatto and Windus).

KEVIN RODDY
for permission to reproduce an extract from K P Roddy 2000. 'Politics and Religion in Late Antiquity: The Roman Imperial Adventus Ceremony and the Christian Myth of the Harrowing of Hell', *Apocrypha.*

SCOTTISH TRUST FOR ARCHAEOLOGICAL RESEARCH

for permission to reproduce extracts from A Crone 2000. *The History of a Scottish Lowland Crannog: Excavations at Buiston, Ayrshire 1989–90*', STAR monograph 4.

SHETLAND AMENITY TRUST

for permission to reproduce an extract from S J Dockrill, et al. 2010. *Excavations at Old Scatness, Shetland, vol.1: The Pictish Village and Viking Settlement*. Shetland Heritage Publications/Oxbow Books.

SOCIETY OF ANTIQUARIES OF SCOTLAND

for permission to reproduce extracts from the following *Proceedings of the Society of Antiquaries of Scotland*:

L Alcock, E A Alcock and S M Foster 1986. 'Reconnaissance excavations on early historic fortifications and other royal sites in Scotland, 1974–84: 1, Excavations near St Abb's Head, Berwickshire, 1980.'

I Armit, E Campbell and A Dunwell 2008. 'Excavation of an Iron Age, early historic and medieval settlement and metalworking site at Eilean Olabhat, North Uist.'

D Christison, J Anderson and T Ross 1905. 'Report on the Society's excavations of forts on the Poltalloch Estate, Argyll, in 1904–05.'

C Hatherley 2009. 'Into the west: excavation of an early Christian cemetery at Montfode, Ardossan, North Ayrshire'.

and for permission to reproduce extracts from L Alcock 2003. *Kings and Warriors, Craftsmen and Priests in Northern Britain AD 550–850*.

A Crone and E Campbell 2005. *A Crannog of the First Millennium AD: Excavations by Jack Scott at Loch Glashan, Argyll, 1960*.

C Lowe 2006. *Excavations at Hoddom, Dumfriesshire: an Ecclesiastical Site in South-west Scotland*.

THAMES & HUDSON

for permission to reproduce extracts from G Henderson and I Henderson 2004. *The Art of Picts: Sculpture and Metalwork in Early Medieval Scotland*. © George Henderson and Isobel Henderson. Reprinted by kind permission of Thames & Hudson Ltd, London.

TAYLOR & FRANCIS BOOKS

for permission to reproduce an extract from D Whitley 1998. *Reader in Archaeological Theory*. Routledge.

UNIVERSITY OF WALES PRESS

for permission to reproduce an extract from L Alcock 1995. *Cadbury Castle, Somerset: The Early Medieval Archaeology*.

YALE UNIVERSITY PRESS

for permission to reproduce an extract from M. Bagnoli 2010: 'The stuff of heaven: materials and craftsmanship in Medieval reliquaries', in M Bagnoli, H Klein, G Mann and J Robinson (eds): *Treasures of Heaven: Saints, Relics, and Devotion in Medieval Europe*.